Who Controls the Hunt?

The Nature | History | Society series is devoted to the publication of high-quality scholarship in environmental history and allied fields. Its broad compass is signalled by its title: *nature* because it takes the natural world seriously; *history* because it aims to foster work that has temporal depth; and *society* because its essential concern is with the interface between nature and society, broadly conceived. The series is avowedly interdisciplinary and is open to the work of anthropologists, ecologists, historians, geographers, literary scholars, political scientists, sociologists, and others whose interests resonate with its mandate. It offers a timely outlet for lively, innovative, and well-written work on the interaction of people and nature through time in North America.

General Editor: Graeme Wynn, University of British Columbia

A list of titles in the series appears at the end of the book.

Who Controls the Hunt?

First Nations, Treaty Rights, and Wildlife Conservation in Ontario, 1783–1939

DAVID CALVERLEY

FOREWORD BY GRAEME WYNN

UBC Press • Vancouver • Toronto

© UBC Press 2018

All rights reserved. No part of this publication may be reproduced, stored in a retrieval system, or transmitted, in any form or by any means, without prior written permission of the publisher, or, in Canada, in the case of photocopying or other reprographic copying, a licence from Access Copyright, www.accesscopyright.ca.

27 26 25 24 23 22 21 20 19 18   5 4 3 2 1

Printed in Canada on FSC-certified ancient-forest-free paper
(100% post-consumer recycled) that is processed chlorine- and acid-free.

Library and Archives Canada Cataloguing in Publication

Calverley, David, author
   Who controls the hunt? : First Nations, treaty rights, and wildlife conservation in Ontario, 1783-1939 / David Calverley; foreword by Graeme Wynn.

(Nature, history, society)
Includes bibliographical references and index.
Issued in print and electronic formats.
ISBN 978-0-7748-3133-8 (hardcover). – ISBN 978-0-7748-3134-5 (softcover).
ISBN 978-0-7748-3135-2 (PDF). – ISBN 978-0-7748-3136-9 (EPUB).
ISBN 978-0-7748-3137-6 (Kindle).

   1. Game laws – Ontario – History. 2. Wildlife conservation – Law and legislation – Ontario – History. 3. Wildlife conservation – Ontario – History. 4. Ojibwa Indians – Hunting – Ontario – History. 5. Ojibwa Indians – Legal status, laws, etc. – Ontario – History. 6. Ojibwa Indians – Ontario – Government relations – History. 7. Hudson's Bay Company. I. Title. II. Series: Nature, history, society

| KEO916.C35 2018 | 346.71304'69549 | C2017-907798-8 |
| KF5640.C35 2018 | | C2017-907799-6 |

Canadä

UBC Press gratefully acknowledges the financial support for our publishing program of the Government of Canada (through the Canada Book Fund), the Canada Council for the Arts, and the British Columbia Arts Council.

This book has been published with the help of a grant from the Canadian Federation for the Humanities and Social Sciences, through the Awards to Scholarly Publications Program, using funds provided by the Social Sciences and Humanities Research Council of Canada.

UBC Press
The University of British Columbia
2029 West Mall
Vancouver, BC V6T 1Z2
www.ubcpress.ca

For Abigail, Eleanor, and Mindi

Contents

Foreword / ix
Graeme Wynn

Acknowledgments / xxv

Introduction / 3

1 First Nations Hunting Activity in Upper Canada and the Robinson Treaties, 1783–1850 / 13

2 Ontario's Game Laws and First Nations, 1800–1905 / 28

3 First Nations, the Game Commission, and Indian Affairs, 1892–1909 / 40

4 Traders, Trappers, and Bureaucrats: The Hudson's Bay Company and Wildlife Conservation in Ontario, 1892–1916 / 51

5 The Transitional Indian: Duncan Campbell Scott and the Game Act, 1914–20 / 72

6 *R. v. Padjena:* Local Pressure and Treaty Hunting Rights in Ontario, 1925–31 / 88

7 *R. v. Commanda*, 1937–39 / 109

Epilogue / 122

Appendices

1 Ontario's Wildlife Legislation, 1877–1937 / 126

2 Chart from the Report of the Vidal-Anderson Commission, 1849 / 128

Notes / 130

Bibliography / 164

Index / 183

FOREWORD
Strains of Liberalism
Graeme Wynn

Seemingly simple questions often require complicated answers. Take *Who Controls the Hunt?* by way of example. David Calverley's efforts to explore and interrogate this apparently straightforward question run to well over one hundred pages, but even he acknowledges that "the question of who controls the hunt has not been entirely answered" (125). This is not to diminish what this book achieves: some questions defy answers, easy or otherwise, and there is much to be learned through engagement with important issues in a long-form argument, even if that argument ends by revealing ambiguity or uncertainty. Calverley's careful examination of interactions between First Nations and the state over Aboriginal hunting and trapping in Upper Canada/Ontario between 1800 and 1940 focuses on a specific series of events and conflicts to show, in telling detail, how the Ontario government and the Department of Indian Affairs undercut Indigenous peoples' treaty rights. In sum, these pages reveal how federal-provincial rivalries, differing government agendas, and various popular and official conceptions of the "Indian problem" affected hunting and trapping rights in northern Ontario. Yet their implications spin outwards and backwards to raise broader questions about legal and constitutional concerns, humanitarian convictions, conservation theories, political ideologies, concepts of liberty, property, and equality, and the ambiguities and tensions (strains) inherent in different strains (forms) of liberalism. These are all issues of fundamental significance to understanding the development of Canada, and of equally vital importance to shaping the country's future.

To begin near the beginning: When John Locke, philosopher, office holder, and intellectual founder of modern liberalism proclaimed, late in the seventeenth century, that "in the beginning all the world was America," he invoked the new world to endorse the old and to validate a particular sociopolitical philosophy. At the same time, he elaborated an ideological position that would have a profound influence on the development of the United States and on evolving relations between First Nations and others in British North America.[1] Coming of age in the aftermath of the English Civil War, Locke lived in tumultuous times marked by conflict between Crown and Parliament and between Catholics and Protestant dissenters. As a young man he saw the abolition of the Anglican Church, the House of Lords, and the Monarchy, and the collapse of Oliver Cromwell's Protectorate; early in his fifties he was in exile in Holland and only returned to England after the Glorious Revolution of 1688 that crowned Protestant William of Orange King.

Challenging the argument of earlier authorities who supported the Divine Right of Kings and defended absolute monarchy as the only legitimate form of government, Locke's *Two Treatises of Government* insisted that "men [sic] are by nature free and equal," and that they have (natural) rights to life, health, liberty, and possessions.[2] Christian faith led Locke to believe that God gave "the World to Men in common," and reason convinced him that people, "once born, have a right to their Preservation." In the beginning, therefore, in the "state of nature" when there was no legitimate government or political society, people shared ownership of the earth and owed one another mutual love, justice, and charity. But they had no means of arbitrating disputes among themselves. In this world of metaphorical kings, all people would live in constant fear and continual danger. So they entered a social contract. By transferring some of their rights to a body politic, they created the means to regulate and preserve property and defend "the common-wealth from foreign injury." By this transfer they established a legitimate government with the power to maintain civil society by enacting and enforcing the laws necessary to limit passion, revenge, negligence, and indifference.[3] In this quasi-historical, evolutionary model, with its culmination in the social contract, Locke challenged the contemporary, widespread, and "dangerous belief that all government in the world is merely the product of force and violence," and reconciled revelation and reason with the claim that all people once lived (as he averred the Indigenous inhabitants of America did) in a "state of nature."[4]

Elaborating on this transition from natural to civil society, Locke faced a pivotal question: If the earth was given to all in common, how does private property come to be? Surely not by the explicit permission of all concerned. People who ate acorns fallen to the ground or munched apples gathered from trees in the wood certainly appropriated those fruits: the nourishment was theirs and theirs alone. But they had not obtained the permission of all humankind before devouring them. "Was it Robbery thus to assume to [themselves] what belonged to all in Common?" No, said Locke. People would starve, notwithstanding God's plenty, "if such consent as that was necessary." Commons were worthless if they could not be used. In this utilitarian calculus, shared tenancy and property rights were not incompatible. Because the earth was given to humans to use, people had to be able to appropriate it. And they did so through their investment of labour. In Locke's eyes, the work involved in acquiring things legitimated claims to them. In this view, "the Fruit, or Venison, which nourishes the wild *Indian,* who knows no Inclosure, and is still a Tenant in common, must be his." The deer belonged to the Indian who killed it.[5]

Beyond rights to plants and animals, Locke concluded that people could also claim property in "the *Earth it self.*" Again, rights were established by labour: "*As much Land* as a Man Tills, Plants, Improves, Cultivates, and can use the Product of, so much is his *Property.*" There was neither illegitimacy nor injury in such enclosure of the commons. By commanding humankind to subdue the earth, God gave people authority to appropriate it. So long as that appropriation rested upon the labour invested by the individual, possessions would be of modest extent. And because the labour of cultivation greatly increased the productivity of land, such enclosure benefited humankind in general. Moreover, the Law of Nature that established property in the first place also prevented energetic and avaricious individuals from engrossing a disproportionate share of the earth's riches. This was, wrote Locke, because God, in his wisdom, made nothing for humankind to spoil or destroy. People could properly claim rights only in what they could use "to any advantage of life before it spoils," and so long as there was enough for others. In this early phase of human development (when "all the world was America"), Locke concluded that

> right and conveniency went together; for as a Man had a Right to all he could imploy his Labour upon, so he had no temptation to labour for more than he could make use of. This left no room for Controversie about the Title, nor for Incroachment on the Right of others; what Portion a Man carved to himself, was easily seen; and it was useless as well as dishonest to carve himself too much, or take more than he needed.[6]

Then came money. When people "agreed, that a little piece of yellow metal ... should be worth a great piece of Flesh or a whole heap of corn," they upset the "natural" order of things by enabling translation of the perishable overplus of cultivation into gold (or silver) that could be hoarded indefinitely.[7] Although different degrees of industry might earlier have enabled some to own more than others, the invention of money opened the way to greater inequality, the eventual dominion of private property, and the labourer's loss of the full value of his or her industry to landlord or capitalist (as Adam Smith and Karl Marx would note later).[8]

Locke deployed the state of nature, in the *Two Treatises*, as an analytical device to account for the introduction of civil government and to define its legitimate functions. Some have taken his references to Indigenous Americans living in the state of nature as merely figurative. But, as Barbara Arneil has shown, Locke's meditations on both "natural man" and property were heavily influenced by England's early engagement with the Americas.[9] Locke's patron, Lord Shaftesbury, was centrally involved in promoting colonies and trade. Locke himself served as secretary to the Lords Proprietors of Carolina and secretary to the Council of Trade and Plantations, and his personal library included dozens of books on the Americas. Far from being an "ahistorical condition" entirely lacking in "transitive empirical content," as John Dunn, author of a book on Locke's political thought claimed in 1969, Locke's ideas about humankind's "natural" state drew heavily, if selectively, from contemporary descriptions of America and his own work in colonial administration.[10] Their influence was profound. By positing a dichotomy between the civil and natural (or savage) states of humankind, his ideas shaped attitudes toward Indigenous peoples for centuries. By attaching property rights to labour in (rather than simple occupation of) the land, they favoured a particular agrarian view of appropriation by enclosure and cultivation that negated Indigenous claims to territory. And by implying an inexorable progression from the state of nature to civil society, they legitimated the conviction that hunters should become farmers – that Indigenes should assimilate by giving "up their own 'habits' and natural state for a civilized society based on a sedentary life, property, and 'regular government.'"[11]

So long as newcomers/settlers were few and the "vast inland" of America seemed to have no end, it was easy for colonizers to believe that their presence caused Indigenous inhabitants no harm and to concede to those inhabitants rights to the fruits and beasts of the earth. "No Body," Locke wrote, "could think himself injur'd by the drinking of another Man, though he took a good Draught, who had a whole River of the same Water left him to quench his thirst. And the Case of Land and Water, where there is enough of both, is perfectly the same."[12] In other words, the basic subsistence activities of hunting and gathering peoples, conducted beyond the limits of the English proprietors' initial toeholds on the continent, did not impinge upon the immediate purposes of those proprietors and could be tolerated.

Widely accepted in the new republic, this uncomplicated understanding changed little as settlers subdued more and more of the colonial earth by tilling and planting through the early years of the eighteenth century. Possessed of money and engaged in trade, rising numbers of newcomers were able to enclose and claim more and more extensive tracts of land; it did not seem untoward that Indigenes, regarded as living in a state of nature and lacking commercial opportunities and thus subject to natural laws against spoilage, were necessarily confined to small parcels, even if they elected to become cultivators. The implied imperative for all Native people was clear in President Thomas Jefferson's dealings with the Cherokee Nation who were given a choice, in 1809, between remaining on their traditional lands by joining civil society (which meant abandoning hunting and becoming cultivators) or relocating across the Mississippi to continue their traditional ways.[13] Two decades on, under the presidency of Andrew Jackson – "Indian fighter and settler politician par excellence" – a US statute outlawed tribal jurisdiction within state boundaries: Tribal members who refused to become citizens would be removed to lands west of the Mississippi.[14]

The fundamental premises upon which Lockean liberalism and such strategies rested were undercut by the US Supreme Court in 1823.[15] This precedent-setting decision rejected the claim that cultivation conferred title and dismissed the view that Indigenous Americans lived in a state of nature without society or government. Yet, these ideas retained strong popular currency both north and south of the 49th parallel in the nineteenth century. In British North America their implementation was complicated, to some degree, by the Royal Proclamation of 1763 (which ostensibly "guaranteed" Indigenes "possession of their hunting grounds" west of the Atlantic drainage divide and forbade the occupation or purchase of these lands by individual settlers – although it allowed Indigenous peoples to concede them to the Crown), and by Indigenous support of British military forces through the half-century thereafter. For all that, challenges to the various agreements by which the Crown acquired parcels of this territory in the 1830s and 1840s were resisted by resort to natural law. Its fundamental tenets were given almost flawless expression by the authors of the 1845 *Report on The Affairs of the Indians in Canada,* who argued that the earth "belongs to mankind in general" and that the "unsettled habitation" of "erratic nations," which failed to cultivate the earth, could not "be accounted a true and legal possession."[16] In this view, colonial officials were caught between the proverbial rock and a hard place – unable to check the tide of immigration and helpless "to guard the Indian Territory against the encroachments of the whites"; they were to be congratulated on arranging the "voluntary surrender" of Indian lands and for adopting "the most humane and most just course in inducing the Indians, by offers of compensation, to remove quietly to more distant hunting grounds."[17]

These early nineteenth-century decades were contentious and complicated years in the globe-spanning engagement of British colonial ventures with Indigenous peoples, as new world opportunities cemented belief in classic liberalism – the idea that individuals should be free "from dependence on the will of others" and possessed of the fundamental right to own private property. Yet widening acceptance of this market ideology was met, variously, by growing political radicalism in rapidly industrializing Britain, rising turn-of-the century concern about the slave trade, and Indigenous resistance to colonial settlement in several of Britain's overseas territories through the 1820s and 1830s. All of these developments heightened a sense of societal responsibility for what has been termed "the plight of distant strangers." Sometimes characterized as recognition of the "white man's burden" but better described as humanitarianism, or philanthropic liberalism, this emergent strain of thought spawned new missionary zeal and generated much debate about the circumstances of Aboriginal peoples in the colonies.[18]

In Upper Canada, the "voluntary surrender" of Indigenous territory began with negotiations between colonial officials and local bands to smooth the way for Loyalist settlers fleeing the American Revolution. Typically, these discussions ended with the transfer of relatively small tracts of land in return for yearly presents. As the likelihood of hostilities with the United States faded, efforts to secure the loyalty of Indigenous inhabitants with annual gifts of guns, axes, food, clothing, and the like seemed increasingly pointless. Then, as a tide of newcomers spilled into the colony, more land surrenders (generally regarded as contracts of sale) were negotiated to facilitate settlement. Soon thirty or so such agreements had been reached, covering most of the productive land in the southern parts of the colony, albeit with some confusion caused by poorly described boundary lines and other uncertainties. In effect, precedent established, and then in

1839 legislation confirmed, that "control over and disposal of lands in Upper Canada" would not occur "until the Interests & rights of the Indians had been extinguished, and the same had been formally ceded to the Crown."[19]

Concurrently, questions emerged about the existence and function of the Indian Department, which traced its roots back to the appointment (for military purposes) of an Indian superintendent in 1755. Officials began to envisage a new administrative structure and purpose for the department. In 1828, the chief superintendent of Indian Affairs for Upper and Lower Canada recommended settling Aboriginal people on farms, providing them with education and religious instruction, and replacing existing annual gifts with presents of farm stock and agricultural implements. These recommendations were accepted by officials in London with certain provisos: costs would not increase; the Indian Department would be transferred from military to civil control so that its budget could be scrutinized by the British Parliament; and Indigenous people would be settled in considerable numbers "in villages with a due portion of land for their cultivation and support." These changes were well characterized by historian Leslie Upton as setting the foundations of "the whole civilization programme."[20] As the secretary of state for war and the colonies summarized the situation in 1830 from his view in Westminster, dealings with the Indigenous inhabitants of the Canadas should henceforth be focused on the "settled purpose of gradually reclaiming them from a state of barbarism and of introducing amongst them the industrious and peaceful habits of civilized life."[21]

In England, discussion of the ways in which encounters with Indigenous peoples across the colonies might best be managed paralleled local initiatives in the Canadas. Early in the century, a group of evangelical Anglicans and social reformers (including parliamentarian William Wilberforce) agitated for abolition of the slave trade and emancipation of slaves – even as they worked to alleviate social ills at home. A few years later, in 1837, concern over the "desolating effects of the association of unprincipled Europeans with nations in a ruder state" led to the founding of the Aborigines Protection Society; the appointment of a committee of the Quaker Meeting for Sufferings to consider the circumstances of "the Indians in Upper Canada;" and the establishment of parliamentary committees to recommend measures to secure "due observance of Justice and the protection of ... [the] Rights" and promote the spread of civilization and Christianity among native inhabitants in areas of British settlement overseas.[22] At the heart of these developments lay the notion of "fair" exchange between colonizer and colonized: in return for their independence and land, indigenes would receive (as Thomas Buxton, a leading humanitarian of the 1830s put it) "all the benefits of knowledge, civilization, education and Christianity that it is in our power to bestow."[23] Indeed, the "River Credit Mission," established by the Methodist Peter Jones in Upper Canada in 1826, was held up as a prime example of what was possible: "About ten years ago," the Mississauga people who lived there (characterized as Chippeways in contemporary reports) "had no houses, no fields nor horses, no cattle, no pigs, and no poultry" but now lived in "about 40 comfortable houses" replete with furniture, crockery and cutlery, and even clocks and watches. They grew wheat, maize, and oats in 200 acres of fields beyond their gardens and had a few barns and stables for their implements and stock.[24]

However, even as this discourse unfolded in the metropolis, its foundations were being challenged abroad. In 1836, a request, from the colonial secretary in London, for information on the social and economic circumstances of the Indigenous population of the Canadas led the lieutenant governor of Upper Canada, Sir Francis Bond Head, to visit many of the Indigenous settlements in his colony. He concluded that they were failing to prosper, and that all Indigenous people living in the southern parts of Upper Canada should be relocated to the Manitoulin islands in Georgian Bay, where they could hunt, fish, gather, and even cultivate in isolation from white settlers. Indigenes, the missionaries who worked among them, and members of the Aborigines Protection Society in England were outraged by Bond Head's conclusions. When Lord Glenelg received Lower Canada's belated response to his 1836 request for information, which recommended the establishment of more reserve lands near white settlements rather than the removal of Indigenous people to remote areas, he rejected Bond Head's approach and reiterated his predecessor's 1830 commitment to civilizing indigenous peoples. "Wandering Indians" were to be settled on land where they would become farmers; they would receive title to their reserves, their land would be protected from creditors, and their education would be encouraged. The fundamental aim of British policy, insisted Glenelg, was "to protect and cherish this helpless Race ... and raise them in the Scale of Humanity."[25]

In this period of vacillating policy, Herman Merivale, professor of political economy in the University of Oxford, brought his considerable intellect to bear on "the Native Question" in a series of lectures delivered in the late 1830s and early 1840s. These lectures reached back to consider the very beginnings of European expansion in the Americas and drew examples from around the globe in an attempt to address "the greatest moral difficulty of colonization."[26] Neither racist nor sanguine, Merivale theorized that there were four possible policy solutions to the Native question: extermination, slavery, insulation, and amalgamation. A philanthropic liberal himself, Merivale shared the humanitarians' abhorrence of the first two of these possibilities. Understanding "race" as a cultural construct, he did not subscribe to the view that Indigenous people were inferior – physically, intellectually, or materially – to Europeans.

The challenge, as Merivale saw it, was to ameliorate the effects of European colonization on Indigenous peoples. Imperial governments needed to act with "tact, prudence and firmness" to ensure the protection and civilization of those whose territories they claimed.[27] Establishing reserves for the exclusive use of Native peoples could insulate them from the "ferocity and treachery" that many colonizers exhibited, but they would provide only a temporary and ultimately unsatisfactory reprieve for all concerned. Increasing numbers of newcomers would "soon press on the limits of the Indian ground," and whites would look askance at reserve land left uncultivated. Indigenous peoples would then be relocated, perhaps more than once, to new reserves in "some distant territory," causing them "a loss of capital and comfort" as well as "insecurity, the despair of permanence, [and] the conviction of approaching annihilation." Amalgamation – by which Merivale meant some form of acculturation or assimilation between white settlers and Native peoples – was also a flawed and difficult option. A "wild and chimerical" idea to some, it offered, in Merivale's assessment, the best hope for the future. But it would succeed only if accepted as an "immediate and an individual process – immediate, if not in act, at least in contemplation." Indigenous peoples had to treated, from the outset, as potential citizens; missionaries and teachers working among them would awaken a spirit of improvement and allow them to realize its benefits. Soon, intermarriage would lead to the development of a new society free of the cultural tensions evident in early colonial encounters.

When the former English public servant Rawson W. Rawson, newly arrived in British North America, was appointed in 1842 to investigate the work of the Indian Department in the newly united Canadas, he and his fellow commissioners brought fresh critical eyes to their task. Their voluminous report offered "a depressing picture of bungled departmental operations, deplorable Indian conditions, and unresolved policy questions."[28] By the early 1840s, the civilizing policies adopted in 1830 were condemned as paternalistic. There were no inherent racial barriers to the advancement of Indigenous peoples, but existing arrangements tended to keep them "in a state of isolation and tutelage and materially retard their progress." These should be replaced, said the commissioners, with new provisions intended to foster a thirst for knowledge and promote industry and self-reliance. Among these were a better system of education, more effective protection of Indigenous land and resources, and a re-organized Indian Department.[29]

None of these were simple matters, although educational reforms were soon implemented with the cooperation of Native peoples, missionaries, and the Indian Department. While it seemed clear that existing approaches to the management of land had been "defective and injurious to the interest of the Indians," it was less clear how the situation could be improved. Better record keeping and more straightforward bureaucratic structures might help. But the most efficacious solution, in the eyes of the commissioners, lay in the classic liberal strategy of individual land ownership and resort to the courts for remedy against trespass. There were complications and ambiguities even here, though. Contrary to the commissioners' recommendations, many Indigenous groups favoured communal over individual ownership of land. And the claim that plundering of reserve fisheries was detrimental because it deprived Indigenous inhabitants of a valuable source of food sat uneasily with the view that the disappearance of game "might be ultimately more beneficial to the Indians," as it would encourage them to take up agriculture. Sweeping changes were made in the Indian Department to save money and to improve efficiency, but organizational problems continued as the influx of a million immigrants to Canada in the 1840s exacerbated tensions between a department (and a colonial legislature) closely attentive to the settlers' interest in economic development and those who believed (with Merivale and the Aborigines Protection Society) that ultimate responsibility for the welfare of Indigenes should rest with the Colonial Office.[30]

These pressures grew more acute in the late 1840s when the establishment of "Responsible Government" passed control of Crown land grants to the provincial executive, and mining concerns began to show interest in the northern shores of the Great Lakes.[31] After the government ignored the provisions of the Royal Proclamation to grant mining leases before land surrenders were negotiated in this area, there were skirmishes between prospectors and Indigenous people, and Indigenous leaders protested against the incursions. Seeking to regularize the settlement and exploitation of this relatively remote and thinly inhabited territory by asserting jurisdiction over it, the provincial government engaged with the governor general and local leaders to conclude the Robinson Treaties in 1850.

These agreements, which form the essential starting point of David Calverley's explication of the vexatious story of First Nations' treaty rights and wildlife conservation in Ontario through the eight decades that followed, hold an important place in the history of settler engagement with Indigenous peoples in Canada. Seen by the commissioner after whom they were named as continuing established practices of treaty making, and widely regarded as creating a template for the later numbered treaties of western Canada because they provided for "annuities, reserves for the Indian, and liberty to hunt and fish on the unconceded domain of the Crown," the Robinson Treaties did more than this.[32] Shaped in significant ways by forceful Indigenous leaders, they "effectively ended Canadian flirtation with US-style removal policy," recognized that Natives and newcomers might coexist in areas covered by treaties, and acknowledged that Indigenous people should benefit from the development of timber and mineral development. Indeed, as James Morrison noted in his 1996 study, "the Robinson treaties provided more to their beneficiaries than all subsequent agreements": annuity payments were to increase as resource revenues rose; broadly defined Indigenous harvesting rights were "not ... subject to government regulation" and included commercial as well as subsistence use; and the extent of reserve lands was not determined by an arbitrary administrative formula.[33]

As the old adage reminds us, however, "there is many a slip between cup and lip." Some reserve surveys encompassed much smaller areas than anticipated and, in time, several bands were pressed to give up parts of their reserve lands in what has been described as "part of a modified *removal* policy."[34] Constitutional disputes, and concern about the costs and implications of the 1850 agreements – as well as a hardening of racialized attitudes across the British Empire after 1860 – "led both federal and provincial governments to unilaterally reinterpret the Robinson treaties" after Confederation.[35] Although resource revenues increased dramatically, annuity payments were increased only once, from $2.00 to $4.00 per person in 1874, and the provinces persistently resisted paying arrears. In 2017, the issue is before the Canadian courts; estimates place resource development revenues from the treaty territories at between $500 million and $1 billion over the years since 1874, and the First Nations involved are asking for a full accounting of these sums before indicating the level of compensation they will consider fit.[36] And in ways that are traced in meticulous and arresting detail through archival records and court cases in the pages of this book, both the Ontario government and the Department of Indian Affairs played their parts in eroding Anishinaabeg treaty rights to hunt and trap in the years after Confederation.

In Calverley's telling, there were two basic causes of this erosion. One lay in the very different understandings of liberty held by Indigenous peoples and governments. For the former, the liberty conferred by treaties meant freedom to hunt and trap, and implied a guarantee of their ability to do so; for the latter, liberty was one of the three critical commitments of colonial society's increasingly robust embrace of the liberal order, along with property rights and equality before the law. Colonial governments were generally steadfast in their devotion to "the rule of law" and made this principle the bedrock of their dealings with Indigenous peoples. But the problems and inequities of this, so far as First Nations were concerned, were many. From his Oxford study, Herman Merivale had perceived some of them. Laws were needed to keep avaricious, self-aggrandizing settlers in check, but English law reflected English culture, and extending it to Native peoples who were "ignorant of it" would leave them vulnerable to being "tried for crimes of which they are not aware."[37] Things became even more troublesome when provincial governments enacted laws – such as those intended to conserve wildlife – and insisted that they applied equally to all, regardless of treaty rights. This placed Native peoples who claimed liberty to continue their traditional approach to hunting and trapping at risk of arrest and punishment (and undermined their traditional conceptualizations of property). It was no longer clear that "the deer belonged to the Indian who killed it."

The second source of difficulties for the Anishinaabeg lay in the most venerable of Canadian political thorns: the division of powers between federal and provincial authorities. After 1867, the Dominion government held responsibility for Indians and lands reserved for them, and Ontario controlled natural resources within its boundaries. When Indigenous interests, including those established by treaty, were threatened by provincial legislation and regulation, the federal Department of Indian Affairs proved to be a weak defender of First Nations' rights. There were many reasons for this. A continuing commitment to the acculturation and enfranchisement of Indigenous peoples – aimed at bringing them to equal citizenship within the liberal order – ate away at the obligation to defend treaty hunting and trapping rights. Honouring this obligation would perpetuate traditional modes of life, and inhibit progress toward this larger goal. Yet it could not be denied completely. Agents reported that

Anishinaabeg were unfairly targeted by provincial officials, and their superiors worried about the costs of maintaining Native peoples if they were forced to abandon hunting and trapping before they were ready to be enfranchised; in this bureaucratic limbo, "it was not in the First Nations' best interests to have their treaty rights fully protected but, at the same time, it was not in their interest to have those rights completely denied" (9). Confronting this dilemma, Deputy Superintendent General of Indian Affairs Duncan Campbell Scott, who shared with many of his contemporaries the view that "the First Nations peoples were a vanishing race, and that government had a duty to minimize the pain of their eventual acculturation" (73), acknowledged the historical and legal accuracy of the Anishinaabeg claim that the treaties protected their hunting and trapping activities. But recognizing this would imply that the Anishinaabeg had a degree of independence from the Canadian state, that they were citizens *sui generis*. This was a conundrum beyond the resolution of those confronting it in the 1920s. Rooted in liberal ideology, it haunts Canadians still.

* * *

Framed as a revolutionary challenge to the old European order in which "the church and aristocracy combined to impose an authoritarian vice on society," and tweaked, critiqued, and reformulated over the decades, classic liberalism was tempered by an humanitarian impulse through the early part of the nineteenth century.[38] Then Darwinian theories of evolution and the fueling of racist attitudes by the Sepoy Mutiny in India sharpened the distinction, made by Locke, between civil and natural (savage) states of humankind. It was this harder-edged form of liberalism that historian Ian McKay held responsible for moulding post-Confederation Canada through "the implantation and expansion over a heterogeneous terrain of ... [the] politico-economic logic ... [of] liberalism." In this view, the country is best understood as "an *extensive* projection of liberal rule across a large territory and an *intensive* process of subjectification," inculcating "a belief in the ... primacy of ... the individual" among those who called Canada home.[39] But – observes McKay with mordant acumen – "Aboriginals, the demographic majority in most of the territory eventually to be claimed by the liberal dominion, were people whose conceptions of property, politics, and the individual were scandalously not derived from the universe of Locke, Smith, Bentham, or Lord Durham." By tracing a particular set of struggles to reconcile First Nations' conceptions of land, society, and treaty rights with the power of the (liberal) state through a century or so, *Who Controls the Hunt?* does much to reveal the ambiguities of liberalism as a political and social ideology – even as it reminds us why this matters for Canadians (and many others) in the twenty-first century.

In its standard form, liberalism lays claim to cultural neutrality and colour blindness: race, religion, and culture are private matters of no consequence to a state intent on treating all equally under the law. Admirable though this may seem in principle and at first glance, in practice and in the long run, liberal rule often proves less than impartial. Political theorist C.B. Macpherson famously found reasons for this in the centrality of liberalism's commitment to "possessive individualism." By making capitalist market relations a first principle, reifying "the individual" as "essentially the proprietor of his own person or capacities, owing nothing to society for them," and insisting that all should be subject to the same rules, this conception of liberalism framed the essence of human existence as "striving for possessions." But by defining people as "infinite appropriators," Macpherson insisted, it enabled those possessed of disproportionate strength and skill to acquire more than their fellows, and thus to control the means of labour, which made it "impossible for many men [sic] to be fully human."[40] Conceived thus, liberalism privileged certain identities and neutered the state, leaving it powerless to counteract the imposition of dominant cultures on minorities. In its indifference to race and culture and its insistence that "special" privileges were incompatible with universalist principle, it not only underpinned but essentially created the conundrum of Anishinaabeg hunting and trapping rights.

Yet Macpherson well knew the ambiguities that riddled liberal ideology and its implementation in policy. Influenced by Marx, John Stuart Mill, and the "new liberals" of late nineteenth- and early twentieth-century Britain, Macpherson eschewed the "narrow, materialistic and distorted sense of humanity" inherent in possessive individualism for a broader, more dynamic, and more nuanced view of liberalism that envisaged the free person as "a doer, a creator, an enjoyer" of "uniquely human attributes."[41] This development-democratic strain of liberalism strove "to ensure that all ... [people were] equally free to realize their capabilities;" it set the promise of liberation against the spectre of marginalization and domination raised by unrestrained possessive individualism.[42] Tangled together, these somewhat different conceptions of liberalism shaped many other facets of Canadian policy through the second half of the twentieth century. Ian McKay offers a telling example in characterizing residential schools as "pre-eminent laboratories of liberalism" and "Christian/liberal manufactories of individuals" in which First Nations children "were 'forced to be free' in the very particular liberal sense of free."[43] Here an indifference to culture ratified the imposition of dominant norms.

In much the same vein, *The Statement of the Government of Canada on Indian Policy* (White Paper of 1969), reflecting Prime Minister Pierre Trudeau's principled opposition to special rights for any group of Canadians and his desire to build a more just society, sought to bring about "the full, free and nondiscriminatory participation of the Indian people in Canadian society" by repealing the Indian Act of 1876 and granting Indigenous people "equal status, opportunity and responsibility."[44] Intended to offer a route to emancipation – "To be an Indian must be to be free" asserted the first page of the White Paper – this document envisaged "the replacement of the collective rights of status Indians with greater integration with the individualistic Canadian mainstream."[45] As David Calverley observes, it was "a perfect liberal statement: true equality for Indians requires them to acculturate and give up additional rights provided by treaty. Once that happens, they will be equal and have full access to all the benefits of the Canadian state" (123). In effect, the liberal ethos decreed that separate could not be equal, that assimilation was appropriate so long as both groups received equal treatment (an improbable possibility), and that the cultural superiority of Western values would prevail.

Indigenous resistance to the proposed repeal of the Indian Act was swift and strong, not because those who were subject to its provisions considered it a good piece of legislation but because (as Harold Cardinal wrote in his riposte to the White Paper) they would rather "continue to live in bondage under the ... Act than surrender ... [their] sacred rights."[46] Maintaining that "recognition of Indian status is essential for justice" and, drawing a pointed distinction between equality in law and equality in fact, Indigenous leaders argued that Indians should be regarded as "Citizens Plus," possessed of rights in addition to those of citizenship by virtue of their position as "charter members of the Canadian community."[47] With the withdrawal of the White Paper in 1970 the government stayed its long-standing commitment to assimilation.

A decade or two later, Canadian philosophers Charles Taylor and Will Kymlicka framed important intellectual challenges to liberal individualism and universalism with their arguments for a "politics of difference" sensitive to minority identities. For Taylor, a leading critic of the atomizing tendencies of liberalism, humans are social and political animals who draw meaning and identity from their contexts, and social institutions are essential to their sense of self; to recognize the claims of different cultural perspectives, he favours a "language of perspicuous contrast" or a form of public discourse that highlights "differences between ... cultures rather than attempting to gloss over or reconcile them."[48] In seeking more just treatment of minority groups Kymlicka also acknowledges "that things have worth for us in so far as they are granted significance by our culture" but is more explicit than Taylor in insisting that group-specific rights are consistent with liberalism, reconciling liberal commitments to autonomy and equality with the benefits of cultural group membership and seeking to rectify the "unchosen inequalities" associated with membership of minority groups within a multicultural society.[49]

As these philosophical commitments have been translated, often haltingly, into policy, so many of the limits of nineteenth-century liberalism have been transcended. Through Supreme Court decisions and the Canadian Charter of Rights and Freedoms, the hunting, trapping and other rights of Canada's First Nations are now legally recognized and more firmly entrenched than at any time in the 150 years since Confederation.[50] Yet the various strains of liberalism manifest across the centuries should remind us that the ideas and principles we use to navigate the world are complicated, mutable, and unsteady points of reference, and that the words and deeds that flow from particular readings of them are both contingent and unstable. Barnaby Commanda, Wilson Ottawaska, Joe Padena, and Paul Quesawa – Anishinaabeg men whose stories are central to this book – might well be amazed by the changes that have occurred since they appeared before the courts for contravening the game laws. But change exacts its price – and it is eternal vigilance. Though we may aspire to shape the future, we cannot determine it. The great contribution of *Who Controls the Hunt?* is, ultimately, to remind us that the struggle at its heart continues. Our challenge is to ensure that all Canadians are free to shape their lives in ways that do not deny others the right to shape theirs.[51]

Acknowledgments

Many people helped me create this book. First, I want to acknowledge Michael Behiels, who provided me with critical insights into this topic, particularly the importance of the Constitution as a way of understanding Aboriginal/state relations. I also want to recognize the archivists and librarians who protect Canada's historical records, and who helped me find my way through those records. I would like to thank two people who directed sources my way: Dr. John Leslie (the former head of the Treaties and Historical Research Centre at Indian Affairs) and Dr. Don Smith of the University of Calgary. Hugh Conn's hypothetical Indian, who begins and finishes this study, came from a letter John sent me. It helped me appreciate how legislative issues play out on the ground. Don sent me several important articles and primary sources that helped to flesh out vital details.

I want to thank Randy Schmidt of UBC Press for keeping me on track but never pressing. Graeme Wynn gave me excellent editorial direction and helped polish some very rough parts of my original manuscript. I also want to thank the two anonymous UBC Press reviewers. Their feedback was exactly what an author needs: clear criticism and helpful suggestions for improvement. In fact, everyone at UBC Press has been first-rate.

Of course, any errors in this book are mine; if I could think of someone else to blame, I would.

Finally, I want to acknowledge three people who aren't here to see the publication of this book. As I approach the age of fifty, I increasingly appreciate how much my understanding of the past has been shaped by others. First, I want to recognize Michael Whatmore, my high school history teacher. My love of history grew from his early encouragement and his own devotion to the study of history and politics. Second, I want to remember Robert Surtees who taught at Nipissing University. I took his course "The Canadian Indian in Historical Perspective" as an undergraduate student in 1990. It sparked an interest in Aboriginal history that has continued for over twenty-five years. Bob continued to mentor me as a new teacher and as a historian. When I undertook this book, his knowledge of sources and willingness to read early drafts were invaluable. His knowledge of Ontario's treaties shaped and continues to inform how I understand Aboriginal history. Finally, I want to thank my uncle, Keith Dick, who offered me intellectual encouragement from an early age and whose critical and insightful way of looking at the world informs my views of both the past and the present.

I also want to thank my wife Mindi and my daughters, Abby and Ellie, for giving me the time to work. I missed a few trips to the zoo, the park, and to Canada's Wonderland to complete this book. When my girls came back from their trips with their stories, they knew where they would find Daddy: sitting at the dining room table typing. Now that the book is finished, I can spend more time with my family.

Who Controls the Hunt?

Introduction

What is the legal position of the Indian?
– Hugh Conn

Testifying before a Senate committee on Indian Affairs in 1961, Hugh Conn, wildlife supervisor with the Department of Indian Affairs, spoke of the complexity of provincial and federal wildlife laws in relation to First Nations hunting rights:

> As the law stands at present, an Indian could walk up to the shores of [a lake] ... He is hungry, not starving, and has food 25 miles away in his cache, but now he needs food for one meal. Swimming in the eddy to his left is a small sturgeon. Off the point, about 25 yards out, is one of those red headed merganser ducks and upstream is a female moose heavy with calf. What is the legal position of the Indian? He cannot catch the sturgeon or shoot the duck, but he can shoot the moose. Is it any wonder we cannot, under these circumstances, explain his position?[1]

As legal scholar Kenneth Lysyk noted six years later: "The native Indian finds himself in many respects subject to laws different, and differently administered, from those which apply to other Canadians."[2] Conn and Lysyk were asking who controlled the hunt.

Neither Conn nor Lysyk addressed the fundamental issue: reconciling the treaty rights of First Nations and the power of the state. A non-Aboriginal hunter faced with Conn's hypothetical problem is, in many ways, in a simpler legal position than an Aboriginal hunter. The state defines non-Aboriginal hunting privileges because non-Aboriginals do not possess any hunting rights; the state determines what they can hunt, how they hunt, and when and where they can hunt. First Nations, in comparison, are unique. Their history and relationship with the Crown sets them apart from other Canadians, and they possess rights other Canadians do not possess.

Early studies of Aboriginal treaties largely focused on the transfer of land from First Nations to the Crown, and the creation of both the treaty system and the Indian Department.[3] Later studies examined how successive colonial and Canadian governments broke treaty rights. Historians and scholars redirected their research in the 1980s as Supreme Court decisions and section 35 of Canada's new constitution reframed Aboriginal issues. They began to examine Aboriginal rights and treaty promises that were either not contained in the legal text of the treaties or understood differently by First Nations. These works laid a foundation for understanding how First Nations have historically related to the Canadian state.

This study considers changes in First Nations/state relations between 1800 and 1940, specifically as they pertain to Aboriginal hunting and trapping activity in Ontario. Specifically, it focuses largely on the Anishinaabeg of northern Ontario, the federal or Dominion government (primarily the Department of Indian Affairs), the Ontario government (in the form of the Game and Fish Commission and its later manifestations, which this study will refer to as the Game Commission), and the Hudson's Bay Company. It seeks to explain how the Ontario government and the Department of Indian Affairs sought to deprive the Anishinaabeg of their treaty rights to hunt and trap. It argues that concepts of liberty, property, and equality, as defined by the dominant Euro-Canadian society, shaped political conflicts over wildlife conservation and resulted in the erosion of treaty rights to hunt and trap. This is not simply a story of paternalism and racism, the concepts that define many studies of First Nations history. Both are present and are important components, but they cannot fully explain the resource issues at stake, the constitutional questions, the impact of conservation paradigms, and historical factors particular to First Nations.

History and treaties placed First Nations outside the normal subject/citizen–state relationship. As the twentieth century began, neither the Ontario nor the Dominion government tried to fit treaties into Canada's evolving constitutional framework. Constitutions, according to legal scholar Patrick Macklem, are meant to distribute power "primarily in the form of rights and jurisdiction ... which systematically benefit[s] certain groups at the expense of others."[4] Canada's 1867 agreement, beyond assigning "Indians" to federal jurisdiction, ignored First Nations. It failed to acknowledge that treaties afforded significant levels of sovereignty to First Nations. Already in a weakened position by 1867, the political power of First Nations continued to recede following Confederation.[5] Canada's early colonial governments once considered treaties to be agreements designed to "distribute constitutional authority between Aboriginal peoples and the Canadian state."[6] By the late nineteenth century, treaties became a process whereby the Dominion government could acquire land, extend Canadian sovereignty, and place a legal and political yoke on the collective necks of First Nations. Canada's constitution had no place for First Nations except as something to be regulated.

First Nations and the Ontario Government/State

At the signing of the Robinson Treaties of 1850, the Crown told the Anishinaabeg that they could continue to hunt as they had "heretofore been in the habit of doing." Concerned more with minerals and timber than wildlife, the Crown believed that this was a small concession. It failed to appreciate, however, that it made a promise with no expiry date. As the economic value of wildlife increased, the Ontario government began to reconsider the promise made by its political ancestor. Eventually the Robinson Treaties and the Anishinaabeg posed a legal and constitutional threat to the provincial government and the liberal principles of liberty, private property, and equality, what Ian McKay labels the "liberal order."[7]

First Nations and governments understood the concept of liberty differently. To First Nations, the treaties secured their liberties. They believed (see Chapter 1) that the treaties guaranteed not just their hunting and trapping rights but also the land tenure system that supported wildlife harvesting.[8] Colonial governments generally shared this perspective until Indian Affairs adopted its policy of acculturation in the 1830s and 1840s.[9] As acculturation slowly took hold, the department's perception of treaties shifted from one of securing alliances to one of removing First Nations as an impediment to development. It was an approach adopted by the Ontario government as it moved to diminish the treaties and extend conservation laws to First Nations. As conflicts over hunting and trapping unfolded, Anishinaabeg leaders wrote provincial and federal officials quoting from the treaties. These documents defined and protected their rights – rights the Ontario government denied them. Occasionally, First Nations wrote directly to the King for help. On the face of it, this action appears quaint and innocent – there was no chance the British monarch would embroil himself in this issue. However, it reflects the Anishinaabeg belief that they had liberties other Canadians did not have – rights protected by treaty and their unique relationship with the Crown.

These rights challenged the liberal concept of equality. Equality is a multifaceted idea. A key element of the liberal understanding of the state is every citizen's equality before the law. Under Ontario's ever-broadening and rigid system of wildlife conservation, all Ontarians were subject to these new laws and regulations. Ontario made no provision for anyone who might possess more rights than the average citizen or who used wildlife in a manner that lay outside of the state's paradigm. First Nations have more rights by virtue of history and their treaties, but Ontario could not allow this to hamper the equal application of its laws. It was an attitude that found its genesis in Ontario's colonial past. Legal scholar Sidney Harring outlines how First Nations increasingly found the law applied to them in eighteenth- and nineteenth-century Upper Canada regardless of their own legal traditions and treaty rights. This application was less forceful in areas removed from denser Euro-Canadian settlement. As the state extended its authority northward, First Nations found their traditional lives disrupted. As conservation laws encompassed northern Ontario, the provincial state refused to allow for the exceptionality of Aboriginal or treaty rights. Instead, these rights became an affront to the dominant concept of equality. Ontario's new conservation bureaucrats expected First Nations to give up their treaty rights and traditional harvesting practices and acculturate. Acculturation was the path to equality.

With regard to property, treaties and the treaty right to hunt threatened provincial control of an increasingly important resource. Unlike minerals and timber, no one can own wildlife (unless they put it behind a fence or in a cage). Only the Crown is legally capable of owning wildlife. Hunters receive state permission to access this property when they receive a hunting or trapping licence. A licence reflects the hunter's acceptance of the state's regulatory system. First Nations existed outside of this regulatory paradigm. The Robinson Treaties protected the Anishinaabeg right to access this resource (or property) both when they wanted and according to their traditional modes of use; however a non-Indigenous hunter had to access wildlife in a manner sanctioned by the state. An Anishinaabeg trapper could set a trapline on his familial territory, but a non-Aboriginal trapper applied for a licence to use a state-created trapline. Another Aboriginal hunter might seek permission from an Indigenous family to hunt on their traditional grounds to avoid cultural sanctions against trespass. A non-Aboriginal hunter trapped or hunted based on open and closed seasons. Anishinaabeg hunters certainly appreciated when an animal's fur was at its best, but they also hunted and trapped for subsistence purposes regardless of state-established schedules. At every turn, the Anishinaabeg faced arrest for exercising their treaty rights and attempting to continue with their traditional approach to hunting and trapping and their traditional conceptualizations of property. Similar patterns of disempowerment occurred elsewhere in North America as the regulatory power of the state displaced traditional approaches to wildlife. Outlining how state-level conservation laws displaced pre-existing folkways in parts of the United States, Karl Jacoby notes that the state took on a "powerful, managerial role, standardizing and simplifying what had been a dense thicket of particularistic, local approaches to the natural world."[10]

This new faith in conservation fused with pre-existing ideas about inferior and superior races and their ways of life. Conservation enthusiasts soon began to single out and denigrate First Nations treaties and hunting practices. Treaty rights, they argued, made First Nations lazy because treaties allowed them to use improper hunting and trapping practices. Many early conservationists referred to traditional First Nations harvesting practices as destructive, and argued that Aboriginal peoples needed to adopt modern, proper, and scientific attitudes towards wildlife. During Ontario's early colonial period, settlers and officials considered First Nations hunting a complementary and at times necessary support for British settlement. Conservation flipped this idea. Now First Nations were a threat to conservation.

There was also the broader constitutional issue. Under the British North America Act, the Dominion government assumed jurisdiction over Indians and lands reserved to Indians and the provinces controlled natural resources within their borders. Ontario was always touchy in this regard, owing in large part to the efforts of its second premier, the provincial rights champion Oliver Mowat.[11] Mowat brooked no Dominion interference in his empire, and was quick to challenge any effort by Ottawa to trespass on Queen's Park's constitutional jurisdiction. It was an attitude that remained long after Mowat left politics, even when the resource was as economically inconsequential as wildlife (relative to the value of other natural resources such as minerals and timber). While the Ontario government perceived the main threat to wildlife to be First Nations and their treaties, it quickly linked the issue of treaty rights to the Dominion government's control over First Nations. Any effort on the part of Indian Affairs to ameliorate the position of First Nations relative to the game laws met with fierce provincial opposition.

Indian Affairs

After 1867, it is difficult to separate constitutional concerns from many Aboriginal issues. As the power of provincial governments grew, jurisdictional problems with the federal government expanded correspondingly. The *St. Catherine's Milling* decision of 1888, in which the Privy Council confirmed a lower court decision establishing provincial (rather than federal) jurisdiction over Crown land beyond reserves, is the most obvious example of an early conflict between Queen's Park and Ottawa. Christopher Armstrong's *The Politics of Federalism* provides a solid explanation for the behaviour of Ontario's bureaucrats during conflicts with their federal counterparts.[12] They were well aware of their powers under sections 92(5) (provincial authority over "the management and sale of public lands belonging to the Province") and 109 ("Lands, Mines, Minerals and Royalties"). Successive Ontario governments refused to admit that a competing interest in the land and its resources possessed any right of access. Armstrong demonstrates that federal bureaucrats and politicians were equally willing to argue with the Ontario government over these concerns, but his thesis falters when applied to First Nations' issues. Unlike their battles with Ontario over the control of natural resources such as mining and timber, federal bureaucrats did not behave aggressively to assert their constitutional control under section 91(24), "Indians and Lands reserved for Indians." Rather than protect treaty rights and its control over First Nations, Indian Affairs operated using the same liberal concepts of equality, liberty, and property that Ian McKay ascribes to the state. Convincing First Nations to acculturate and adopt these principles (leavened with a heavy dose of Christianity) was the impetus behind the department's civilization policy, and it affected its willingness and ability to protect treaty rights from Ontario's conservation laws. To protect treaty rights would work against Indian Affairs' own policies. Ontario's denial of First Nations treaty rights to hunt and trap forced First Nations to look for wage labour. Furthermore, protecting treaty rights amounted to recognition by Indian Affairs that treaties created a *sui generis* class of citizens, over whom the Dominion government had limited jurisdiction. Recognizing the treaty harvesting rights of the Anishinaabeg meant recognizing a level of independence from the Canadian state. If treaties overrode the Ontario government's jurisdiction over wildlife, a legal precedent would be set that threatened the foundation of federal Indian policy.

Indian Affairs, however, could not ignore the problem created by Ontario's game laws. Indian agents' reports showed that the provincial enforcement officials unfairly targeted the Anishinaabeg. Agents noted that the Robinson Treaties should offer protection, and that restricting Anishinaabeg hunting rights cost Indian Affairs money in increased assistance programs. Indian Affairs, however, saw a problem only with the pace of the restriction. Ontario's game laws were fast-tracking acculturation before First Nations were fully prepared to abandon hunting and trapping: it was not in the First Nations' best interests to have their treaty rights fully protected but, at the same time, it was not in their interest to have those rights completely denied. Indian Affairs favoured slowly whittling away at Aboriginal hunting rights and easing them out of traditional pursuits. Once acculturated, First Nations could be enfranchised and brought fully into the Canadian state. Acculturation offered equality.

Indian Affairs' policy became the maintenance of acculturation while working to convince the Ontario government to show the Anishinaabeg some leniency. This allowed Indian Affairs to accomplish three goals: keep acculturation and enfranchisement at the forefront of its policy, afford (or try to afford) First Nations some protection, and deny the treaties any legal weight. In this context, acculturation takes on a different hue. Indian Affairs did push back against Ontario's prosecution of the Anishinaabeg, and it occasionally pursued legal action against the province, but there were limits to how far it could proceed without undermining its own policy of acculturating First Nations across Canada.

The state is not monolithic, however. Indian agents, usually portrayed as the front-line troops of paternalism, often defended treaty hunting rights. As the actions of the Ontario government became increasingly punitive towards First Nations, Indian agents' efforts to protect bands in their agencies grew apace. Agents saw communities in their charge losing the ability to support themselves through traditional harvesting, and they found it difficult to conceal their frustration from their superiors. This sentiment slowly filtered upward to senior bureaucrats, including the often-vilified Duncan Campbell Scott. Compared with his predecessors, Scott made a substantial effort to seek legal protection for First Nations treaty rights to hunt. After his retirement, the policy he started continued and gained strength. Indian Affairs became increasingly forceful in its efforts, although its efforts were always more focused on maintaining its bureaucratic control over First Nations than on protecting their treaty rights.

Historiographical Issues

Over the last fifteen years, wildlife conservation (and conservation in general) has become an increasingly dominant theme in Canadian historical writing. What is clear from these studies is that local circumstances shaped and directed approaches to conservation. Each province developed its own legal structure to regulate wildlife and how First Nations fit into that structure. Describing a single history of wildlife conservation and First Nations is therefore difficult.

If there is a consistent element to this history, however, it is in the generally negative impact conservation laws had on First Nations. Frank Tester and Peter Kulchyski's study *Kiumajut* is an excellent examination of the conservation regime in the Canadian Arctic and its impact on the Inuit.[13] Using Jean-Paul Sartre's concept of the totalizing regime, they argue that wildlife conservation in the High North reflected ethnocentric assumptions that discounted Aboriginal concepts of land, land use, and wildlife management. Government officials believed that a scientific approach to wildlife would ensure its long-term viability. Mixed into this were the paternalistic goals of the federal government: that the Inuit needed to live as Euro-Canadians (in permanent settlements) and adopt wage labour.[14] Denigrating and then replacing Inuit concepts about the land and its resources were part of the state's efforts to acculturate the Inuit.[15] However, Kulchyski and Tester acknowledge that state actors varied in their attitudes, that they sometimes contradicted official state policy, and that they occasionally joined in resistance against the state.

Some historians portray conservation as a Canadian success story. Animal species and ecosystems under threat received protection and regulation. Governments set aside thousands of square kilometres for parks and preserves and protected Canada's wilderness heritage. Conservation was not a success for everyone, however. The Migratory Birds Convention Act, for example, created many difficulties for First Nations that relied on annual migrations of ducks and geese as a source of food.[16] Historians of national and provincial parks often overlook the fact that these lands were once the traditional harvesting grounds of First Nations.[17] While Ontario's provincial records are scarce on this issue, an examination of Indian Affairs files show that the province not only cared little for the rights of Aboriginal peoples but actively worked against them. One important provincial source, the early reports of the Ontario Game and Fish Commission, shows that successive bureaucrats did not care about treaty rights, and often denigrated treaty rights and First Nations in their official reports. Provincial parks and game preserves often meant that First Nations families lost access to traditional hunting territories, and game wardens and officers arrested those who attempted to re-enter land designated as protected. Mark David Spence notes regarding US national parks and First Nations removal that there is a "widespread cultural myopia" among Americans who believe that these lands were never occupied.[18] It is a perspective that continues to dominate the Canadian scene.

Outline of the Book

This book begins with a contextualization of how the Anishinaabeg of northern Ontario hunted and trapped in the mid-nineteenth century, and how the Robinson Treaties reflected Anishinaabeg resource use. Chapter 2 outlines the origins of Ontario's Game and Fish Commission in 1892 within the broader context of North American conservation. It also situates Ontario's conservation policies within the "Empire Ontario" mentality of the late nineteenth century. Chapter 3 examines the first application of the Ontario Game Act to the Anishinaabeg, their reaction to it, and the lukewarm response of Indian Affairs. It outlines why Indian Affairs, within the broader framework of Dominion/Ontario relations, was unwilling to protect Anishinaabeg harvesting rights. Chapter 4 continues this analysis by describing the Hudson's Bay Company's (HBC) challenge of the Game Act between 1910 and 1914, and the impact this process had on Indian Affairs and the Game Commission. Chapters 5 and 6 outline the efforts and partial success of the Anishinaabeg in influencing the debate at the local level. Chapter 5 outlines how the Anishinaabeg gained allies among some local officials and elites in their attempts to protect their treaty rights. Chapter 6 continues this analysis by examining several issues that restricted not only the Anishinaabeg's physical right to hunt but also their traditional system of land and resource management. Duncan Campbell Scott figures prominently in both chapters as his growing understanding of local Anishinaabeg circumstances affected Indian Affairs policy. Chapter 7 outlines the events surrounding *R. v. Commanda*, and how the failure of Indian Affairs to appeal this decision paved the way for three more decades of indecision about hunting rights.

Lastly, a note on terminology is needed. Throughout the book, I use the terms Anishinaabeg (for the Ojibwa) and Haudenosaunee or Six Nations (for the Iroquois). Although this book is not concerned directly with the Cree, there are references to Treaty 9 in this study. Treaty 9 is composed of several distinct groups or nations: the Cree, the Oji-Cree, and the Anishinaabeg. The Muskegog Cree Council of Treaty 9 adopted the name "Mushkegowuk" in 1987. However, some communities prefer the term *Ininiw*, which means human being. (This term itself has different pronunciations depending on the local dialect.) I use the term Mushkegowuk to refer to the Cree of Treaty 9, recognizing that there are two other nations in the area, and there continues to be discussion about terminology.[19]

I recognize that these were not the terms used by the people studied in this book. Government officials usually used the term "Indian" and did not bother indicating what nation someone belonged to. During this time, most First Nations groups also used the term Indian in their correspondence. I decided contemporary terminology is more appropriate and more precise. Unless specifically noted in the text, "Anishinaabeg" refers to those who reside in the Robinson Treaties area, not the Anishinaabeg of southern and central Ontario.

Other words such as "Indian" are used when they appear in a document or when referring to historical institutions (i.e., the Indian Department or Indian Affairs), past occupations (i.e., Indian agent), or the legal concept of a "status Indian" or a "treaty Indian." I use the term "First Nation(s)" in this study except in the aforementioned exceptions or when the word "Indian" seemed a more appropriate term. The term "Aboriginal," under section 35 of the Constitution Act, 1982, includes the Métis and Inuit. Obviously, this study is not concerned with the Inuit, but the term "Aboriginal" should not be extended to encompass Métis claims to Aboriginal harvesting rights. Métis harvesting claims constitute a separate historical and legal question.[20] In this study, "Aboriginal" refers only to First Nations.

Resolving ambiguity with the words "hunting," "trapping," and "harvesting" is also necessary. This study is concerned with the two first activities only. "Harvesting" is a more generalized term that applies to First Nations use of natural resources. It can refer to shooting deer, trapping muskrat, fishing for pike, gathering blueberries, harvesting wild rice, or cutting down trees. When used in this study, "harvesting" refers to hunting and trapping. Fishing is not considered here. Studies already exist regarding First Nations fishing activity in Upper Canada/Ontario.[21]

I

First Nations Hunting Activity in Upper Canada and the Robinson Treaties, 1783–1850

> *They would still have the free use of all territory ceded to [Her Majesty], to hunt & fish over as heretofore, except such places as were sold to white people and others by the Govt. & occupied in such a manner to prevent such hunting.*
>
> *– William Benjamin Robinson, 1850*

In September 1849, the government of the Province of Canada appointed Thomas Anderson and Alexander Vidal as government commissioners to investigate Anishinaabeg land claims on the north shores of Lakes Huron and Superior.[1] Previous governments of Canada had refused to enter into a treaty with the Anishinaabeg and allowed mining to take place on these lands without securing a treaty. Seeking to defuse the resulting tension, Canada's new governor, Lord Elgin, sent Anderson and Vidal to rectify the situation. Both men possessed considerable knowledge of the region and the people who lived there. Anderson was a former Indian Department superintendent from Manitoulin Island.[2] Vidal was a provincial land surveyor with experience in the north. Starting at Fort William on the north shore of Lake Superior, they worked their way back to Sault Ste. Marie. As they travelled, they met groups of Anishinaabeg at Hudson's Bay Company (HBC) posts and they sought information about both Anishinaabeg hunting territories and their hopes regarding a treaty. It became clear that a treaty was both necessary and desirable, and the commissioners argued in their report that a treaty would placate the Anishinaabeg. In return for allowing the British to use the land, the assembled chiefs wanted monetary compensation for both the land and resources, and promises that they could continue to hunt, trap, and fish as they had in the past. Such a price, Vidal and Anderson stated, was more than suitable. Canada would gain what it wanted and the Anishinaabeg, they wrote, "must be gainers."

That awkward phrase, "must be gainers," reflects how both the colonial government and the Anishinaabeg perceived the forthcoming Robinson Treaties. The government had no interest in interfering in the Anishinaabeg's harvesting activity, system of land tenure and management, or modes of governance. What Lord Elgin and the administration wanted was security of resource development through the application of British concepts of property ownership to the region. The treaty was the legal vehicle through which the state could extend its control over the north and its resources, and protect the property rights of investors who purchased mining licences in the region.[3] Previous administrations, such as Governor Metcalfe's, had trodden on the treaty process and caused violence and conflict. Lord Elgin's arrival and the election of a Reform government resurrected the long-established legal requirement of treaty negotiation established by the Royal Proclamation of 1763. Despite this change in policy, the Elgin government was motivated by the same desire as the Metcalfe government: to secure access to resources in the region.

Similar concerns motivated the Anishinaabeg and shaped their understanding of the treaty. They were as concerned about property and resource rights as the Crown, although their concerns differed substantially. Anishinaabeg leaders understood the legal importance of a treaty and its importance as a prelude to developing a relationship with the Crown. A treaty (or treaties, as it turned out) would guarantee their property rights to wildlife in two ways. Well aware of precedents set by other treaties, the Anishinaabeg believed it would secure future access to wildlife and other resources they depended upon. A treaty would also protect how the Anishinaabeg organized and used the land. A treaty meant that the Crown recognized their land tenure system, such as familial hunting territories. In broad terms, a treaty set parameters for their relations with the state and vice versa.

However, the devil was in the details and these can be understood only by examining the evolution of the treaty system in relation to the expansion of the colonial state in Upper Canada, and by considering how First Nations understood these treaties. It also requires understanding the evolution of wildlife use in the colony in relation to the development of Indian policy and the changing settler perception of First Nations and their use of wildlife.

Early Treaties of Upper Canada

From the Crown's perspective, early treaties, those signed between the late eighteenth century and the 1830s, served a dual purpose. First, they established an orderly means of bringing First Nations into the British fold through the prevention of misunderstanding and conflict. Disputes over land and resources often arose between settlers and First Nations. While some early colonies had generally favourable relations with Indigenous peoples, others, such as Virginia, often came into conflict with them over issues of land and settlement. Britain created its first Indian Department in 1755 to maintain good relations with First Nations, primarily because of their value as military allies. The Indian Department's mandate expanded in 1763 with the issuance of the Royal Proclamation, which established the broad outlines of the treaty system still used in Canada today.[4] Often referred to as the "Indian Bill of Rights" because it represented Crown recognition of First Nations land rights, the proclamation also created the system whereby those rights could be alienated and British settlement facilitated. As settlement spread and immigrant populations grew, the slow dispossession of First Nations and the erosion of their land and resource rights occurred. Over time, British concepts of private property (and private ownership of resources) came to dominate the discourse, both legal and general, in Upper Canada. Faced with a colonial administration steeped in this paradigm, First Nations faced a difficult, if not impossible, battle.

Not all was doom and gloom at the founding of Upper Canada, however. At first, the treaties worked to the mutual advantage of all parties. Most studies of this early treaty period rightly note that Britain's strategic dependence on First Nations after the American Revolution meant it had to negotiate in good faith with them. Thousands of Aboriginal warriors stood ready, given the proper incentives, to protect the colony if relations with the United States soured. This need lasted for several decades, and the foresight of early colonial administrations paid off when hostilities between Britain and the United States resumed in 1812.[5] Disagreements occurred and problems emerged, but the co-dependency of the British and the First Nations meant that neither side could afford to completely ignore the interests of the other.[6]

Beginning with Governor Frederick Haldimand, the early governors did their best to maintain good relations with First Nations. Altruism rarely motivated colonial administrations. Haldimand and his successors wanted one thing: land. Without land, the arriving settlers had nowhere

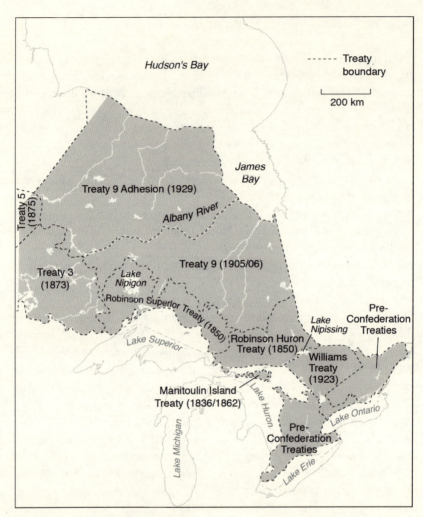

First Nations/Crown treaties in Ontario

to live. However, low rates of immigration and the abundance of land in Upper Canada meant that there were minimal conflicts between settlers and First Nations during the colony's infancy. Backwoods farms were small, and settlements (such as York, Niagara, and Kingston) sat lightly upon the land. There was little disruption of First Nations traditional use of the land. Indeed, the government encouraged First Nations to hunt, trap, and fish and sell the meat and furs to the settlers. Accordingly, early treaties cannot be considered an extension of state authority over First

Nations. Despite language in the treaties about First Nations being subjects of the Crown, First Nations retained their autonomy in what they did and how they did it.

There are few references to wildlife harvesting in the early treaties. Treaties are detailed only in their description of the land being "surrendered," a reflection of the state's concern with settlement and property and disinterest in wildlife and Aboriginal hunting. However, careful analysis of the gifts given to First Nations indicates where Aboriginal concerns lay. First, in return for entering into these treaties, First Nations received compensation generally in the form of material goods such as cloth, metal items, and other sundries.[7] In 1783, for example, Governor Haldimand sent Captain William Redford Crawford to negotiate with the Mississauga chiefs of the Bay of Quinte for a section of land along the north shore of Lake Ontario on which to settle the Crown's Six Nations allies.[8] To obtain the land from the Mississauga, the Crown agreed to provide "[gun] powder and ball for winter hunting, 12 laced hats and red cloth sufficient for 12 coats."[9] Had the Mississauga agreed to restricted hunting in the treaty, it is unlikely they would have received gun powder and ball for hunting. Similar evidence from other treaties signed before 1850 further supports the argument that the Crown never intended to restrict First Nations harvesting.[10]

Aboriginal chiefs and headmen often expressed concern about the impact of settlement on their harvesting activity.[11] At other times, local Anishinaabeg wanted the distribution of treaty presents and annual gifts rescheduled to help them with their winter hunting activity.[12] Such statements and presents did not protect Anishinaabeg hunting and trapping from the long-term impact of settlement, however. As towns and farms grew and lands were cleared and fenced, the Anishinaabeg slowly lost access to their traditional territory. Settlers whose farms occupied traditional Aboriginal hunting and fishing locations refused to grant access to the newly displaced Anishinaabeg. Many chiefs complained to the colonial authorities in York that their bands could no longer hunt or fish.[13]

Until 1814, war and the threat of war gave the First Nations of Upper Canada some influence with the government when such concerns arose. So long as relations between the United States and Britain were strained and Canada remained a convenient target for the republic's displeasure, First Nations remained an important part of the colony's defence. After the Treaty of Ghent ended hostilities in 1814, First Nations transformed from allies into liabilities. The threat posed by the United States shifted from military invasion to the slow infiltration of republicanism. Postwar administrations hoped that increased settlement from the British Isles would combat this perceived menace.[14] Land quickly filled with new settlers, its price increased, and it became necessary to obtain more through treaties. As more immigrants arrived, the size and scale of the Crown's treaties with First Nations grew accordingly. Southwestern portions of the colony filled quickly, and the steady arrival of new settlers led the government to look north to the Bruce Peninsula in the search of land.

At the same time, the paradigm governing Indian Department policy, specifically that of maintaining Aboriginal warriors as allies in case of any future conflict with the United States, ended. By 1830, civilizing First Nations became the Indian Department's new mantra, more specifically, transforming them into farmers and Christians.[15] To this end, the Indian Department created model communities to remove First Nations from the corrupting influence of whites (such as traders exchanging alcohol for furs), and tried to settle them in specific areas with access to farm instructors and Christian missionaries.[16] Some, such as Upper Canada lieutenant-governor Sir Francis Bond Head, considered the policy futile.[17] However, his minority opinion did not last, and the new civilization/acculturation policy persisted until well into the twentieth century (some might argue into the twenty-first). Government officials and settlers increasingly perceived First Nations as a barrier to colonial progress. Removing Aboriginal peoples as an obstacle to resource development and locating them on reserves became the focus of treaty creation.[18] While Canada's policy was more humane than the removal policies of the United States (as evidenced by the treatment of the Cherokee along the Trail of Tears), the state certainly saw treaties as a means of facilitating the creation of reserves and securing "valuable" resources for private investors. As the treaty system moved north, minerals and timber (rather than land for farming) became the resources that increasingly attracted the attention of politicians and investors.

The Robinson Treaties

The Robinson Treaties fall easily within this context. The driving force behind these treaties was not land for settlement but rather land for resource development. Copper, iron, and timber brought prospectors and investors north. Mineral discoveries in the early 1840s along the north shore of Lake Huron and Lake Superior led the government of the Province of Canada to issue mining leases and ignore the Royal Proclamation. As early as 1845, the Crown Lands Department issued regulations governing the licensing of prospectors around Sault Ste. Marie. By 1846, thirty-four companies had government permission to prospect for minerals and ore along the north shore of Lake Superior even though no treaty existed.[19] It took almost five years of Anishinaabeg petitions, some violence, several reports by government officials, and a change in colonial administration before the Crown met Anishinaabeg demands for a treaty. During this period, it was clear that some members of the government perceived the Anishinaabeg as a barrier to the colony's progress. Treaties were not necessary, in their opinion, and the claims of the Anishinaabeg were irrelevant. Progress through mining and logging would not be held back by the demands of a people for whom the colony had no further use. Even when the Reform government assumed power and recognized the need for a treaty (admittedly slowly), a treaty was still a vehicle for protecting state interests in the north. A treaty served the interests of government and investors because it secured their property rights. Rhonda Telford outlines the pressure government agents exerted on the Lake Superior and Lake Huron chiefs to sign the treaties.[20] The Crown's anxiety that a treaty be secured and mining leases protected is understandable considering the money at play in 1850 and the projected future value of the region.

Opposed to this were the Anishinaabeg, who possessed a clear appreciation for their unique relationship to the colonial state and to the Crown. Treaties, from the Anishinaabeg perspective, were not a tool of subjugation but a vehicle to codify and regulate their relationship to the Crown and protect those things they considered important. With regard to wildlife, the Robinson Treaties offered the Anishinaabeg strong protection of their rights. Mainly concerned about mineral and timber rights, the government cared little about wildlife. Vidal and Anderson raised no objections about hunting rights in 1849, and William Robinson was similarly disposed in 1850.

As early as 1840, the Anishinaabeg petitioned the government about mineral development and white prospectors taking resources from the north without their permission.[21] By 1845, there were a number of operations working in the north. Early in the fall of that year, Lieutenant Harper travelled to Sault Ste. Marie in the steamship *Experiment* to investigate complaints of Americans cutting timber on the Canadian side of the border (an issue the Anishinaabeg also brought to the government's attention). Harper reported to his superiors that mines and prospectors were operating in the region even though none of them possessed legal title to the land or the resources. First Nations, Harper reported, recognized only the Hudson's Bay Company's right to operate in the north.[22] Unsure about or unhappy with Harper's report, the government's Executive Council asked Captain Thomas Anderson to comment on the lieutenant's assessment. Anderson concurred, writing that the "Indian title to the Land on the North shores of Lake Huron on the route from Penetanguishene to the Sault Ste. Marie has never been extinguished."[23]

None of this pleased Denis Benjamin Papineau, commissioner of Crown lands. Papineau ignored both recommendations for a treaty.[24] Historian James Morrison has hypothesized that Papineau's hostility towards land claims stemmed from personal factors. First, his property in Canada East was the subject of a land claim. Faced with this problem, Papineau was not inclined to support Aboriginal claims to land anywhere. Furthermore, the British employed Haudenosaunee scouts against French Patriotes during the rebellions in Lower Canada, and Papineau's prejudices might have influenced his outlook. Morrison may be correct, but other factors were likely at play. Politicians at the time did not labour under conflict-of-interest laws. William Benjamin Robinson, the man eventually chosen to negotiate the treaties, was an executive director of one of the illegal operations in the region. When the Reform government took over, these links continued. Morrison notes that senior cabinet ministers were linked to northern resource development companies.[25] It is also likely that Papineau sincerely believed that the Anishinaabeg had no legal right to the land: it was unoccupied (from his perspective) and therefore open to private ownership. Papineau also argued that the Anishinaabeg in the Sault were immigrants from the United States who settled there following the War of 1812.[26]

Papineau's ignorance and intransigence led to continued Crown intrusions in the region. In the spring of 1846, the government sent Alexander Vidal to survey mining properties in the Sault area. Many chiefs on the Canadian side of the border understood the need for a treaty. Two Sault Ste. Marie chiefs, Shingwaukonse and Nebenaigoching, possessed a strong understanding of treaty precedent, and impressed upon Vidal the legal need for a treaty.[27] Shingwaukonse and other chiefs had been taking part in treaties with the American or British governments since the 1820 US treaty at Sault Ste. Marie.[28] He and Nebenaigoching claimed all the land around the Sault, and stated correctly that the government had no right to either sell mining licences or even send Vidal to survey the properties without a treaty. One month later, the chiefs who represented nations from Michipicoten on Lake Superior to Thessalon on the North Channel of Georgian Bay forwarded a joint petition to the governor of Canada.[29] They clearly understood the changing situation in the north, what it meant for their people, and the legal necessity of a treaty to protect their access to wildlife. Some prospectors, the chiefs noted, wrongly claimed "that some of our land had already been sold" to them. Treaties, they stated, already existed for both Michilimackinac and St. Joseph's Island; those agreements allowed the Crown to build military installations. The chiefs also knew about existing treaties with the Anishinaabeg of the Saugeen Peninsula, Rama, Rice Lake, and the Credit River. A treaty, they observed, was not a simple land transaction. It was an agreement between sovereign peoples. They asked for a treaty "in the same form and manner as has always been the custom between our nation and the British government."

Papineau and the Tory administration ignored these petitions. Not until the accession of the Baldwin-Lafontaine Reform government and the appointment of Lord Elgin as governor of Canada was any action taken to deal with the Anishinaabeg's claims. Elgin had a particularly critical view of his predecessor, Sir Charles Metcalfe. Given the period, Elgin was well acquainted with patronage and kickbacks, but even he found the actions of his predecessor and the government excessive. Writing to Colonial Secretary Earl Grey, Elgin noted that

> Metcalfe's Gov[ernment] of Jobbers gave licenses to certain mining companies in that quarter [Sault Ste. Marie] without making any arrangements with the Indians, and I have been occupied for the last two years in getting some compensation for them.[30]

To that end, Elgin dispatched Thomas Anderson northward yet again in the spring of 1848 to investigate the situation.[31] Anderson convened a meeting of Anishinaabeg leaders at Sault Ste. Marie. Chiefs and headmen travelled from as far away as Fort William. Anderson reported the Anishinaabeg's desire to protect their harvesting practices, and their concerns about mining and its impact on wildlife. He stated that the "damage done by the burning of the Forest and the blasting of Rock by the mining companies" caused greater environmental damage than the selective fires set by the Anishinaabeg to encourage certain animal and plant species.[32] Warning Elgin that the Anishinaabeg "will give serious annoyance until their rights be extinguished," he recommended treating for the largest area of land in the history of the colony: all land north of the Midland District to the height of land, and from the western end of Lake Superior to the Ottawa River in the east.[33]

While Anderson validated Anishinaabeg claims to the region, Elgin wanted to know the potential mineral and timber value of the area as well as the potential cost of the treaty in annuity payments. He also needed to know the precise boundaries of the Anishinaabeg territories and their population. In contrast to the previous administration, Elgin's desire for specificity cannot be classified solely as an attempt to stall. Obviously valuable ore deposits were found along portions of the lakeshore, but government knowledge of the interior and its natural resources was virtually nonexistent, and there was also little knowledge of the First Nations who resided in the north, particularly those whose territory was further inland. Budget cuts in the 1830s limited the ability of Indian Affairs to gather data about "remote" areas of the colony. J.B. Macaulay's 1839 "Report on the Indians of Upper Canada" made virtually no reference to the Anishinaabeg of the Upper Great Lakes. Governor Bagot commissioned a further investigation in 1842, titled the *Report on the Affairs of the Indians of Canada*.[34] Its sole statement about the northern Anishinaabeg consisted of two paragraphs that left the general impression that these were "wandering Indians" and of little consequence. This lack of information led Elgin to send Vidal and Anderson northward yet again in 1849 to "[visit] the Indians on the North Shores of Lakes Huron and Superior, for the purpose of investigating their claims to territory bordering on those Lakes, and obtaining information relative to their proposal to surrender their Lands to the Crown with a view to the final action of the Government on the subject."[35] This report is known as the Vidal-Anderson Report.

The Vidal-Anderson Report reflects the government's preoccupation with the region's resource potential. The government's interest lay solely with mining and logging. Settlement, apart from that associated with mines and logging camps, was not part of its plan for the north. The Anishinaabeg's interest, however, lay with obtaining compensation for both the incursions into their territory and the resources extracted, and with securing their way of life. This meant protecting their access to traditional resources, their land base, and their system of land management. Based on what Vidal and Anderson said to the assembled chiefs, the government had no interest in restricting either Anishinaabeg harvesting or the cultural practices that supported hunting. Understanding the content of the Vidal-Anderson Report, therefore, is vital to understanding the Robinson Treaties. It situates the Robinson Treaties as an agreement between two nations, each of which brought its own understanding to the treaties and the process whereby they took these perceptions into account.[36] As legal scholar Jeremy Webber has noted, early treaties were the result of "mutual adaptation, in which the structure of the relationship was formed as much from compromises on the ground as abstract principles of justice."[37] In 1849 and again in 1850, the Crown applied an abstract principle known as a treaty, but the content of that treaty reflected the reality on the ground and in the minds of the Anishinaabeg.

Starting at Sault Ste. Marie in September 1849, Vidal and Anderson proceeded directly to the HBC post of Fort William and retraced their journey back to the Sault. At each of the HBC's lakeshore posts (Fort William, Pic, Michipicoten, and Sault Ste. Marie, and then onward to points along the North Channel and Lake Huron), they met with groups of Anishinaabeg and sought the following information at each gathering: the extent and boundaries of each band's territory, its nature (swampy or forested, types of timber and rock, and so on), and the band's expectations regarding compensation should a treaty be offered.[38] Their evidence was provided in their report as both a chart and a map. Vidal and Anderson were clearly trying to ascertain the cost of any future treaty in relation to the economic return the government could expect in the form of mining and timber development (see Appendix 2 at the end of this book for the chart from the Vidal-Anderson Report).

Their report to Lord Elgin is telling. It reveals how the state perceived the treaties and how the Anishinaabeg understood the matter. Vidal and Anderson thought that the Anishinaabeg placed too high a value on the territory (some chiefs asked for one hundred dollars per annum for every man, woman, and child in their band).[39] The problem, the commissioners outlined, was that the most "valuable" land lay along the shoreline where all the minerals and accessible timber were concentrated; they considered the interior worthless.[40] Anishinaabeg chiefs did not share that assessment. Vidal and Anderson wrote that "there was a general wish [among the Anishinaabeg] to cede the whole [so long as] their present place of abode [and] their hunting and fishing [are] not interfered with" and reservations were set aside.[41] The Anishinaabeg saw ceding all the land as a way to protect themselves from poor hunts in the future and to lighten the credit they took on at HBC posts. Ceding only the lakeshore would help families that lived in those areas without doing anything to help families that resided in the interior.[42] An economic motivation cannot be dismissed, but it does not take into account broader concerns. First, the Anishinaabeg probably believed that extending the treaty inland would protect family territories in the interior. Many families that resided on the lakeshore moved inland during the autumn to occupy winter trapping and hunting grounds. On its face, a treaty would protect their continued use of those territories. Furthermore, the Anishinaabeg probably had enough foresight to realize that mining and logging would not remain confined to the lakeshore for long.

Vidal and Anderson considered the Anishinaabeg's request a small concession in light of the state's interest in the more "valuable" resources on the lakeshore. The Anishinaabeg had their own, and better, idea about the resource value of the north. They knew white miners and loggers were benefiting from their land, and they wanted to benefit as well. Vidal and Anderson understated the Anishinaabeg's interest in minerals and timber in their report. Reflecting the hubris of the time, they wrote that the Canadian state and private investors could develop the mineral and timber wealth of the north with their "superior intelligence and industry" as these resources "never were nor could be of any particular service to [the Anishinaabeg]."[43] In their opinion, the Crown could obtain "all that is known of value" by treaty, while the Anishinaabeg would "retain undisturbed possession of their hunting grounds."

After Vidal and Anderson presented their report, events in Sault Ste. Marie hastened Lord Elgin's decision to negotiate a treaty with the Anishinaabeg. A group of armed Anishinaabeg, Métis, and whites forcibly occupied the Quebec Mining Company's location at Mica Bay on 19 November 1849.[44] Some historians portray the government's response as heavy-handed and a possible variable in the treaty negotiations that followed. Considering the inefficiency of the government's response, this is a questionable interpretation. Elgin responded by sending troops north to Mica Bay, but bad weather forced them to turn back during the final leg of their journey. These soldiers never arrested the accused, who instead surrendered to authorities in the spring of 1850. Elgin refused to prosecute. He sympathized with the Anishinaabeg and noted that years of indifference by the previous government had driven them to desperation.[45] Two prominent chiefs, Shingwaukonse and Nebenaigoching, were released from jail in Toronto and returned to the Sault.[46] When the treaty negotiations began in September 1850, Elgin dispatched soldiers to Sault Ste. Marie on the understanding that these "coercive measures" would not prejudice the "immediate and equitable adjustment of all Indian claims."

William Benjamin Robinson was chosen by the Executive Council to negotiate with the Anishinaabeg. His familial connections to the Family Compact, the elite Tory families who ruled Upper Canada, made Robinson an odd choice, considering that a Reform government was in power.[47] Perhaps he was a compromise choice because of his links to the former government and the companies operating in the north. Robinson was a former superintendent of a mining operation at Bruce Mines (on the north shore of Georgian Bay). Instructed by the Executive Council to secure a treaty for the whole area, but to avoid paying an excessive amount for it, Robinson left by steamer for Sault Ste. Marie on 19 April 1850.[48] Arriving on 1 May (and having completed the final twenty-five miles of the journey on foot due to a late spring ice breakup), Robinson met with the Sault chiefs and informed them of the upcoming treaty talks.[49] Robinson spent two weeks at the Sault writing letters to HBC post managers and local missionaries, asking them to spread word of the forthcoming talks.

Robinson departed for Toronto on 13 May and returned to the Sault on 14 August. Peau de Chat and other Lake Superior chiefs arrived on 21 August, and those from Michipicoten appeared on 2 September. Formal negotiations with all the chiefs and headmen began on 5 September. In his diary, Robinson recorded the promises he made to the Anishinaabeg:

> [I] addressed them, explaining my appt to them, & finished by proposing to pay them $16,000 (£4000) down in specie and an annuity forever of £1000. Explained to them the benefits of a perpetual annuity instead of a present pay[ment] only. Also told them they might make reasonable reservations for their own use for farming &c &c, & that they would still have the free use of all territory ceded to [Her Majesty], to hunt & fish over as heretofore, except such places as were sold to white people and others by the Govt. & occupied in such a manner to prevent such hunting.[50]

While two of the Lake Superior chiefs, Peau de Chat and Totomenai, agreed to the terms, Shingwaukonse asked for another day to consider. Robinson agreed, and the council was adjourned. The following day, Shingwaukonse told Robinson that he wanted ten dollars per head as a perpetual annuity for every member of his band, and a reserve "from Partridge pt below the Sault to Garden River & thence to Echo Lake for a reserve about 15 miles [of lake] front."[51] Robinson told Shingwaukonse that he could not provide such an annuity, and "that they [would] have the same privileges as ever hunting & fishing over the whole territory & to reserve a reasonable tract for their own use." Shingwaukonse's proposed reserve would encompass nineteen mining locations.[52] Robinson could not agree to the request. He informed the chief that since the majority of those assembled wanted to sign, he would proceed without him.

Peau de Chat and the other Lake Superior chiefs assembled on 7 September. Robinson read the treaty aloud and George Johnson, the official interpreter for the treaty, and William Keating, a mining promoter, government surveyor, and former Indian Department employee, translated it to them.[53] Peau de Chat and the others stated that they understood the terms and "were perfectly satisfied & said they were ready to sign it."[54] Peau de Chat said he did not "wish to dictate to the Chiefs of the other Lake how they were to act," but that he and the other Lake Superior chiefs were there only to represent the interests of their bands and they "had done what [they] thought best." After his speech, Peau de Chat along with three other chiefs and five "principal men" signed the two copies of the Robinson-Superior Treaty in open council.

Shingwaukonse was not prepared to accede to Robinson's terms. After the signing, he restated the terms upon which his band would enter into the treaty. Robinson repeated that the demands were excessive, but that he would not pressure anyone into signing. He told the remaining chiefs that "those who signed [would] get the money for their tribes & those who did not sign [would] get none, & I [would] take the remainder of the money back to Toronto, give it to the govt. and take no further trouble about the treaty matter."[55] Robinson then distributed half of the annuity money (eight thousand dollars) to the Lake Superior chiefs to disburse among their bands.

Two days later, Robinson reconvened the meeting to finalize the Robinson-Huron Treaty with those Lake Huron chiefs willing to sign. Shingwaukonse and Nebenaigoching made one final demand: they would not sign the treaty unless the government pledged to give the Métis in the area a free grant of one hundred acres each.[56] Neither chief had raised Métis concerns earlier. This request, in light of the chiefs' earlier appeal for a larger reserve, indicates a further attempt to extend control over a large area of land. If Robinson agreed, the land chosen by the Métis would have been attached to the proposed reserve, giving the local Anishinaabeg control over an extensive area. Robinson confirmed that "certain old residents [could retain] ... free & full possession of their lands on which they now reside," but told both chiefs that he was authorized to treat only with the Anishinaabeg. They were, he stated, free to give portions of their reserve and annuity money to the Métis if they chose.[57] Robinson then had the treaty read aloud and translated. Shingwaukonse and Nebenaigoching were the first Lake Huron chiefs to sign.

The terms of both treaties are identical apart from the land described in them. The written text of the treaty must be considered in light of other promises, however. The Anishinaabeg agreed to voluntarily surrender, cede, grant and convey unto Her Majesty, Her heirs and successors forever, all their right, title and interest in the whole of the territory above described, save and except the reservations set forth in the schedule hereunto annexed.[58]

Clearly the Anishinaabeg did not surrender all of their rights to the land. Based on the Vidal-Anderson Commission, Robinson's diary, and Robinson's official report to the government, the Anishinaabeg believed that the treaty protected their harvesting rights. The treaty document itself notes that the Anishinaabeg retained a substantial interest in the land and the wildlife. The Crown promised

> to allow the said Chiefs and their tribes the full and free privilege to hunt over the territory now ceded by them, and to fish in the waters thereof as they have heretofore been in the habit of doing, saving and excepting only such portions of the said territory as may from time to time be sold or leased to individuals or companies of individuals, and occupied by them with the consent of the Provincial Government.[59]

For some time after the treaties' creation, the Anishinaabeg hunted and trapped as they had and maintained their hunting territories. At least with regard to wildlife, the treaty largely worked. The Anishinaabeg became, as Jeremy Webber explains, "members of at least two communities at the same time – their original society, which continued to govern most of their relations, and, for a much more limited set of questions, the community of all inhabitants, Aboriginal and non-Aboriginal."[60] Unfortunately for the Anishinaabeg, the community of all inhabitants was lopsided. While the Crown yielded to the legal need for a treaty, it did not uphold its end of the bargain as the north changed and the Anishinaabeg began to seek protection under the treaty. Mining and logging remained the most profitable ventures in the region and accordingly attracted most of the state's attention, but wildlife slowly drew the gaze of those who saw profit in the exploitation of a resource that Vidal, Anderson, and Robinson had disparaged. While the Anishinaabeg had "been gainers" in the treaty, at least with regard to wildlife, their victory was short-lived. Before fifty years had elapsed, the children and grandchildren of the Anishinaabeg who signed the Robinson Treaties witnessed the state's trampling of their treaty rights to hunt and trap.

2
Ontario's Game Laws and First Nations, 1800–1905

Indians ... bear a strong resemblance to wolves.
– Ontario Game Commission Report, 1905

Based on their treaties with the Crown, First Nations in Ontario believed they possessed unrestricted hunting and trapping rights. By the end of the nineteenth century, the Ontario government had completely undermined this idea. Pressure from angling and hunting clubs, concerned citizens, and businesses that catered to the growing sport hunting market led Ontario to form the Royal Commission on Game and Fish in 1890 to investigate the state of wildlife in the province. Its conclusions were dire. Wildlife in Ontario, it stated, faced a "merciless, ruthless and relentless slaughter" at the hands of hunters.[1] Left unregulated, Ontario's wildlife and the burgeoning sport hunting market faced a bleak future. In response, the Ontario government amended the province's old conservation laws and passed "An Act to Amend the Act for the Protection of Game and Fur-bearing Animals" (also known as the Game Act) in 1892.[2] It marked the government's most comprehensive effort to bring the province's wildlife under state regulation. Hunters and trappers now faced a range of closed seasons, bag quotas, and outright hunting bans when going after animals as diverse as fowl, deer, moose, and fur-bearing animals.[3] By establishing the Game Commission as the province's first permanent wildlife regulatory body, the Game Act created a new licensing system to regulate hunters (domestic and foreign), and a new system of game wardens (called game overseers) patrolled the province to ensure that hunters complied with the new legislation. Those who broke the law faced arrest and fines. The commission would not tolerate anything that threatened its mandate to protect the province's wildlife. First Nations quickly found themselves targeted by the province.

Ontario's new game laws recast the relationship between First Nations, their treaties, and the state. Treaties the Crown once sought in order to acquire land and resources now menaced its new regulatory system. Treaties subverted the power of the state to regulate and profit from wildlife. However, the legislation alone did not create this new perspective; it reflected the decades-long development of a new conservation paradigm based on the utilitarian value of wildlife.

Colonial Conservation and First Nations

Conservation laws during much of Ontario's colonial period were either nonexistent or ineffective. Everyone, colonist and Aboriginal alike, was free to hunt as he or she wished. Wildlife was part of what is often termed the "commons": a resource that is free and open to everyone. Furthermore, most settlers believed that wildlife such as deer, moose, partridge, and other game was virtually limitless.[4] So long as settlers had relatively open access to such abundance, they saw no need to limit or regulate Aboriginal access.

Early settlers made widespread use of wildlife. Elizabeth Simcoe, wife of Upper Canada's first lieutenant-governor, John Graves Simcoe, kept a diary during her years in Upper Canada. She noted the abundance of wildlife, particularly pigeons, and the propensity of early settlers to fish and hunt.[5] Settlers' letters recount tales of farmers firing into massive flocks of pigeons, swinging sticks in the air, or stringing nets to catch and bludgeon their evening meal.[6] William Radcliff, who settled near Adelaide in the early 1830s, stated that when he went hunting, he could "without failure, bring back one, two or three deer."[7] He also observed that settlers always carried their "fowling piece" while walking along a road or trail to shoot at partridge that came bursting out of the underbrush.[8] Thomas William Magrath, in long letters to Thomas Radcliff of Dublin in the late 1820s, outlined his and his brother's hunting ventures along the Credit River for deer, raccoon, bear, ducks, and other game.[9] J.L. Warnica recalled his early settler days near Lake Simcoe in the 1840s as a time when "the forests, which then covered the land, were filled with game."[10]

Settlers who could not hunt looked elsewhere for a supply of fresh meat. Residents of Upper Canada's small settlements often relied heavily on First Nations to supply game. When Lieutenant-Governor Simcoe arrived in York, he described the inhabitants as "wretched beyond discription

[sic]" due to a lack of flour and fresh meat. He quickly realized that the Anishinaabeg and the Haudenosaunee could supply both York and other fledgling settlements.[11] Writing to Henry Dundas, Simcoe proposed convincing the First Nations "who live near the settled parts of Upper Canada ... to bring the produce of their hunts to those towns and settlements which are about to arise in their vicinity."[12] Eighteenth-century accounts of Niagara's weekend market reveal that local First Nations were already putting Simcoe's idea into practice. Observers recount how the neighbouring Six Nations community would "range the woods for different sorts of game" for their own families and sell "the over plus ... to the white inhabitants of the neighbourhood." One observer noted "many loads of venison coming into the market of Niagara, and [that] it is rare to find in the season a house without the same."[13]

Abundance did not last, and successive colonial governments realized that growing scarcity affected the ability of settlers to support themselves.[14] Game laws began appearing in Upper Canada as early as 1821 for deer and 1823 for salmon.[15] Although they applied to the entire colony, these laws likely reflected growing scarcity in more settled areas rather than the less populated western and northern parts of the colony. In 1845, the legislature passed an act restricting the hunting of wildfowl, snipes, grouse, and quail. A petition to the Legislative Assembly warned that these birds were scarce and settlers needed them as a source of food.[16] By 1851, the province had enacted closed seasons for deer. By 1860, game laws were so comprehensive that they covered deer, moose, and elk as well as wildfowl, fur-bearing animals, and the taking of eggs from the nests of wild birds.[17]

At no time, however, was there any legislated attempt to restrict the hunting rights of First Nations. In several instances, the various Game Acts contained specific clauses exempting First Nations in the province from game restrictions. The previously mentioned 1845 legislation protecting snipes and quail noted that "nothing in this Act contained shall extend to or be construed to extend to the people usually called Indians." Similar wording was found in the 1851 legislation. In 1829, the colonial legislature passed "An Act the Better to Protect the Mississauga Tribes, Living on the Indian Reserve of the River Credit." This legislation made it an offence for anyone other than a band member to hunt or fish on the reserve without the consent of three headmen.[18]

Two factors explain this exemption. First, wildlife had ceased to be a subsistence activity for settlers by the mid-nineteenth century. As farms grew and became increasingly productive, hunting became a supplementary activity.[19] Wildlife was becoming scarce enough to attract the attention of legislators, but not enough to enact serious restrictions. Second, declining wildlife worked in the Indian Department's interest. Some officials hoped that reduced wildlife would eventually force First Nations to settle and adopt farming. In 1845, the Bagot report recognized the increasingly meagre supply of game in the colony but hypothesized that "its entire extinction ... might be ultimately more beneficial to the Indians than its most rigid preservation ... As the Game is destroyed the Indians take to the cultivation of land for sustenance."[20] Thomas Anderson, who later took part in the 1849 commission with Alexander Vidal, made similar observations in the Pennefather report of 1857. Anderson noted that Mohawks on the Bay of Quinte who hunted often left the reserve for up to two months in the autumn; prolonged absences made acculturation more difficult.[21]

Ontario's Game Act, 1892

When wildlife attracted the attention of the state, it put in place a system for maximizing profit and revenue by regulating hunting and protecting wildlife. Two factors converged to bring the Game Act into being. First, the act marked Ontario's jurisdictional victory over Ottawa. Second, Ontario's conservation laws exemplified a melding of the two paradigms that dominated conservation in North America: the utilitarian and the transcendental.

Late in the nineteenth century, Ontario fought and won a series of legal battles with the federal government and secured provincial control over other resources such as minerals, timber, and water (specifically the development of rivers and streams).[22] The best known of these legal decisions, and the one that affected First Nations rights most directly, was the *St. Catherine's Milling* decision in 1888.[23] Concerned with the granting of federal timber licences within the Treaty 3 area, which the Ontario government claimed jurisdiction over, this ruling undercut the legal standing of treaties in relation to provincial control of natural resources. Ontario premier Oliver Mowat argued before the Judicial Committee of the Privy Council (JCPC) that the Anishinaabeg possessed no title to the land or resources because "there is no Indian title at law or equity. The claim of the Indians is simply moral and no more."[24] Writing on behalf of the JCPC, Justice Watson noted that the Anishinaabeg never possessed any title to the land. Title rested with the Crown as soon as it claimed the land. Any right the Anishinaabeg had was usufructuary (a right of use), and this right passed directly to Ontario, not the Dominion government, when Treaty 3 was created. Despite the best efforts of Prime Minister John A. Macdonald's successive Conservative governments, Mowat's conception of Confederation and the constitution won.[25] Within a broader historical context, *St. Catherine's Milling* was part of a trend as courts in Canada and the JCPC were largely hostile to the concept of treaty rights.[26]

Constitutional decisions did not determine how Ontario would regulate wildlife, however. Economic utilitarianism, the dominant conservation paradigm in late-nineteenth- and early-twentieth-century North America, directly influenced Ontario's new conservation regime.[27] This approach first emerged in the United States, where the decline in wildlife became apparent sooner than in Canada.[28] However, melded with this materialist approach to conservation was the lingering and alluring appeal of transcendentalism. Best represented by the work of Henry David Thoreau, transcendentalism appealed to those who thought that urban living upset a natural balance in people, who needed access to the wild to remain whole human beings. Having the opportunity, Thoreau explained, to withdraw occasionally to a wilderness refuge enabled one to balance the spiritual, civilized, and primitive parts of one's personality. This was not simply therapy but was essential to maintaining a balance between the "higher, or as it is named, spiritual life ... [and] a primitive savage one."[29] Even within transcendentalism, however, there was a kernel of utilitarianism as it imbued nature with positive qualities from which humanity benefited.[30] The economic value of wildlife remained in the foreground, but the spiritual benefits remained, albeit subdued.[31]

The ethereal benefits of wilderness tourism had a long pedigree dating back decades before the 1892 Game Act. Tourists seeking a respite from the mental and physical breakdown Thoreau cautioned against headed by steamer to Lakes Huron and Superior in the 1860s to marvel at the vast forests, steep cliffs, and raging rivers.[32] Lake Nipigon became a destination for sport anglers in the 1870s and 1880s.[33] The development of railways facilitated this growth in tourism. The building of the Temiskaming and Northern Ontario Railway in 1902 opened the Temagami region.[34] Government survey crews commented on Temagami's tourism potential in 1900, remarking that the region "is an excellent field for lovers of sport and without a doubt, when this country is known to the sportsmen, it will be invaded by them 'en masse,' and districts hitherto untrodden by the foot of man will become the haunts of the pleasure seeking Nimrod."[35]

Canadian sporting magazines such as *Rod and Gun* actively promoted the physical and mental benefits of camping, hunting, and fishing for the many nimrods living in southern Ontario. In the north, one writer claimed, "the brain-fagged denizens of our great cities may find rest, real rest, from the clash and clang, the hurry and worry of the ten months of grind in the treadmill of business life."[36] Summer lodges and camps catered to the wealthier markets of Toronto and other urban areas, where families hoped time in the bush would transform their boys into men of character.[37] It was a sentiment shared by the Game Commission. True sportsmen, it reported in 1897, sought to preserve game in order to protect "those field sports which have done so much to develop both physically and mentally the better men of this country."[38]

While the commission paid lip service to the loftier goals of hunting and camping, its main concern was economic.[39] In its inaugural report, it warned of the impending crisis if action was not taken to protect game:

> Where but a few years ago game was plentiful, it is hardly now to be found; and there is great danger that ... even those animals which have been so numerous as to be looked upon with contempt, will soon become extinct. In many places where game animals formerly abounded, large cities stand today. The clearing of land, the cutting down of the forests, the introduction of railways, the ravages of the wolves, the indiscriminate hunting of the human assassin, and the use of dynamite and net, have all contributed to the general decrease of the game and fish of this land. This is ... a deplorable state of affairs, not only from the sportsman's but from an economic point of view.[40]

"Sportsman" and "economic" were analogous in the commission's mind. Utilitarian management of wildlife, directed by scientific "facts" as the commission understood the concept, was its guiding principle.[41]

To formulate its policies, the commission held public meetings and distributed questionnaires to learn about the state of wildlife in the province. However, the questionnaires reflected the paradigms of economics and profit that guided the commission through its formative years and established the path it would follow for decades to come. Animals deemed valuable (beaver, deer, moose, and other larger game animals) were singled out for special protection. Unprofitable animals, such as porcupines and raccoons, did not receive the protection of the government. No one took hunting vacations to shoot raccoons. Deer received more attention than any other species. There were forty-three deer questions compared with three for moose, elk, and caribou combined. Some questions were concerned with issues of biology. The fundamental nature of these questions speaks to the commission's ignorance about the species. Respondents were asked when breeding, calving, and rutting seasons started and ended. The commission wanted to know when does were old enough to breed, when they gave birth, and whether a doe heavy with young should be hunted.[42] Considering these questions in conjunction with others posed by the commission reveals that its concern for deer biology was economic, not scientific, in origin. Commissioners asked railway and steamship operators, for example, how many "sporting, camping and angling" passengers they carried each year, and the dollar value of such traffic.[43]

So concerned was the commission with the economic viability of deer that it ignored the concerns of Ontarians who hunted. Domestic hunters complained to the commission in 1892 that foreign hunters took so many deer that they could not secure their own supply. Their solution was to prohibit foreign deer hunting until after local hunters had had their season and, if deer were scarce in an area, to prohibit foreign hunters altogether. This sentiment did not sit well with the commissioners:

> It must be remembered that foreign sportsmen put much money into circulation and very materially help the residents and business men in sporting localities, and your Commissioners have therefore to recommend that if it is not thought wise to entirely prohibit foreigners from killing deer in the Province, a permit should be obtained, and a fee paid for the privilege.[44]

Foreign hunting was too lucrative. It brought tourist dollars into the province, and provided a small revenue for the commission through the sale of hunting licences. Over a decade after its initial report, the opinion of the commission remained unchanged. In 1905, it noted that the "money spent in the country by visitors coming here for the purpose of hunting, shooting and fishing, can only be measured by hundreds of thousands of dollars annually ... The mere market value of game as an article of commerce is a trifle compared with the amount of money expended in pursuit of it." In 1906, the commission predicted that the amount of money spent by foreign tourists would "increase tenfold in a few years, if the attractions remain, namely an abundant supply of game and fish."[45]

Licensing and regulating foreign hunters proved sufficiently successful and lucrative that the Game Commission extended it to domestic hunters in 1896. Prior to this, all Ontario residents could hunt two deer each season.[46] Eventually, the commission realized that the honour system was not a solid foundation for a conservation program. Domestic sport hunters were now required to purchase a two-dollar licence from the commission, and settlers (those living in unorganized townships in northern Ontario) had to purchase a twenty-five-cent permit.[47] Domestic licences, according to the commission, not only curtailed the "slaughter of deer by almost one half," but also "furnished a very handsome revenue."[48] By 1898, fees from deer licences alone covered most of the commission's operating expenses. In that year, 3,559 standard domestic deer hunting licences were issued, along with 2,065 settlers' permits.[49] Ontario's chief game warden informed *Rod and Gun* in April 1900 that the number of settlers' permits issued increased to 2,615, and in total there were 6,500 deer hunters shooting during the deer season.[50] More importantly, the warden noted, "an abundance of sport means lots of sportsmen, and a great deal of money annually disbursed by hunters for guides, transport, etc., finds its way into the pockets of the settler."

With safeguards in place to regulate hunting, the commission turned its attention to the depredations of what it termed vermin. Vermin were any animal the commission identified as predators. More specifically, vermin killed animals sought by hunters. Commission reports listed hawks, owls, weasels, coyotes, and foxes as vermin, but the most destructive of all was the wolf. Vying for the infamous distinction of chief destroyer of wildlife were First Nations. Before proceeding to why the commission singled out First Nations as the target of its conservationist wrath, it is important to understand why wolves were considered the most destructive of all animals because the commission drew a parallel between the two.

There was already a long-standing European folk tradition depicting wolves as inherently violent creatures that killed out of an uncontrollable primal blood lust.[51] They killed farmers' sheep and cattle, and they competed with hunters for the same quarry: deer. Contemporary science reveals that wolves rely primarily on small animals as a source of food, and that their hunting of large prey (such as deer and moose) is beneficial to the local ecology. The commission lacked that kind of detailed information, and it made no effort to fully understand the biology and ecology of the species it purported to protect. It relied instead on the anecdotal evidence of its questionnaires to identify wolves as the chief destroyers of deer. Based on this, wolves were described in the 1892 report as "noxious animals," possessed only of "detestable qualities," and completely lacking in courage, which was "absolutely foreign [to their] nature."[52] The wolf was deer's mortal enemy "and the destruction wrought by him is great and merciless ... [deer are] easily overtaken by the band of snapping cowards." Invoking an image reminiscent of the Carpathian Mountains in Bram Stoker's *Dracula,* the commission described the wolves' natural environment as "somber pine forests ... rugged mountains ... and snow covered wastes." Wolves, the report continued, spent their time "skulking" about their mountain retreat, waiting to descend on farms and villages to attack helpless cattle and sheep. If such easy quarry were not available, they turned their attention to deer.

Rod and Gun magazine, a staunch supporter of all that the commission did, shared these sentiments. Its editors called on all provinces to put a bounty on wolves. Such a step was necessary, the editors warned, as deer were a commercially valuable resource and "we cannot afford to satisfy the hunger of the remaining [wolves] by feeding them on venison."[53] Wolves were not beloved creatures. They were an uncontrollable factor in the state's efforts to regulate wildlife.

Given the invective directed at wolves, it is revealing that First Nations were considered analogous. It reflected the commission's belief that First Nations were not just destructive in their use of game but immoral as well. In its 1905 report, the commission stated that "Indians ... bear a strong resemblance to wolves" in the way they hunted. Specifically, they did not "recognize ... close seasons, age or sex. Cow or calf moose is always preferred when required for food, and killed accordingly, irrespective of season or condition."[54] The 1906 report stated that First Nations wasted what they killed and took only the hides of animals, leaving the meat to rot.[55] Perhaps even worse than the dehumanizing 1905 analogy, the commission equated First Nations with an ecological invasion, stating that only those parts of the province not "infested by Indians" saw any increase in game populations.[56]

By comparing First Nations to wolves, the commission made First Nations subhuman and closer to animals. However, the parallel between wolves and First Nations was concerned more with the supposed impact of their hunting than the motivation behind it. Wolves kill out of bloodlust, but commission reports characterized Aboriginal hunting as lazy. Multiple factors informed this belief. First, there was the concept of the sportsmen. "Real" hunters do not take the easy kill. Hunting is a contest between hunter and prey, and a successful hunt testifies to the hunter's skill. First Nations lacked that quality, the commission believed, and the anecdotal information gathered from its questionnaires supported this belief. The commission inquired about two hunting practices it considered immoral: crust hunting and "marsh" or "jack-light" hunting. The former consisted of running down deer or moose in deep snow. The animals flounder as they break through the crust of ice on the surface.[57] Once tired they are easily killed. Marsh or jack-light hunting involved the use of a light to attract animals to the hunter's location. In the questionnaires, the commission asked which "class" of society engaged most in these practices. Of the 468 responses, 309 singled out farmers while 113 accused First Nations.[58]

Although farmers received the bulk of the blame, the commission reports singled out First Nations. Why? Treaties, the commission maintained, kept First Nations in an infantile state because they protected hunting and trapping rights. In its second report in 1893, the commission noted that "where these protected children are domiciled it is almost impossible to bring home to these people the proof of their crime" due to the adverse effects of treaties. In 1894, the commission reported receiving complaints from Ontario residents regarding excessive First Nation hunting. However, it was "almost impossible to bring home to these people the proof of their evil doing, or to punish them by reason of the special privileges which they enjoy as wards of the Crown."[59] Commission chair H.S. Osler echoed this sentiment in 1905, recommending the removal of the section of the Game Act that exempted First Nations by virtue of a treaty promise.[60] Edwin Tinsley, the province's chief game warden, believed that the easy money First Nations made from hunting game and selling the meat to lumber camps, summer hotels, and tourists was the cause of the problem.[61] First Nations, Tinsley said, should take on wage-paying jobs and end their dependency on hunting for their livelihood. He saw such activity as evidence of an inherently lazy people who "should be made to either work or starve, and not be allowed to lead lazy, loafing lives, destroying valuable assets of the Province with impunity."

Tinsley's statement requires some consideration because it encapsulates the various factors that converged in the Commission's attempt to deprive First Nations of their treaty rights. In reverse order, Tinsley states that wildlife is a provincial asset, an asset over which the province has constitutional jurisdiction. These assets are also valuable, a reflection of the utilitarian paradigm that dominated conservationist thinking and approaches during this period. Finally, First Nations are lazy, and if they cannot work (or acculturate), they should starve. Within the final assumption lay a possible solution to the problem: a civilization program to teach First Nations how to hunt properly. Wolves cannot be changed; it is in their nature to be violent. However, if First Nations are "protected children," the solution is obvious: remove the protection and educate them as one would a child. To this end, in 1895 the commission suggested sending a competent man well versed in the Indian languages, to make a tour of the Indian reserves in the northern portion of the Province, for the purpose of convincing the Indians that they are acting very foolishly and very much to their own detriment, in the useless and indiscriminate slaughter of game.[62]

Ontario never initiated a hunting education program for First Nations; instead, it worked actively to neutralize any protection offered by treaties despite the clear protection given to First Nations in the original 1892 Game Act:

27(1) ... nothing herein contained shall be construed to affect any rights reserved to or conferred upon Indians by any treaty or regulation in that behalf made by the Government of the Dominion of Canada with reference to hunting on their reserves or hunting-grounds.[63]

Despite the unambiguous wording of the clause, the government, enforcement officers, and provincial courts ignored this clause when hunters took game on their traditional territories. Why judges and magistrates overlooked the clear wording of the legislation is impossible to determine.[64] Considering the hostility towards Aboriginal hunting, one wonders how section 27(1) even made it into the commission's founding legislation. H.S. Osler, an early head of the commission, recommended removing the exemption in 1905, but it remained in place until the legislation was amended in 1913.[65]

For First Nations, the issue was moot. They were being arrested for hunting off reserve regardless of section 27(1). Disenfranchised and derided by Euro-Canadian society, Aboriginal people were easily singled out by the Game Commission as detrimental to its conservation plans. The state could easily break treaty promises regarding hunting and trapping, regardless of how explicit they were.

In one century, First Nations in Ontario went through several stages in relation to wildlife and hunting. First, they were welcome providers of wild game to Upper Canada's fledgling settlements. Later, they were hunting a resource the state cared little about. Finally, with the advent of the conservationist movement, they became a menace to the viability of an important economic resource. In all of these stages, there is a consistent theme: as long as First Nations do not conflict with Euro-Canadians' perception and use of wildlife, there is no problem. Once wildlife became a useful and valued resource, Aboriginal hunting became problematic. From the perspective of the Game Commission, First Nation hunting was not simply a threat to conservation but bordered on barbarism. So convinced was the commission in the rightness of its cause that it vilified First Nations. Aboriginal hunting was not simply (from the commission's perspective) wrong in a technical sense; it was an immoral act. Treaties were not just political problems to be overcome as the province sought to implement conservation laws, but a threat to the entire conservation paradigm. Treaties were the root of the entire problem, and First Nations were the manifestation of that problem. Treaties enabled a simplistic and childlike group of people to decimate the province's resources. They prevented the state from applying its laws effectively, and allowed a segment of society to exist outside of the laws that applied to all other citizens. This rigid view dominated the Game Commission for decades. As the politics around Aboriginal hunting in Ontario developed, it became clear that the commission's goal was to defeat any threat to both conservation and (by extension) the province's control of wildlife as a natural resource. Treaty rights were not a factor that the Game Commission could work into its equation. Such rights, and the First Nations who wanted to exercise them, were wild cards in the commission's well-planned, scientific approach to conservation. First Nations existed in a constitutional no man's land due to their treaty rights: they were bound to most laws of the province, but they existed within a special legal framework since they were a Dominion responsibility and possessed a unique relationship with the Crown. It was a no man's land that Ontario intended to occupy.

3
First Nations, the Game Commission, and Indian Affairs, 1892–1909

Indians had the right to kill moose under the Robinson Treaties.

— *Chief Semo Commanda*

Semo Commanda, chief of the Nipissing Reserve just west of the town of North Bay, was angry. His brother Barnaby Commanda and another band member, Wilson Ottawaska, had been arrested for hunting moose out of season in violation of a province-wide ban. Barnaby Commanda had shot a moose for himself and his family, and agreed to sell some of the excess meat to a Canadian Pacific Railway (CPR) survey crew working in the area. He enlisted Ottawaska's aid in transporting the meat to the crew. Joseph Rogers, an inspector working with Ontario's Department of Crown Lands, learned of the incident, arrested both men, and brought them before the local magistrate. At their trial in August 1898, both pled guilty to hunting moose.[1] Commanda paid a fifty-dollar fine, and the court confiscated the moose meat and his rifle. Ottawaska could not afford to pay the fine and was sentenced to thirty days' hard labour in the Sudbury jail.[2] Chief Commanda dictated a letter to George Chitty, the local Indian Affairs timber agent, and sent it to Indian Affairs in Ottawa. The arrest, the chief contended, was an outrage as "Indians had the right to kill moose under the Robinson Treaty."

While Indian Affairs grudgingly accepted that the Robinson Treaties protected Anishinaabeg hunting and trapping rights, it was unwilling to protect those rights if it required a legal conflict with the Game Commission. Conflicting and complementary interests on both the provincial and federal levels coalesced in such a way that Anishinaabeg complaints remained unaddressed. From the Game Commission's perspective, treaty rights threatened a valuable provincial resource. The commission considered First Nations to be uncivilized and savage, a random force that would plunder Ontario's wildlife if left unchecked. Further influencing this assessment was the commission's opinion that treaties only enabled First Nations to hunt recklessly. Ontario's position, therefore, was firm: no exceptions would be made for First Nations regardless of any treaty they might have with the Crown or the explicit wording of the Game Act.

Indian Affairs was in a more difficult position. It had no developed policy relating to provincial game laws. As it dealt with the first arrests and the issues, its policy became one of convincing Ontario to show some leniency towards First Nation hunters while at the same time encouraging those same hunters to respect the game laws. It was a hopelessly confused approach. Indian Affairs could not effectively counter the commission since its own policy towards First Nations continued to be one of "protection, civilization and assimilation."[3] It did not want to encourage traditional hunting among First Nations and it amended the Indian Act in 1890 to permit the Governor-in-Council of Manitoba and the North-West Territories to apply wildlife conservation laws to them.[4] Indian Affairs believed that parents who continued to follow traditional pursuits were "retarding the education of [their] children" by keeping them out of school during hunting and trapping season.[5] Given its own low opinion of Aboriginal hunting, it was difficult for Indian Affairs to convince provincial officials that First Nations deserved special treatment.

Even if Indian Affairs wanted to adopt a more aggressive policy regarding treaty hunting rights, it lacked the physical and political resources to challenge Ontario. In the 1880s, Indian Affairs headquarters in Ottawa employed only thirty-eight people, including janitors and box packers.[6] Those assigned to bureaucratic endeavours were split among three branches: Accounts, Lands and Timber, and a Secretariat.[7] Specialized legal offices did not exist. Physically small (it filled a cluster of offices in the East Block of Parliament), Indian Affairs was equally irrelevant to the Dominion government's larger policies. It was part of the Department of the Interior, subordinated to the greater concerns of Conservative and Liberal administrations preoccupied with railway construction and western settlement. When Clifford Sifton became minister of the interior in 1896, his interests lay with western settlement and immigration.[8] Sifton once proposed selling uncultivated reserve land in western Canada to settlers whenever he pleased. Officials told Sifton that Indian Affairs could not simply sell reserve land without a vote by all the adult males in a band.[9]

With Wilfrid Laurier at the helm, it was unlikely that the Dominion government would jump back into the constitutional fray and challenge provincial autonomy. The previous Conservative government had pricked the provinces sufficiently (Ontario in particular) over the question of provincial rights. Former Ontario premier Oliver Mowat was Laurier's first minister of justice (July 1896 to November 1897). There was little chance that Mowat would drop his mantle of defender of Ontario's rights and challenge the legality of Ontario's new game laws. If any political support for Indian Affairs existed, it would not be found in a Liberal administration.[10]

Senior officials exacerbated bureaucratic inertia at Indian Affairs. Bureaucrats usually ran Indian Affairs with minimal interference from their political masters. Lawrence Vankoughnet was firmly in charge during his tenure as deputy superintendent general (1874–93).[11] Institutional apathy was also the norm at the department, and Vankoughnet's officials took little interest in their work.[12] His successor, James Smart (1896–1905), could not devote his attention entirely to Indian Affairs as he was made responsible for the entire Department of the Interior.[13] Sifton saddled Smart with these additional responsibilities of reducing expenditures and cutting staff.[14] Consumed with western settlement and immigration, Smart left the day-to-day running of Indian Affairs to its ubiquitous secretary, J.D. McLean.

McLean remained in his position until the 1920s and laid the policy groundwork for Indian Affairs' response to hunting claims. One year before the Commanda/Ottawaska arrest, he asked the Department of Justice for an opinion regarding treaty rights to hunt in relation to the Ontario Game Act. Acting deputy minister Augustus Power, advised that the Ontario legislature was well within its constitutional jurisdiction when regulating wildlife and applying those laws to First Nations.[15] Power conceded that the Game Act of 1897 explicitly exempted First Nations, but in light of the Ontario government's interpretation of the legislation, he counselled against appealing any convictions.[16] He cautioned that the Ontario government would simply amend the legislation, and First Nations would be in a worse predicament.[17] One year later, E.L. Newcombe, the newly appointed deputy minister of justice, offered McLean similar advice, and confirmed the attorney general's interpretation of the Game Act.[18] Neither Power nor Newcombe suggested that treaties were relevant to the issue. Given such advice, McLean's reluctance to challenge Ontario's game laws becomes easier to understand. Justice officials saw no legal solution to the problem. McLean also served an indifferent minister in a government that was unlikely to challenge Ontario's constitutional jurisdiction.

Indian Affairs' impotence became apparent in the Commanda/Ottawaska arrest. It was Chief Commanda who retained two North Bay lawyers, Browning and Leask, to ascertain the band's treaty rights. Working pro bono, they wrote to Clifford Sifton and outlined the local legal confusion surrounding the hunting rights of the Nipissing Band.[19] Both the local Indian agent and the deputy game warden in North Bay had informed the Nipissing Band on earlier occasions that treaty Indians could hunt moose and sell the meat if they used the money for personal necessities, a view rejected by the magistrate. Sifton passed Browning and Leask's letter on to Smart, who passed it down to McLean. McLean's advice to Commanda's lawyers was to appeal directly to the magistrate for leniency.[20] McLean did follow up with Ontario's Attorney-General, who responded unequivocally that the Game Act "only protects Indians in the same way it protects settlers, and that ... such was the intention of the Act."[21]

There was a legal argument supporting First Nations' entitlement to hunting and trapping. In the *St. Catherine's Milling* decision (1885), the Judicial Committee of the Privy Council (JCPC) decided that Aboriginal tenure was "a personal and usufructuary right dependent upon the good will of the Sovereign," and that the Crown possessed "a substantial and paramount estate ... underlying the Indian title."[22] However, the ruling implied that this title was linked to hunting, trapping, and fishing, since the Royal Proclamation of 1763 had reserved land to the First Nations for their use as hunting grounds.[23] The *St. Catherine's Milling* decision certainly left open the possibility of challenging Ontario's Game Act. If Aboriginal title centred on traditional harvesting activity, and this activity was dependent upon the "good will of the Sovereign" (i.e., the Dominion government), then the question of whether the province could affect something which had been specifically protected by a treaty, reserved to the Anishinaabeg, and allocated to the Dominion government as a constitutional responsibility remained unanswered.

This interpretation found further legal support in *Ontario Mining Company v. Seybold*.[24] This 1901 case was concerned with a portion of Reserve 38B (Treaty 3) that the band surrendered to the Dominion government in 1886. The Dominion then granted a portion of that land to the Ontario Mining Company in 1889. Almost concurrently, the Ontario government granted the same portion of land to another mining company. Canada's Supreme Court ruled that once the Dominion effected the surrender of that portion of Reserve 38B, sole proprietary ownership passed to the province. It also stated that the surrender did not abrogate any existing treaty rights to engage in traditional harvesting activity.²⁵ The Supreme Court referred specifically to the JCPC's earlier decision in *St. Catherine's Milling* and section 109 of the British North America Act to explain that Ontario's interest in the land was subject to restriction:

> It was decided by this Board in the *St. Catherine's Milling Co.'s Case* that prior to that surrender [Treaty 3, 1873] the province of Ontario had a proprietary interest in the land, under the provisions of s. 109 of the BNA Act, 1867, subject to the burden of the Indian usufructuary title, and upon extinguishment of that title by the surrender the province acquired the full beneficial interest in the land *subject only to such qualified privileges of hunting and fishing as was reserved to the Indians in the treaty.*²⁶

In other words, Anishinaabeg interest in wildlife persisted following a formal land surrender, if this interest was noted and protected under the terms of the treaty.

Despite legal precedent, Indian Affairs was advised to negotiate with the Game Commission.²⁷ McLean and his superior, Deputy Minister James Smart, adopted an interesting tactic in their negotiations. At the heart of the strategy was avoiding conflict and confrontation with the Game Commission. McLean and Smart tried to convince the commission that leniency for First Nations hunters was in its interest. Allowing First Nations to hunt for food or obtain a bit of money would prevent a band from hiring its own lawyers to fight any future conviction. If a band were successful in court, a legal precedent would exist that supported treaty hunting rights.

McLean first applied this strategy when he followed up on the Commanda/Ottawaska conviction. Never in his letters to Ontario provincial secretary E.J. Davis did McLean mention that Indian Affairs was challenging Ontario's game laws. Instead, he warned Davis that Chief Commanda might appeal the conviction because of the Robinson Treaties, and that the Game Act itself protected "Indian [hunting] rights reserved to them by treaty."²⁸ McLean also stated that Commanda's sale of the moose meat could be justified within the parameters of the legislation: an Indian could sell meat from an animal killed for personal use if the money was used to obtain necessities for himself and/or his family.

McLean warned that a victory for Commanda was not in the Game Commission's interests. It would neuter Ontario's game laws when applied to treaty Indians and make it impossible to regulate First Nations hunting. McLean's message to Davis was the necessity of keeping power and control over First Nations with the Game Commission and Indian Affairs. Reflecting his desire to effect a compromise, McLean proposed that First Nations be allowed to hunt at all seasons on public lands for their own personal use, but suggested that Ontario prevent First Nations from selling meat commercially by "making stringent provisions to prevent the purchase from them, by anyone, of game during the closed season." Prosecuting buyers circumvented the treaties, and any First Nations argument about a right to sell meat commercially was bound to fail in court. McLean also asked that the fine paid by Commanda and his confiscated gun be returned without the band's having to turn to a court of appeal (by this point Ottawaska had already served his thirty-day sentence).

McLean's letter was the first in an effort to push to provincial officials towards a more relaxed policy towards First Nations. If it did not work, Indian Affairs was willing to press further. McLean's letter was passed to J.M. Gibson, Ontario's commissioner of Crown lands. Gibson bypassed McLean and wrote to James Smart, contending that a local CPR survey crew had employed Commanda and Ottawaska full-time to hunt (something both men admitted in court).[29] Successful conservation, the commissioner concluded, demanded that no provincial official, from local game wardens and magistrates to senior civil servants, show any leniency towards those who had broken the law.

Smart and McLean had anticipated the province's response, and had already gathered further information from Indian Affairs' timber agent in the North Bay area, George Chitty. Chitty was supportive of Chief Commanda; he helped the chief compose the initial letter to Indian Affairs at the time of the arrest. Chitty now provided McLean with information that Gibson and the province chose to ignore. First, Commanda shot the moose for his and his family's personal use and sold only excess meat for a price and an additional transportation charge of $1.50 per day. With this evidence in hand, Smart pressed the issue with the commissioner of Crown lands.[30] He drew Gibson's attention to irregularities in the case and the potential for an appeal. First, Commanda and Ottawaska had pleaded guilty only to hunting out of season, not to selling moose meat. If this was the charge, Smart continued, then he failed to understand the conviction because the Game Act exempted treaty Indians from the legislation. The magistrate also failed to refer to any section of the Game Act when he sentenced the two men. Smart further contended that the proceedings were unfair. The magistrate acted improperly during the trial because he elicited a statement from Commanda and Ottawaska that they worked for the CPR survey crew to supply meat. In so doing, the magistrate abandoned the role of adjudicator and took up that of the prosecutor. This action denied Commanda and Ottawaska a fair trial. Furthermore, both men may have been duped, inadvertently or otherwise, into stating that they were employed by the survey crew, because neither possessed a sound knowledge of English and no interpreter was employed at the trial. Smart therefore posed a simple question: if neither man properly understood the charges brought against them, and if they were not warned that any admissions they made, elicited by no less than the magistrate, could be used against them, did they receive a fair trial? With the legal ball firmly in Gibson's court, Smart concluded that Indian Affairs was willing to wait until the commissioner found a convenient time to discuss the matter.

Months passed without a response from Gibson. In the meantime, the game laws were strengthened and increased pressure was brought to bear on the Nipissing Band. The commission sent inspector Joseph Rogers to investigate Anishinaabeg hunting along the North Channel of Georgian Bay.[31] In the spring of 1899, Rogers reported that men from the Nipissing Reserve were the chief culprits in overhunting.[32] When questioned by Rogers, hunters said that "they would do as they liked, [and] that the Ontario Government could not do anything about it." Further indicting the Nipissing people, Rogers's report detailed an entire distribution system. Rogers concluded that the only way to stop this slaughter was to arrest and convict several of the offending Anishinaabeg and punish them as severely as possible.

Rogers's recommendation found a ready ear at the Department of Crown Lands, and sparked another round of correspondence between Gibson and Smart. Smart attempted once again to raise the possibility of an appeal, but after months of stalling this possibility was increasingly remote. With Rogers's report in hand, Gibson denounced Anishinaabeg complicity in decimating the northern moose population. He advised Smart that the Game Commission would take sterner action against the Nipissing Reserve.[33] Some members of the band, he maintained, believed that the "big Government" in Ottawa would protect them from the Game Act, and too many moose were being killed as the Nipissing hunters believed themselves exempt from provincial laws. Gibson put forth one option for the Nipissing Band: adhere to the moose ban, and in a few years a short season would be opened. This would provide them with the opportunity to find work as guides for visiting sportsmen. Indian Affairs' only role in this, Gibson concluded, was convincing the Nipissing Band that "their true and permanent interests are in protecting the deer and moose."

Smart's response was weaker than his original letter. He knew that Indian Affairs was limited in what it could do. He drew Gibson's attention to the confusion regarding the legal position of the Anishinaabeg.[34] Regarding the Nipissing Band's belief that the government in Ottawa would protect them, Smart assured Gibson that Indian Affairs was not encouraging this attitude, but the First Nations needed clarity about "what constitutes a breach of the game ordinances." This led Indian Affairs to occasionally give the accused the benefit of the doubt, and the bands had misconstrued this as support and protection. He argued that non-Aboriginals interested in obtaining meat and pelts had exacerbated the situation by convincing members of the Nipissing Band, who Smart contended were easily duped, to break the game laws.[35]

The Ontario government eventually realized that its own legislation was part of the problem and amended the Game Act. The specific textual changes to the Game Act (it was amended four times between 1900 and 1905) did not directly target First Nations or their treaty rights, but considering the attorney general's earlier statement that First Nations and settlers were analogous, they are important. Section 32(1), which dealt with "Indians and settlers killing, etc., for food," was amended in 1900. It stated that First Nations and settlers residing in unorganized townships or territories could still kill game for their own use as food, or for necessities. Furthermore, it said the act would not affect "any right specially reserved to or conferred upon Indians by any treaty or regulations in that behalf made by the Government of the Dominion of Canada with reference to hunting on their reserves or hunting-grounds."[36] In this regard, the 1900 amendment was the same as the 1896 version; however, there now existed an additional condition "that no settler shall hunt, take, kill or have in his possession any moose, reindeer or caribou except in any year when the same may be lawfully killed according to the provisions of this Act."[37] While the wording clearly indicated that this condition applied only to settlers, considering earlier statements made by the attorney general and the commissioner of Crown lands, it is clear that "settlers," from their perspective, was analogous to "Indians."

The Game Act of 1900 further affected the Anishinaabeg by banning the hunting of some animals and creating restricted hunting seasons for others. While a moose season was created (from 1 to 15 November for 1900 and every third year thereafter), the act was also amended to ban all beaver and otter trapping throughout Ontario until 1 November 1905.[38] After that date, the beaver and otter season would be open from 1 November to 31 March; however, when 1905 finally arrived, the beaver and otter ban was extended to 1910.[39] Apart from any treaty rights, the province gave no thought to the Anishinaabeg, who relied on beaver not just as a source of furs (for trade) but also as a source of food.

When another member of the Commanda family (Francis) was arrested in the early winter of 1906, Indian agent George Cockburn asked Indian Affairs whether it could secure Commanda some leniency. Secretary McLean's response reveals that Indian Affairs had effectively conceded to Ontario the right to determine the nature and extent of treaty hunting rights. McLean informed Cockburn that "the Department is not aware of any exemptions in favour of Indians in the province of Ontario from the operation of the statutes other than those granted by the statutes."[40] McLean concluded that his department was "powerless to protect Indians from the consequences of their own disregard or defiance of lawful [provincial] authority."[41]

Lacking support from their superiors, some Indian agents began to cooperate with bands and chiefs in dealing with both the Game Commission and Indian Affairs. In 1909, Frank Ogima of the Fort William Band was arrested for killing a moose out of season.[42] Ogima's arrest was not an isolated incident in the area, and it brought the matter of hunting rights to a head with his band. William McDougall, the local Indian agent, told the bands under his authority that they could hunt for food. McDougall's instruction, in light of events, was clearly at odds with Indian Affairs' directives. McDougall and Fort William chief Moses McCoy both wrote letters to McLean. Chief McCoy's letter (with which he almost certainly received assistance from McDougall) drew McLean's "attention to the hardships which are imposed upon the Indians of the Robinson-Superior Treaty by the present game laws in the Province of Ontario."[43] Not only did the Game Act prevent the Anishinaabeg from hunting, McCoy said, but their fishing was restricted on both Lake Nipigon and the Nipigon River.[44] These restrictions, he argued, meant that the province denied the band an important part of their livelihood. McCoy quoted the portion of the Robinson-Superior Treaty relating to hunting rights, and he asked McLean to have the game law restrictions removed so the Anishinaabeg could "hunt for a living as we have heretofore been in the habit of doing and as promised in the Treaty."[45]

McDougall's letter supported and reiterated Chief McCoy's arguments. He sent McLean extracts from both the Robinson-Superior Treaty and the provincial Game Act related to hunting. He also highlighted an important element of Ogima's case: Ogima had killed the moose during an open season but he did not possess a valid licence. McDougall noted that the issue was whether "an Indian has a right to kill moose or deer in an open season without a hunting license."[46] It was an issue of some frustration for both the agent and the Fort William Band. McDougall pleaded that "the Dept. should take a definite stand either to say the Indian has no further right than a white man or protect him in so far as his rights go." McLean's response offered neither the agent nor Ogima any hope. The game laws, McLean said, apply to First Nations as well as to other Ontarians "except in so far as the Indians are specifically exempted [in the legislation]."[47] Since the Game Act explicitly exempted treaty Indians, McLean's advice was useless. Indian Affairs was unwilling to challenge the validity of the Game Act when applied to First Nations.

Ogima's case went to trial. The Fort William Band secured the pro bono services of two Fort William lawyers, Langworthy and McComber. McLean did write to the two lawyers. First, he counselled that it would be "worse than idle" to encourage the Fort William Band or any band to resist Ontario's game laws. He also warned that local magistrates consistently ruled against First Nations arrested for hunting out of season, and an appeal would certainly fail.[48] McLean was not incorrect. The presiding magistrate was so unaware of the legal issues that he wrote to Ontario's game and fish commissioner and asked whether the game laws applied to First Nations hunting off reserve. The commissioner replied that "Indians off their reserve are amenable to the laws which have been enacted for the protection of game and fish the same as anyone else."[49] Unsurprisingly, Ogima was found guilty.

By 1910, Indian Affairs had concluded that First Nations were subject to Ontario's game laws and that it would not make any attempt to protect those rights. McLean and Smart cajoled Ontario bureaucrats into being lenient towards First Nations, but their unwillingness to support legal appeals and to challenge the Game Commission created a hollow and insubstantial policy.

McLean and Smart were not entirely unsympathetic to the hunting rights of Commanda, Ottawaska, or Ogima. They wanted to negotiate, but they were constrained by the lack of political support they could expect if they advocated a legal challenge. Prime Minister Wilfrid Laurier was not someone who would challenge provincial rights. His justice minister, Oliver Mowat, was not supportive. More pressing political concerns consumed Laurier's attention; Aboriginal issues simply carried no weight in Ottawa.

Indian Affairs' own policies further prevented it from challenging the Game Act. Allowing First Nations to challenge legislation, defend their treaty rights, and establish their own political agenda was anathema to Indian Affairs' assimilationist policies. McLean understood that the game laws imposed hardship on Aboriginal hunters, but would not support any effort to alter those laws if it empowered First Nations. If there was to be a challenge to Ontario's new conservation laws, Indian Affairs was both ill equipped and ill disposed to throw down the gauntlet. Within its conception of state/Aboriginal relations, Indian Affairs could not take steps to protect a people it wanted to acculturate.

4
Traders, Trappers, and Bureaucrats: The Hudson's Bay Company and Wildlife Conservation in Ontario, 1892–1916

> *Before too long the Company's exportations from Hudson Bay ... may expect the interest of some one party or another having a sentimental regard ... for the preservation of Beaver.*
>
> – C.C. Chipman, HBC Commissioner, 1905

In 1892, C.C. Chipman, the Hudson's Bay Company's Canadian commissioner in Winnipeg, informed the London-based Board of Governors about Ontario's new wildlife conservation laws. If enforced, Chipman warned, they would affect the Company's Ontario operations "from Mattawa to Rat Portage."[1] Proposed closed seasons for certain fur-bearing animals, Chipman said, would reduce the annual beaver catch by a quarter and reduce the muskrat trapping season by one month, which "practically precludes the spring hunts of Musquash when the fur is at its best." Chipman's concerns were prescient. Over time, it became apparent that the Company's old way of doing things would no longer work in Ontario's new conservation regime.

Prior to the imposition of Ontario's conservation laws, an organic relationship had evolved between the Hudson's Bay Company and First Nations. Through centuries of cross-cultural trading, diplomacy, and interaction, both the HBC and Indigenous peoples developed a mutually supportive system. Like any relationship, it was at times rocky and one-sided. However, the system of trade that developed with the Anishinaabeg permitted traditional hunting practices to continue. It also allowed the Anishinaabeg to sell what they harvested to the Company. This trade was sustained as much by the traditions of the Anishinaabeg as by the HBC's business practices. It is impossible to separate them, as the Company had to adapt to the regions and First Nations it traded with while First Nations had to compromise with the realities of European business.[2]

As the power of the regulatory state moved north, this relationship changed. Problems emerged, but not with the treaties themselves or with Indian Affairs' policies. Indian Affairs had limited interest in affecting Aboriginal hunting except as it pertained to convincing First Nations to acculturate and take up either farming or wage labour. Ontario, however, was a different matter. Its concern over wildlife, its attitude towards First Nations, and its reflexive response to any perceived threat to its jurisdiction led the province to wield its regulatory powers without compromise or compassion. When this occurred, the relationship between the HBC and First Nations fractured. Previous practices (such as trading in furs during closed seasons) became illegal. The fur trade managed to escape serious provincial scrutiny for over ten years after passage of the Game Act. That grace period ended in the early 1900s when the Game Commission turned its attention to trading posts and began to actively prosecute HBC post managers. Eventually, the Company came to believe that its only course of action was to challenge the game laws. Treaties provided an ideal vehicle for driving that challenge forward.

The Company's interest in the treaties was entirely selfish. If successful, the legal challenge would benefit the Anishinaabeg, but this was tangential to the HBC's concern: protecting its control over the northern fur trade. Company officials were prescient enough to realize that conservation laws would affect their trade beyond Ontario as other provinces passed their own legislation. To prevent this, Company lawyers put forth a novel legal argument that would not resurface again for decades: the Robinson Treaties protected Anishinaabeg commercial harvesting. Robinson's 1850 promise that the Anishinaabeg could continue to hunt and trap as they had been in the habit of doing encompassed their historical relationship with the HBC. Prior to 1850, the Anishinaabeg were in the habit of trapping furs and selling them to the HBC (or any other trader). A commercial treaty right to sell furs meant that the province could not restrict purchasers from acquiring those furs. Prosecuting and preventing the HBC from carrying on its historical trade with the Anishinaabeg infringed an important treaty right. With its substantial resources, the Company was in a position to pursue this novel legal argument in the courts.

Understanding the HBC's case provides insight into how two facets of the Canadian state, the Ontario government and the Dominion government, treated and perceived First Nations and their treaty rights. It demonstrates how a large corporate entity, the Hudson's Bay Company, sought to use one level of government against the other in order to achieve its aims. The relationship among the three parties was a complex one. Company executives sought to enlist Indian Affairs in their efforts, but Indian Affairs' assistance was lukewarm at best and always oriented towards its goals of acculturation. When it became apparent that an HBC victory could set a legal precedent for treaty rights and place First Nations outside of the Dominion government's regulatory control, Indian Affairs' assistance disappeared and the Company was left to its own devices. Formidable as its resources were, those of the province of Ontario were greater. The province was also more motivated. The Game Commission had a singular vision of conservation and where First Nations fit into that paradigm, and it shared the Ontario government's sensitivity to any attempt to limit its jurisdiction. It could not countenance an HBC victory, which would not only place First Nations trapping beyond provincial regulation but also remove the Company from the regulatory regime; in essence, the Company would become a regulatory agency in its own right. What right would the Ontario government have to interfere in the historical HBC/First Nations relationship if it was protected by treaty? To prevent such an outcome, the Ontario government engaged in stalling, harassment, and eventually manipulation of the judiciary to block the Company.

In this context, some of the arguments advanced by Tina Loo in *Making Law, Order, and Authority in British Columbia, 1821–1871* are applicable.[3] However, the nature of the HBC adds a unique element that expands and complicates her argument. Loo maintains that the expansion of the British Columbian state, via legal regulation of the province's resources, supported the imposition of a European-style economy. In one sense, her argument applies to the situation involving the HBC and the Anishinaabeg. As Ontario's regulatory system extended north, the historical fur trade changed because of the imposition of outside authority, not local factors. However, the HBC was already a corporate entity in the European style. Locally, it remained sensitive to the realities of Aboriginal life, but the Company acted as a corporation on the national and provincial scale. The combination of First Nations rights, treaties, the paradigm guiding conservation, and Ontario's reluctance to brook interference in its regulatory system created a unique situation. The HBC existed both inside and outside of the European corporate system of the period because its local operations were based more on its historical relationship with its primary supplier, the Anishinaabeg.

For a few years the HBC's fur-trading operations in Ontario escaped notice, or at least prosecution. First Nations hunters were being arrested, but this did not affect Company profits. Chipman hoped during this early period that the Dominion government might challenge Ontario's Game Act on the basis that it was *ultra vires* when applied to First Nations, but saw no need for the HBC to become actively involved.[4] This challenge never occurred, but in the meantime, northern Ontario changed considerably. Fred LaRose accidentally discovered silver in Cobalt in 1903 and started one of the biggest rushes in Canadian history. Agricultural settlements in Haileybury and New Liskeard, in a region known as the Little Clay Belt, brought farmers into the north. Mining and farming led the Ontario government to build the Temiskaming and Northern Ontario Railway, which facilitated the arrival of thousands of Euro-Canadians into a region where few previously lived.[5] Fur traders were not ignorant of what this meant. As Chipman wrote in 1905, "before long the Company's exportations from Hudson Bay ... may expect the interest of some one party having a sentimental regard ... for the preservation of Beaver or other wild animals they may think to be disappearing."[6] Chipman was right. As the province's authority extended north, so too did its desire to exert that authority. Within a few years, Ontario's attorney general and the Game Commission began to actively arrest and prosecute HBC employees, confiscate thousands of dollars' worth of furs, and levy correspondingly punitive fines.

At first, Chipman tried to deal with incidents of fur seizures and fines personally. The first fur seizure in Ontario occurred in 1906. Provincial game wardens in Ottawa apprehended a shipment of furs from the Lake Superior District bound for St. John, New Brunswick.[7] Chipman met with Ontario's minister of public works in Toronto and smoothed matters over: the Company's post manager submitted an affidavit to the attorney general stating that the furs were trapped in season but were shipped out late, and the furs were released. Three years later, however, the Company faced another charge. In July 1909, fifteen beaver and thirty-nine otter skins were taken from the Company warehouse in North Bay. This seizure was more costly. Chipman retained the services of a prominent Toronto law firm, McCarthy, Osler, Hoskin & Harcourt.[8] In a meeting with North Bay's Crown prosecutor, Leighton McCarthy stated that the furs were trapped in Quebec (North Bay is approximately sixty kilometres from the Quebec border). His efforts failed, however, and the prosecution went ahead. The Company was found guilty and the court levied a fine of sixty dollars per beaver pelt (the otter skins were a separate charge) on the manager of the Company's North Bay warehouse.[9] McCarthy had the fine remitted, but it was clear that the Company was no longer immune to fur seizures and prosecution. McCarthy recommended to Chipman that the Company come to an arrangement with the Game Commission and other provincial officials, but he cautioned that success was unlikely.[10] Two years earlier, the Company's chief trading rival, Revellon Frères, failed to convince the Ontario government to modify the Game Act.[11] McCarthy had advised Chipman at that time that trying to negotiate with provincial officials was difficult if not impossible; in light of the recent seizures, however, he felt that some effort was required. Legal action is always uncertain. A good case can fall apart, and determining how a judge might rule is impossible. Furthermore, poking the state with a legal challenge might exacerbate the situation. McCarthy warned Chipman, however, that legal action might be necessary if negotiations failed.

In March 1910, the Company's storage warehouse at Biscotasing (on the Canadian Pacific Railway line northwest of Sudbury) was raided. This was more serious than the North Bay raid: provincial officers confiscated several thousand furs and arrested George Train, the warehouse manager. A Sudbury magistrate imposed a fine of almost $6,400. McCarthy represented the Company's interests in Sudbury, and advised Chipman that the fine was excessive and that the Company should appeal the ruling.[12] Train's arrest and the earlier fur seizure in North Bay were the catalysts that sparked the Company's legal challenge.

An analysis of McCarthy's legal arguments offers insight into how a well-trained senior lawyer perceived treaty hunting rights in the early twentieth century, when few legal precedents supported this concept.[13] McCarthy constructed four arguments to present in court, although ultimately only two were of any significance. The less important arguments were that the Ontario Game Act was *ultra vires* of the Ontario legislature because it dealt with a matter of criminal law (a Dominion responsibility), and the sale of Rupert's Land to Canada in 1870 guaranteed the Company the right to carry on its trade unhindered. Neither carried much weight. Provinces are allowed to legislate within their constitutional jurisdiction, and to levy fines to enforce those laws. People found guilty under the Game Act did not have a criminal record. McCarthy's second argument, if accepted, would create a corporate body that existed and operated independently of any provincial regulation: the Hudson's Bay Company would assume considerable power within the historical boundaries of Rupert's Land. It was unlikely that any court would establish such a precedent. McCarthy also overlooked the fact that the location of both fur seizures was south of the boundary established by the HBC's 1670 charter, and therefore outside of the land given to it by King Charles II.[14]

Canada's constitutional division of powers and the Robinson Treaties formed the basis of the Company's appeal over the next several years. Regarding the constitution, McCarthy argued "that any Act attempting to regulate the Indian's privilege of hunting is *ultra vires* of the Ontario Legislature" since the Dominion government retained constitutional jurisdiction over "Indians and Lands Reserved for Indians."[15] More important, however, was his interpretation of the Robinson Treaties. First, McCarthy made the obvious point: the Robinson Treaties explicitly protected Anishinaabeg hunting and trapping activity. Although not a popular argument, even among those at Indian Affairs, it was crucial to McCarthy's next idea. McCarthy extended this argument to encompass the historical relationship between the Anishinaabeg and the HBC. First, he noted that the beaver skins in question were trapped by members of the Nipissing Band. Under the terms of the Robinson-Huron Treaty, and reflected in section 8 of the Game Act, the Anishinaabeg retained "the privilege of hunting" as they had "heretofore been in the habit of doing." Anishinaabeg hunting and trapping, McCarthy contended, historically encompassed trade with both other First Nations and European fur traders. If the acts of hunting and trapping encompassed the acts of trading or selling, McCarthy concluded, the Anishinaabeg had a treaty right to sell and "the Company had the right to buy" those furs.

Undertaking the appeal was risky, and McCarthy warned Chipman that failure would carry a high price. If successful, the case would afford the Company protection from provincial game laws across Canada. If the Ontario government won, it would signal to the other provinces that they could apply their game laws to the fur trade, and would severely affect the HBC's business. However, acquiescing carried the same consequences as failure. Accordingly, Chipman forwarded McCarthy's concerns to the Board of Governors and advised that inaction was not an option as both British Columbia and Quebec had game laws similar to Ontario's.[16] Failing to act in Ontario meant that the other provinces could apply their game laws with impunity. Pressing forward, challenging Ontario, and hoping for the best constituted the only option left for the HBC. It wasn't exactly the good fight, but it was the only fight the Company had left to give.

Success in the courtroom required success in the backroom. McCarthy and Chipman understood that challenging the Game Act was both a legal and a political action. They were defying the power of the state. This required allies. Chipman always hoped, even before the decision to challenge

Ontario, that Indian Affairs would challenge the constitutionality of Ontario's conservation laws. In this scenario, Indian Affairs would assume all the risks and costs while the HBC would reap any potential benefits. Before undertaking the appeal, Chipman instructed McCarthy to open a dialogue with Indian Affairs in hopes of gaining political support. There was also the added possibility that Indian Affairs might pry some concessions from the Game Commission that would benefit the Company. Much to their dismay, however, McCarthy and Chipman learned that when First Nations are added to the political mix, the result was unpredictable. As became apparent during his tenure at the HBC helm in Canada, Chipman was never an enthusiastic supporter of a legal challenge. His correspondence on this subject and his willingness to ultimately let the legal challenge lie fallow under his leadership reveals that he wanted to use the legal threat as a lever to pry concessions from the Game Commission or, at worst, as a legal club with which to beat the commission.

Before departing for Chelmsford (the location of the appeal), McCarthy opened correspondence with Frank Pedley, deputy superintendent general of Indian Affairs, in an effort to convince the department to take part in the appeal.[17] McCarthy wanted Pedley to send a representative to the hearing. There was no legal benefit to this request, but it would make a political statement. McCarthy knew Indian Affairs' position regarding Ontario's game laws and treaty rights.[18] He knew that this first appeal was important, and was experienced enough to realize that the solution to the problem might be political rather than legal. Advertising an alliance between the HBC and Indian Affairs, he reasoned, would increase his chance of success. Perhaps the Ontario government would balk at the prospect of facing a large corporation in league with the Dominion government and would seek some form of accommodation with the HBC. McCarthy's efforts were successful: Frank Pedley himself and a representative from the Department of Justice travelled to Chelmsford.

If McCarthy hoped their presence would unnerve the local prosecutor, one Mr. Drayton, he was mistaken. Drayton approached McCarthy with the possibility of directing the appeal to a higher provincial court as a "stated case." Such a court, he said, provided a more appropriate venue to adjudicate the constitutional issues McCarthy wanted addressed. McCarthy refused but the issue was forced by the magistrate, Judge Kehoe, who gave Drayton his change of venue. The nature of the case indicates that Kehoe was not an impartial observer. First, a local magistrate at this period in Ontario's history was probably beholden to the party in power, as such positions were usually distributed based on patronage. Allowing a potentially damaging case to proceed on appeal would not augur well for Kehoe's future. It is also probable that Drayton knew the personality of the local judges and reckoned that Kehoe would be uncomfortable ruling on constitutional issues. Magistrates were not well-schooled lawyers. They had limited or no legal experience. Kehoe may have legitimately felt unqualified to hear the case. Faced with the prospect of his case falling apart, McCarthy agreed to refer the issue to the next sitting of the Ontario Divisional Court in October 1910.[19]

McCarthy did achieve a minor success: he had certain facts of the case admitted as evidence. He informed the Company's Board of Governors that these admissions "were a great deal better than we could have by any possibility hoped to prove."[20] First, both he and Drayton agreed that the furs in question were trapped by members of the Anishinaabeg tribe, who were "entitled to all the benefits of the Robinson treaties." Furthermore, the Anishinaabeg acted on their initiative when they trapped these furs, not as employees of the HBC. Such a point supported McCarthy's contention that the Anishinaabeg were only trapping in a manner consistent with their traditional activities. Furthermore, McCarthy established the fact that the Anishinaabeg and their ancestors had "for centuries been in the habit of hunting animals of the kind in question in the territory in question ... and the said Governor and Company of Adventurers of England trading into Hudson's Bay have for the purpose of its trade for the past two centuries or more been trading with them and purchasing such skins." McCarthy also convinced Drayton that George Train was in possession of those furs in his capacity as an HBC employee engaged in trade and barter. Finally, McCarthy had the HBC's 1670 charter and its 1869 Deed of Surrender with the Dominion of Canada admitted as evidence.[21]

The chain of events following the agreement in Chelmsford indicates that Ontario's attorney general, J.J. Foy, had no intention of waiting for the stated case to work its way through the courts. He began a deliberate strategy of stalling, harassment, and intimidation to convince the Company to drop its case. Shortly after McCarthy and Drayton reached their agreement, further arrests were made and local magistrates found HBC employees guilty. Only two months after the Chelmsford hearing, provincial enforcement officers raided the HBC's Montizambert Post. Officers confiscated 65 beaver, 78 otter, and 1,961 muskrat pelts. Post manager R.C. Wilson was arrested. A fine totalling $6,500 was levied against the Company.[22] The raid had all the appearance of a politically motivated act. McCarthy tried to convince Foy to delay Wilson's prosecution and to combine his case with Train's in the upcoming stated case. Foy refused to delay, but agreed to consider Wilson's case as part of the stated case if Wilson were found guilty.[23] Wilson's guilt was a foregone conclusion, but there was more to the incident than a simple infraction of the Game Act. Foy harboured resentment against the HBC. When one of McCarthy's partners, Osler, wrote to Foy regarding the Wilson arrest, he received a terse reply. Noting that the HBC promised in 1909 to "discontinue illegal activity," Foy considered the HBC's actions at Biscotasing and Montizambert to be a breach of that promise. He told Osler that the HBC should "try [and] obey the law and not give the Crown the trouble of prosecuting such cases."[24] Foy's use of the word "trouble" implies a belief that the HBC was both guilty and duplicitous: it knew it was breaking the law, had lied to the government in the past, and believed it should be able to carry on its trade with impunity.

Faced with such intransigence, McCarthy turned to Indian Affairs for help. Close examination of the correspondence between McCarthy and J.D. McLean reveals considerable collusion between both men, even though Indian Affairs never had any legal standing in the case. Indian Affairs provided such aid as it could while at the same time remaining safely behind the scenes (and free of any provincial claims of Dominion interference). McCarthy, for example, sent a draft copy of the Company's arguments in the upcoming case to the Department of Justice, which advised him that the Game Act was constitutionally sound except when applied to First Nations.[25] It was a break with the advice given to Indian Affairs in the 1890s, and one has to wonder where this new idea came from. Perhaps the confidentiality of the correspondence and the hope that the HBC challenge might finally settle the matter caused the department to be more forthright. It counselled McCarthy not to challenge the Game Act in its entirety, but concentrate on its application to treaty Indians. The courts would be more likely to rule the act unconstitutional in this limited context. McCarthy accepted the recommendations and made the appropriate alterations to the Company's case while still preserving the essence of his earlier arguments.[26] He forwarded a revised draft to the Department of Justice in late October 1910, and received the deputy minister's approval.[27] McCarthy's confidence grew as he worked through the case. He boasted in a letter to C.C. Chipman that his arguments had "so shaken the confidence of the law officers of the Crown in the constitutionality of their own *Game Act* that they are not very anxious to proceed with the stated case."

Indian Affairs' optimism grew as well; there was now hope that the case might finally overcome provincial inertia. A reinvigorated J.D. McLean became practically fiery, for a bureaucrat, in his demands for leniency from provincial officials. Despite the looming HBC case, provincial officers continued to arrest any First Nations person who hunted out of season. Francis Commanda's arrest in November 1910 for possessing pelts and partridge out of season provided McLean with the opportunity to press Ontario for change. Commanda was arrested while returning to the Nipissing Reserve from his hunting grounds, which lay to the north in an unorganized territory (i.e., land that was not surveyed into townships and that possessed no municipal government). Brandishing the legal club provided by the HBC, McLean sent a strongly worded letter to Edwin Tinsley, the superintendent of game and fisheries.

Interestingly, McLean's letter paralleled McCarthy's legal arguments, perhaps in an effort to pressure the Game Commission. First, it drew Tinsley's attention to sections 8 and 9(j) of the legislation. These sections stated that the Game Act would not "affect any right specially reserved to or conferred upon Indians by any treaty," and that the lieutenant-governor could exempt First Nations or "bona fide" settlers residing in northern parts of the province "from any of the provisions of the Act."[28] Tinsley responded as his predecessors had in the past: that First Nations possessed special hunting rights only when hunting on their reserves or hunting grounds that had been set apart for them.[29] Uncharacteristically, McLean persisted. He asked Tinsley to provide a list of the grounds and territories set apart for First Nations to hunt and trap on, knowing full well that the Game Commission could not answer. Furthermore, he took the unusual step of outlining the historical context within which the Robinson Treaties were created in 1850:

> There can be no doubt but that the Commissioners who negotiated the treaties with the Indians under the authority of the Government, and the Indians with whom the treaties were made both understood, rightly or wrongly, that the promise so solemnly made would be kept, that the Chiefs and their tribes would be allowed "the full and free privilege to hunt over the territory ceded by them."[30]

Historical context, previously anathema to McLean, now figured prominently in his letter. McLean concluded that Commanda and others like him were merely exercising rights "of which they could not be deprived." No Indian Affairs official had ever adopted such a strong tone with a game official over hunting rights. Tinsley's response to McLean no longer exists, but a series of letters between the Game Commission and McLean shortly afterwards indicates that the commission took the stated case seriously.

Kelly Evans, a bureaucrat in the office of the Game Commission and founder of the Ontario Game Protective Association (a sport hunting group concerned with game conservation) was undertaking an investigation into the state of game and fish in the province at this same time. This report (examined in more detail in Chapter 5) constituted the commission's first thorough examination of Ontario's game situation since 1892. Despite almost two decades of unopposed game regulation, and corresponding violation of treaty rights, Evans adopted a conciliatory approach in his inquiries with Indian Affairs. Writing to McLean for information, he noted his surprise when he discovered there were some concerns regarding First Nations and game conservation. Considering the matter's lengthy history, Evans's surprise seems contrived. He claimed that he was "particularly anxious not to clash in any way with the general policy of [Indian Affairs] ... and the Dominion government in regard to Indian rights and privileges." He asked McLean for clarification on several questions:

1. Have Indians any rights greater than white men in reference to hunting, fishing, or trapping in territories other than their reservations?
2. Have Indians the right to trade fish, game, or furs, during the close seasons, which have been caught or taken on their reservations?
...
3. In the event of a license being exacted for fur trappers, as a provincial regulation, could this be collected from Indians when trapping on their reservations?[31]

Considering the brazen and dismissive attitude of provincial officials less than a year earlier, Evans's letter reflected a new timidity. Never before had any provincial official raised these questions except in a rhetorical manner only to dismiss them. Clearly, the HBC case gave the Game Commission cause for concern.

McLean was not blind to this change in attitude, or to the fact that Evans's letter was an effort to elicit information about Indian Affairs policies. Obviously, Evans wanted to discover Indian Affairs' official position on these matters in order to determine the extent to which it supported the Company's efforts. An improperly or ambiguously worded response on McLean's part could impact either the upcoming case or any future negotiations. To exploit this turn of events to the full, he forwarded Evans's letter to McCarthy. McCarthy knew political gold when he saw it. Winning the case in court was only part of the battle; he realized that a negotiated settlement between the HBC and the Ontario government was the likely outcome. McCarthy believed this was a potential turning point for a case now stalled for ten months: the province was feeling anxious and looking for a political compromise not just with Indian Affairs but also with the Hudson's Bay Company. With the Game Commission on the metaphorical ropes, McCarthy offered McLean "confidential and unofficial" advice on how to handle Evans. He advised McLean to argue four points in his reply to the latter: (1) that the official policy of Indian Affairs was that Indians have greater hunting rights than "white men"; (2) that the Ontario legislature had no jurisdiction over Indians; (3) that Indian treaties permitted Indians to hunt, trap, and fish off their reservation; and (4) that only the Dominion government could restrict Indian hunting and trapping and, most importantly, restrict the trade in game, fish, or furs.[32] All four of these points matched what McCarthy hoped to hear from the Ontario Court of Appeal.

McLean's reply to Evans, however, marks a break in the alliance between Indian Affairs and the HBC. When analyzing Indian Affairs policy and how it shifted over time, one must be attuned to subtleties of language and nuance. Upon quick reading, McLean's response to Evans seems supportive of McCarthy and the HBC, and it was in many ways. Close examination, however, reveals a distancing from the Company's legal position. McLean adopted a supportive tone, but only insofar as it complemented Indian Affairs' own agenda. It seems that the four points expounded by McCarthy were too much for McLean. Indian Affairs policy was still one of acculturation. It was not within its ethos to argue that treaties gave First Nations additional rights.

Two features in McLean's letter distinguish Indian Affairs' policy goals from those of the Company. First, Indian Affairs wanted the Company to succeed but not at the cost of undermining government policy. Therefore, when McLean responded to Evans that "with every show of reason under the British North America Act the sole right of legislation, in so far as concerns Indians, is vested in the Dominion Government," he was attempting to use the HBC case as a bulwark against provincial encroachment into Dominion jurisdiction.[33] McLean had little interest in the case apart from its utility. It could potentially help Indian Affairs re-establish control over First Nations while at the same time protecting it from any provincial charges of interference in Ontario's jurisdiction. While the HBC certainly sought an ally in Indian Affairs, the government also sought to achieve certain goals by having a private corporation act as its proxy. When those goals diverged, the relationship ended.

To this end, McLean said that only subsistence hunting deserved leniency. Throughout his letter, he deliberately avoided any indication of support for commercial hunting or trapping. Indeed, the letter contains only one reference to commercial hunting and trapping, and it undercut the HBC's position: "So far as it can properly be done they [Indians] should be made to conform to the same laws and regulations as white men" when hunting commercially.[34] McLean claimed that Indian Affairs actively discouraged First Nations from taking game and fish during close seasons (even from their reserves) for the purposes of sale or traffic. From his perspective, First Nations who harvested commercially were less likely to acculturate than those who farmed or worked for wages.

Unaware of the fissure in his pact with McLean, McCarthy continued to prepare the Company's case and confidently assured HBC officials that all was well, noting in April 1911 that "it is unlikely that the Government will make any further seizures against the Company pending disposition of the Stated Case."[35] His optimism was misplaced. Scheduled for adjudication in the early autumn of 1910, the case remained undecided in 1912. This was not entirely to the Company's displeasure, as arrests of post managers subsided during this period of détente between both parties, but the easier state of affairs lulled the HBC into a false sense of security. Chipman was unconcerned; perhaps his pending retirement caused him to let some issues slide.

His successor as fur trade commissioner, R.H. Hall, felt differently. Unlike Chipman, Hall was unimpressed by the business customs of HBC post managers. He believed that the Company was hurting itself by engaging in questionable trading practices. For example, Hall knew that post managers were buying illegal furs that were either trapped outside the proper season or purchased from trappers who exceeded their pelt quotas. To avoid arrest, managers also hid their furs in the bush, burying them in caches. Hall feared that such actions were unwise, whether or not the Company agreed with the game laws. Ontario's Game Commission and enforcement officers would not ignore them, and this would fuel the commission's animosity towards the Company. Hall recommended that the Company try not to attract the attention of provincial enforcement officials.

His fears were borne out in the spring of 1912 as game enforcement officials and provincial detectives descended on HBC posts and warehouses in northern Ontario. Detectives in the Temagami and North Bay area posed as fur buyers and arrested all trappers who sold them illegal furs. Provincial officers raided the Company warehouse in Biscotasing and climbed through the rafters looking for illegal furs. Although nothing was found, HBC employees in the region feared that officers knew that post managers hid their furs. Arrests seemed imminent. One Company employee warned Hall that he might soon "be placed in circumstances that may put the Company to extraordinary expenses."[36] Hall also received word from the manager at the post on Lake Abitibi (on the northern Ontario/Quebec border) that his fur shipments to Montreal faced seizure.[37]

Hall had predicted this turn of events. Only a few months into his new position, he had warned the Company's directors in London that Ontario's game laws put the Company's fur trade in jeopardy; trying to coexist with those laws, Hall cautioned, was not an option. Further jeopardizing the Company's operations was the existence of disgruntled employees. The Biscotasing raid occurred because an angry former employee told detectives about the HBC's illegal trading. Hall wanted to expedite the stated case, believing that it would settle all outstanding legal questions. Unfortunately, his predecessor had allowed the case to stall. Secure in his belief that the Ontario government had been taught a lesson by the threat of a legal battle, Chipman had instructed McCarthy not to devote too much energy to the matter. When Hall asked about the status of the case after the Biscotasing raids, he received an exasperated reply from McCarthy: "If ... you are being hampered in carrying on the Company's business, and it would be to your advantage to have this question definitely settled of, win or lose, then you should so instruct us and we will use our most active endeavours to have the form of the Stated Case agreed upon and argued."[38]

Hall was a different commissioner from Chipman, however. He disagreed with his predecessor's approach to the Company's fur-trading practices and informed McCarthy "that it is bad [Company] policy from every standpoint to violate the law, whether that law is constitutional or not," and regardless of whether this policy had the approval of the Company's governor and directors.[39] Such a policy did nothing to help the Company determine its rights either under the Deed of Surrender or the Robinson Treaties. Unwilling to simply continue hoping for uninterrupted trade, Hall initiated negotiations with the governments of Manitoba, Saskatchewan, and Alberta to make arrangements that would permit the Company to carry on its trade and allow these governments to enact meaningful conservation laws. Ontario was the only province that still posed a political and legal problem because it refused to negotiate. Only a favourable court ruling, Hall reasoned, would aid the Company. McCarthy warned Hall, however, that "nothing is so uncertain as a law suit," and that perhaps it was better to leave Ontario alone and "let sleeping dogs lie."[40]

Sleeping dogs eventually wake up. Company warehouses had already been raided in early June 1912, and before the month ended provincial authorities targeted other trading posts. Montizambert Post, on the north shore of Lake Superior, was raided and $2,600 worth of furs confiscated (in addition to a potential fine of $1,500). Hall's concerns about an unhappy employee were borne out once again. A local trapper who frequented the post was angry with the Company and informed police officers about the secret fur cache ten miles from the post.[41] The Montizambert Post manager warned others that constables were conducting raids. Fort William manager John Routledge quickly transferred otter and beaver skins, and twenty pounds of beaver castoreum, to his private residence.[42]

Maintaining the status quo was no longer an option, and Company officials resumed their efforts to have the stated case brought forward. Sir Augustus Nanton, chairman of the Canadian Committee of the Hudson's Bay Company, met with Premier James Whitney to convince him to expedite the hearing of the stated case.[43] Nanton reported that it was only with "great difficulty [that] the Gov't would consent to [the] stated case being brought before the courts as soon as possible," and that all fur seizures would cease until then.[44]

The Company also instructed its London solicitors, the firm of Younger and MacKinnon, to review McCarthy's work and offer their opinion regarding the Company's chances of success in the stated case. In a lengthy memorandum, they agreed with McCarthy's definition of the legal questions central to the case. Furthermore, since the Company was not seeking to declare the entire legislation *ultra vires,* but only its application to First Nations with treaty rights to hunt and trap, the HBC stood a reasonable chance of success. Younger and MacKinnon agreed with McCarthy that section 8 of Ontario's Game Act guaranteed treaty First Nations their hunting rights, noting that "without let or hindrance by the Provincial Legislation an Indian may kill as he likes as much as he likes." While the legislation did not provide the same protection to the sale of furs by Aboriginal trappers, both men noted that to restrict the right to buy would "in effect deprive the Indian of the power to sell."[45]

Pleased by what he learned from both Nanton and the London solicitors, McCarthy sought to put one more piece into place before proceeding with the stated case: open support from Indian Affairs. Up to this point McCarthy, Chipman, and others had corresponded with McLean and Pedley at Indian Affairs, but the opinion of the minister was unknown.

McCarthy hoped that Indian Affairs would have legal counsel present when the stated case was heard.[46] Nanton travelled to Ottawa in August 1912 to meet with Robert Rogers, the minister responsible. His report back to McCarthy was not encouraging.[47] First, Rogers stated that he knew nothing about the HBC's legal challenge. This was a surprising assertion, since one would assume that his officials had advised him about McCarthy, the Hudson's Bay Company, and the reason for Nanton's meeting. Rogers's professed ignorance notwithstanding, he promised to take up the matter with his officials. He also asked McCarthy to send him the particulars of the case, and explain why Indian Affairs should be involved or even interested. Nanton recognized that Rogers was reluctant to involve Indian Affairs in this matter. He informed McCarthy that "Mr. Rogers ... desired that there should be no interference with any rights the Indians were entitled to, but that he did not want to oppose the Ontario Government unless the Indians' interests would be detrimentally affected."

There are several possible reasons for Rogers's reluctance to commit his department to the case. First, as noted earlier, Indian Affairs senior bureaucrats believed that unrestricted commercial hunting and trapping by First Nations hindered the department's aims of civilizing and acculturating First Nations. Second, Department of Justice officials had earlier warned Indian Affairs officials that directly challenging Ontario's Game Act would only cause the provincial legislature to amend the law and apply it more aggressively. Finally, one must not overlook the political ties between the governments of Premier James Whitney and Prime Minister Robert Borden. The Tory premier supported both Borden's 1911 election campaign and his handling of the politically charged Naval Bill issue. Borden's victory also helped Whitney, who took advantage of a favourable government in Ottawa to press for both federal subsidies for the expansion of the Temiskaming and Northern Ontario Railway and a decision regarding Ontario's northern borders with Manitoba and Quebec. The relationship between the two governments was so cozy that one Liberal MP noted from the opposition benches that "Ontario has given a large majority to the present government, and it has only to present its claim [to Borden's government] and get any amount of money it may require."[48] Perhaps if Wilfrid Laurier's Liberals had won the 1911 election Nanton would have met with a more receptive minister at Indian Affairs. As it stood, the Borden government was not about to lose an important political ally.[49]

Politics further affected the HBC case as the date of the stated case slowly approached. Despite Whitney's assurance that the case would be expedited, delays continued. Deputy Attorney General Cartwright, for example, took his summer holidays in August 1912, and the government did not assign anyone else to continue preparing the case during his absence.[50] The hearing was postponed until November. Another delay occurred when Ontario's chief justice, William Meredith, could not be part of the appeal court because he was in England. Meredith, leader of the provincial Conservatives in the 1870s and 1880s, had a close relationship with Whitney. For example, when Meredith adopted a controversial policy against separate Catholic schools in Ontario in 1889, his newly elected MP James Whitney remained loyal even as Catholic Conservatives defected and drifted towards the Liberal Party. The two men developed a close political relationship after that, and Meredith provided Whitney with help when Whitney became leader of the Conservative Party. In 1910, for example, Whitney asked Meredith to investigate worker compensation legislation.[51] Given this relationship, one can understand why Attorney General J.J. Foy refused to proceed with the case unless Meredith was present on the bench.[52] The case was deferred again until August 1913. In the meantime, the province continued to raid HBC posts and shipments. For example, six bales of "fine furs" and one bale of muskrat pelts (worth $15,000) were seized from a CPR train at McIntosh Station (just north of present-day Kenora). Hall sent an outraged letter to Premier Whitney, asking how "in view of our conversation" such a seizure could take place.[53] Although the furs were returned, the incident reveals how the provincial government abused its powers to pressure the HBC to drop its case.

Finally, on 10 February 1913, the Ontario Court of Appeal heard the case. Chief Justice Meredith was present, as were Justices Maclaren, Magee, Hodgins, and Kelly. No court transcripts exist, but McCarthy was clearly confident in his arguments. He informed Hall that the court was initially predisposed to the province's view but that he succeeded in moderating the court's opinions, "if not bringing them absolutely to our view."[54] Perhaps his confidence stemmed from the court's response: it reserved judgment to consider the arguments.

Win or lose, the legal die was cast. Regardless of the outcome, an appeal was inevitable. The Company's directors instructed Younger and MacKinnon to prepare for an appeal to the Judicial Committee of the Privy Council if necessary. McCarthy, however, grew increasingly anxious as the months passed and the Court of Appeal withheld its decision. In frustration, he attempted to ascertain the court's position. Whom he spoke to is not known, but he learned that the justices were having difficulty with the questions raised by the case. McCarthy's concern now was time:

would the court render a decision early enough to permit an appeal to the JCPC that summer?[55]

Another two months passed, and in the meantime the province began applying well-timed pressure on the HBC. In late May 1913, provincial enforcement officers raided HBC posts at Missanabie and Montizambert. McKenzie, the officer in charge of the Lake Superior District, wrote to Commissioner Hall that these "seizures are being made for some purpose."[56] There were very few contraband furs at the posts given the time of year, and each post manager reported that no search warrants were produced: the officers simply entered and began searching. J.S.H.S. Stranger, the Montizambert Post manager, said that the lead officer during the raid, Constable Edwards, had stated that "the Government had given him direct orders" to search the post.[57] Before McCarthy could meet with provincial officials to inquire about the raids, both managers appeared before a magistrate, who found them guilty. While the value of the furs and the corresponding fines were small, the events indicated that something was afoot. The provincial government was unwilling to stay the prosecution of these employees even though the Court of Appeal's ruling was pending.

Finally, on 12 June 1914, one year and four months after it was presented (and four years since the original appeal in Chelmsford), the Court of Appeal issued its decision: it decided not to provide a ruling. Fortuitously, the Whitney government amended the Game Act at the same time. Retroactive charges could now be laid against offenders. These events can only be considered duplicitous and indicative of political and judicial collusion to force the HBC to drop its legal challenge. N.H. Bacon, who replaced Hall as fur trade commissioner the previous June, realized what was happening. If the HBC appealed the decision, the Game Commission could "enter into the fight and simply walk into every one of our posts in Ontario, [and] fine us for every contraband pelt that has gone through the books."[58] Faced with this threat, the Company was effectively deprived of the ability to appeal.

The Court of Appeal's refusal to issue a clear ruling explains the province's actions. Bacon noted to Nanton that the rationale behind the court's ruling was that it "realized that [it] cannot deliver a judgment other than one which would be picked to pieces by the Law Lords in England."[59] Perhaps there is some truth in that observation. What emerged fifteen years later, however, provides greater insight into this ruling. In 1930, Justice Hodgins, who had sat on the court that heard the HBC challenge, adjudicated a case involving two Pic River Anishinaabeg men, *R. v. Padjena* (see

Chapter 6). In a statement to the lawyers involved, Hodgins noted that he and the other justices in the HBC decision refused to rule because "it might injuriously affect the real interests of the Indians." Hodgins did not explain this statement any further. Given his decision in *Padjena*, it is not as paternalistic as it appears at first reading. It would seem that Hodgins and the other presiding justices thought the HBC was not acting in the best interests of the First Nations but was manipulating the intent of the treaties to protect its commercial enterprise. There is certainly some truth to this; however, it does not fully explain why the court did not simply rule on points of law regardless of the motivation behind the case. Hodgins, however, also noted that it was Chief Justice Meredith who "suggested that the parties get together and come to some settlement."[60] It was Whitney's long-time political mentor and friend who seems to have convinced his fellow judges to provide the provincial government with the best possible decision. If the court ruled in the Company's favour, the province faced a very difficult situation. However, if it ruled in the province's favour, the province faced further appeals and the chance of losing before the Privy Council (a disastrous outcome from the government's perspective). The best outcome for the province, therefore, was a court that refused to issue a ruling. This, coupled with well-timed retroactive legislation and raids by enforcement officers, prevented the HBC from initiating any further legal action.

There was little else for the Company to do but negotiate with the government to secure the best possible terms. Nanton, McCarthy, and Bacon met in Toronto in June 1914. Although McCarthy still believed that Ontario's Game Act was *ultra vires*, he realized that the courts were no longer a viable option for the Company. Other provinces, such as Quebec, intended to enforce their own game laws and McCarthy informed Nanton and Bacon that the Company could not afford to mount a legal challenge against all of Canada's provinces. He also feared that the provinces might collectively pressure the Dominion government to pass national wildlife legislation to restrict First Nations commercial hunting and trapping, thereby removing the *ultra vires* argument altogether.[61] As it turned out, however, Premier Whitney died, and things were further "cleared and made somewhat easier by the serious illness and incapacitation of J.J. Foy."[62] William Hearst became premier and W.J. Hanna replaced Foy. McCarthy believed that these men were more open to negotiation.

McCarthy met with Premier Hearst in late autumn of 1914. He noted in a letter to the London directors that the meeting went well. Hearst, he said, was amicable and agreed to pursue negotiations "in the best interest of the Province and the Company." Two years later, Bacon noted that the arrangement reached between the province and the Company should "enable the Company to carry on its business ... except in cases of any flagrant offence against the law, which will meet with my severe disapproval."[63] The Company would now take out fur-trading licences for its managers, clerks, and trippers (Company employees who went out into the bush to collect furs from trappers). All fur shipments now required permits and trading coupons attached to them, and posts had to supply written fur returns on an annual basis to the Department of Game (as the Game Commission was renamed). Game officials, in return, granted leniency to remote posts that required more time to both ship furs and produce fur returns. The province also enacted special regulations regarding "Treaty Indians living north and west of the French and Mattawa Rivers and Lake Nipissing" (within the Robinson Treaties, and Treaties 3, 5, and 9). These new regulations exempted Anishinaabeg and Mushkegowuk trappers from purchasing a trapping licence if they possessed a certificate (provided by Indian Affairs) attesting to their Indian status. Although they were limited to ten beaver and/or otter skins per season, this restriction could be circumvented by an Aboriginal trapper's assumption of the quota of his other family members. Hence a man with a wife and three children could take fifty beaver and/or otter skins in a season. To ensure that only the HBC had access to First Nations-trapped furs, the province further legislated that only those traders with "Royalty Coupons" could purchase furs from treaty Indians. Bacon noted that "the parties to whom this privilege is to be granted will be very limited."[64] In essence, the Company convinced the province to help it push independent fur traders out of business.

Six years after its initiation, the HBC case had done nothing to help the legal position of First Nations trappers in northern Ontario. Initially, the case had the potential to compel recognition of treaty harvesting rights in Ontario. However, the paternalism of Indian Affairs policies, political machinations between the Whitney and Borden governments, and manipulation of the courts by Premier Whitney and Chief Justice Meredith prevented the Ontario Court of Appeal from rendering the decision that it believed was legally correct. Fully committed to its conceptualization of wildlife, First Nations, and treaties, the Ontario government used whatever legal and political weapons it had to protect its jurisdiction. However, altruism was not foremost in the minds of HBC officials and directors either. Interested only in protecting the Company's fur-trading operations, Chipman and others sought only to use the Robinson Treaties to their advantage. Although a victory would certainly have aided the Anishinaabeg, the Company itself cannot be considered an early defender of treaty rights: its chief concern (like that of any business) was profit. The only losers in this entire saga were the Anishinaabeg. Without any real allies, they would continue to rely upon their own limited devices in order to gain recognition of their treaty rights.

5

The Transitional Indian: Duncan Campbell Scott and the Game Act, 1914–20

There was an Indian at the best point of a transitional state, still wild as a lynx, with all the lore and instinct of his race undimmed, and possessed wholly by the simplest rule of Christian life.

— *Duncan Campbell Scott, 1906*

There was a fundamental shift in Indian Affairs policy regarding First Nations hunting rights in Ontario during the First World War as local events in northern Ontario and changes in Indian Affairs administration converged. Hunters from reserves along the Upper Great Lakes faced more rigorous application of the game laws by provincial enforcement officials. In letters to both local Indian agents and senior bureaucrats in Ottawa, Anishinaabeg hunters, chiefs, and band councillors wrote of being singled out for harassment and arrest by game officials and police officers. So bad was the harassment that even Indian agents complained to their superiors that the Anishinaabeg faced discriminatory treatment from game officials and local magistrates. Compounding this problem, from the agents' perspective, was the unwillingness of provincial officials to reach a compromise when an Anishinaabeg hunter was clearly taking game for subsistence purposes. Negotiating was clearly a futile endeavour that led both Indian agents and other Indian Affairs officials to develop a more empathetic ear for the Anishinaabeg's situation. Indian agents were generally more willing than their superiors in Ottawa to take the side of the bands in their agency due in large part to their proximity to the problem. However, even senior officials slowly came around to seeing something of the Anishinaabeg side of the problem.

Duncan Campbell Scott's ascension to the position of Deputy Superintendent General (DSG) of Indian Affairs was the beginning of this new attitude. Scott is a generally maligned figure in the history of Indian Affairs. His ideas and the policies he enforced are considered part of Indian Affairs' (and Canada's) racist treatment of First Nations. Many contemporary Aboriginal issues, all tied to Indian Affairs' civilization policy, have some link to Scott's tenure as DSG. Scott's views on treaty hunting rights were far more nuanced than one would expect, however. Although the department's policy of leniency did not end during his tenure, and his desire for the eventual acculturation of First Nations never wavered, his perspective on the hunting and trapping issue provides crucial insight into Aboriginal policy.

Analyzing Scott and the actions of Indian agents in northern Ontario provides a different view of the role state agencies played in the lives of First Nations. The liberal goal of acculturation – having First Nations adopt the cultural beliefs and practices of the dominant Euro-Canadian society – did not begin or end with Scott. Studies of Scott, notably E. Brian Titley's *A Narrow Vision,* are correct in ascribing to him a fervent belief in the civilizing mission of the British Empire and Indian Affairs' obligation to carry out this duty in Canada.[1] Often forgotten in the contemporary desire to disparage this odious policy are the twin beliefs that buttressed it: that the First Nations peoples were a vanishing race, and that government had a duty to minimize the pain of their eventual acculturation. Advocates of acculturation, therefore, were motivated by two ideas: they believed in the superiority of Euro-Canadian culture, but they also sincerely thought that the Aboriginal way of life was doomed. Achieving the goal of acculturation was desirable, therefore, for two reasons: elevating First Nations, but also trying to ensure that the process had as few negative effects as possible. During the early twentieth century, popular magazines carried articles about the "white man's burden" to provide a painless cultural death for First Nations.[2] This misplaced altruism certainly did not help First Nations, as its final objective was their cultural demise. Numerous books and articles already list and analyze the gross injustices suffered by Aboriginal peoples at the hands of Indian Affairs. However, the approach of Indian Affairs to Aboriginal hunting stands in stark contrast to the Game Commission's methods, which remained harsh, unchanging, and dismissive towards First Nations. Scott personified this new paradigm. His personal views of First Nations led to the formulation of a unique policy that began a new approach to the question of treaty hunting rights.

Scott's opinions regarding hunting rights can be traced back to his time in northern Ontario. Unlike previous DSGs, Scott had some experience with the Mushkegowuk and Anishinaabeg in that part of the province. In 1899, he travelled north to distribute Robinson Treaty annuities to northern treaty bands. In the summers of 1905 and 1906, he treated with the Mushkegowuk and Anishinaabeg for their land as a member of the Treaty 9 Commission.[3] Scott and the commission (which included a representative of the Ontario government, Daniel G. McMartin) travelled by canoe through much of northern Ontario. Mushkegowuk and Anishinaabeg guides supplied by the Hudson's Bay Company, a medical doctor assigned to examine the health of the Mushkegowuk and Anishinaabeg, and two Royal Canadian Mounted Police officers appointed to protect the treaty money and act as "military" representatives of the Crown accompanied them. During these travels, Scott witnessed first-hand the importance of hunting and trapping to First Nations who lived in the north, and the hardships they would endure if such activity were restricted. These insights stayed with him after his appointment as DSG in 1913, and led him to adopt a more aggressive policy to secure greater leniency for (and some recognition of) treaty hunting rights.

Scott did not issue a new directive when he assumed control of Indian Affairs nor announce a new strategic plan. Rather, his opinions regarding First Nations and non-Native society appear in his poetry and other literary work. Some scholars think that Scott's poetry and writing are not useful sources in examining his Indian policy.[4] However, in *Floating Voice: Duncan Campbell Scott and the Literature of Treaty 9,* Stan Dragland provides evidence that Scott's literary output is useful and illuminating.[5] Noting that Scott wrote almost no Indian poems prior to his first treaty trip in 1905, Dragland argues that this journey provided a creative spark.[6] After 1905/1906, the Anishinaabeg and Mushkegowuk ceased to be a bureaucratic abstraction for Scott. They became real people, and he soon developed a concept that Dragland terms the "transitional Indian": First Nations who adopted some facets of European/British culture, but retained most of their traditional culture and practices.[7] Scott's transitional Indian concept first appeared in his 1906 article for *Scribner's Magazine* titled "The Last of the Indian Treaties," in which he wrote of his encounter with Charles Wabinoo at Fort Albany in 1905:

> His name was Charles Wabinoo. We found it on the [treaty] list, and gave him eight dollars. When he felt the new crisp notes he took a crucifix from his breast, kissed it swiftly, and made a furtive sign of the cross ... There was

an Indian at the best point of a transitional state, still wild as a lynx, with all the lore and instinct of his race undimmed, and possessed wholly by the simplest rule of Christian life.[8]

Scott's poetry contains similar allusions and references to First Nations at a transitional phase of civilization. In "The Onondaga Madonna," Scott writes of an Indian woman who is a member of a "weird and waning race, / The tragic savage lurking in her face," and of blood that still "thrills with war and wildness in her veins."[9] While Scott portrays this woman as a "full-blooded" Indian, both "wild" and "savage," she is tragic as her race is ultimately doomed. In her arms is "the latest promise of her nation's doom," her child. He is Métis as he is "paler than she," but the "primal warrior" still gleams in his eye. He is another step towards her people's fate; aware of this, the child sulks "burdened with his infant gloom."

Scott's poetry and other writing are distasteful to modern readers for their racism. During his time as DSG, however, his literary ideas found expression in his Indian policies. Anishinaabeg who wrote to Scott (either directly or through their Indian agents) to complain of Ontario's game laws were the transitional First Nations he conceptualized. Wage labour only supplemented their continued reliance on hunting and trapping. Even converts to Christianity retained elements of a traditional hunting and trapping lifestyle since it was a necessity in the north, something Scott alluded to in his *Scribner's* article and the story of Charles Wabinoo.[10] He certainly looked forward to a time when the last vestiges of traditional Anishinaabeg culture would be gone. Until that day, he realized the necessity of securing some leeway for the Anishinaabeg as they followed their traditional pursuits. Bureaucrats before Scott sought leniency for Native peoples too, but Scott was the first to pursue a deliberate policy of obtaining concessions from the Ontario government.

Ontario's wildlife bureaucrats were not as nuanced as Scott in their perception of treaty rights, nor did they feel beholden to the Anishinaabeg of northern Ontario for signing treaties that opened up northern lands for mining, logging, and settlement. Shortly before Scott's tenure as DSG began, Kelly Evans of the Ontario Department of Game and Fisheries published his report on the state of game and conservation in the province. Evans's 1912 report followed a pattern and logic reminiscent of the Game Commission's founding 1892 report: wildlife constituted an important economic resource for Ontario, and all First Nations, regardless of any existing treaty, had to abide by all provincial conservation laws. Unlike

Indian Affairs policy, which underwent a slow evolution, the Game Commission remained static. Echoing the commission's founding report, Evans noted that "one of the principle [sic] factors in the destruction of game is the Indian living in wilder regions."[11] While Scott was concerned about game laws that affected First Nations and prevented them from obtaining a sufficient living, Evans's only concern was the impact of such activity on one of Ontario's natural resources. Evans believed that First Nations did not suffer any injustice if they were fined or imprisoned for selling wild meat or furs, and that it was the best way to prevent First Nations from overhunting. Their predilection for overhunting, according to Evans, had already destroyed all of the game on their reserves. Furthermore, Evans contended that the inability of First Nations to follow "proper" conservation practices (i.e., those established by the provincial government) now drove them to hunt on Crown land. This opinion in itself reveals Evans's ignorance of First Nations. Obviously, he possessed limited knowledge of reserves as a suitable land base. Northern reserves were small and an insufficient resource base for a community reliant on hunting. Evans also ignored, or was unaware of, the promise in the Robinson Treaties that the Anishinaabeg could continue to hunt on unoccupied Crown land. This was of little concern to him, however, as he believed that First Nations' refusal to adopt agriculture was the general reason for their inability to support themselves. What was the cause of this refusal? According to Evans, it grew from the general loathing of First Nations to "undertake prolonged or steady work."[12]

Evans concluded that it would be a "manifest injustice to the general public" not to apply conservation laws equally to all residents of Ontario. His perception of the issue found full expression in the actions of the Ontario government during and after the First World War. Provincial efforts to limit Aboriginal hunting reveal how the liberal belief in equality led to the unequal treatment of First Nations. Treaties and the very fact of being Aboriginal placed First Nations so far outside the dominant paradigm of conservation that they were not even accorded equal treatment before the law. During this period, the Game Commission followed a much stricter and harsher policy of enforcement against treaty Indians. In the past, local officials operated within the confines of the law. If an officer arrested a First Nations person for breaking the game laws, the officer at least had evidence of an infraction (putting aside the question of treaty rights). Commanda and Ottawaska, for example, did have moose meat in their possession. By 1914/1915, local officials started ignoring the need for evidence or warrants and initiated a campaign of targeting First Nations.

Evans's report had clearly influenced the province's stricter approach to First Nations' hunting. His solution to the problem of treaty rights was to equate treaty Indians with northern settlers. Settler families in northern Ontario were allowed to take a combination of one moose or caribou and one deer, or two deer during the allotted open season if they had a hunting permit. First Nations would have the same privilege in place of their treaty right. One moose, however, was clearly insufficient to feed an entire family (of, say, four or five people) until the next moose season. Settlers chose their plots for farming. Hunting supplemented what they grew on their farms. White settlers also had a much easier time securing wage labour, seasonal or permanent; hunting was also a supplemental activity in this context.[13] Reserves in northern Ontario were generally not selected by bands with farming in mind and were largely or completely unsuited for agriculture.[14] Providing First Nations with the same privileges as settlers was clearly insufficient.

Although there is no systematic measurement of Anishinaabeg food requirements during the winter (or any other part of the year), evidence from Quebec during the same period provides some insight into the nutritional requirements of a Mushkegowuk family living on the land in the winter. J.W. Anderson, a long-time HBC employee in the late nineteenth and early twentieth centuries, recorded how much the Mushkegowuk family of Robert Peetawabano, in Mistassini (northern Quebec), hunted over two winters, in 1912–13 and 1913–14. During the first period, Peetawabano's family acquired "430 lbs of moose meat, 6022 rabbits, 7300 fish, 100 ptarmigan, 59 beaver, 53 marten, 9 otter, 26 muskrats, 9 mink, 10 ermine, 40 ducks, 3 black bear and 18 loons." The next winter, his family harvested "3306 fish, 1642 rabbits, 67 beaver, 8 otter, 21 marten, 4 mink, 3 ermine, 66 ptarmigans, 140 ducks, 3 owls, 2 weenisk, a red fox, 2 yellowlegs, 1 gull, 2 caribou, 3 black bear, and 55 muskrats."[15] Anderson noted that the Mushkegowuk ate everything except the martin, mink, ermine, and fox (which were consumed only in difficult circumstances). The large quantity of game, he explained, was related to the fat content of each animal. Rabbit meat, for example, is not very fatty, and large numbers of rabbits had to be consumed in order to get enough calories. Bear and beaver meat, in contrast, were "strong meat" according to the Mushkegowuk. Considering that meat was their main source of nourishment, and being out in the cold necessitates that a person consume more food to stay warm, the amount of hunting required to sustain a family is not surprising. Evans, however, could not understand that hunting for food was a primary activity for the Anishinaabeg of northern Ontario. He did know that moose, deer, and bear were the quarry most sought by sport hunters, and when the two interests clashed, First Nations always lost.

Close seasons and hunting restrictions for smaller game only harmed the Anishinaabeg further. When big game were scarce, families relied on small game and fish to supplement their supplies. Evans and other provincial conservation officials, from the local game warden to senior bureaucrats, were unable to see beyond an animal's economic value. While Anishinaabeg hunters certainly understood the value of a beaver pelt, they also appreciated the value of such animals for their meat. These different perceptions of fur-bearing animals came into conflict in the autumn of 1916 when two Fort William Band councillors, Alexander McCoy and Frank Peltier, wrote Scott to complain about Ontario's game laws. While restrictions on moose hunting were also causing problems, both men noted that limits on the trapping of beaver and otter had "taken food out of the mouths of the Indians" and treated band members like common thieves when they hunted or trapped for food.[16] They indignantly noted that the Robinson-Superior Treaty should protect them against "the actions of game wardens and Magistrates in the District."

One incident profoundly affected the Fort William Anishinaabeg and their concern for their treaty rights: the death of Pierre Hunter. The circumstances surrounding the death, combined with the callous indifference of provincial bureaucrats, provides a stark and shocking example of the racism and discrimination endured by the Anishinaabeg at the hands of provincial officials. It also helps explain how events in the north drove Dominion officials from Scott to local Indian agents to adopt a more aggressive and empathetic policy towards the Anishinaabeg and their treaty rights. Although Hunter was from Sioux Lookout (within the boundaries of Treaty 3), his fate resonated with Anishinaabeg throughout northwestern Ontario. Arrested for hunting moose out of season, Hunter served thirty days of hard labour at the Port Arthur Industrial Farm. Released in the winter of 1916 with one dollar in his pocket for good behaviour, he faced a solitary two-hundred-mile walk back to his home. Surprisingly, he made it, but died four weeks later of unknown causes.[17] Ontario's provincial secretary, W.J. Hanna, took little interest in the case when Scott contacted him at the instance of the local Anishinaabeg and their Indian agent. Hanna argued that an Indian "is ... at home in the bush" and that such a trip could not have led to Hunter's demise. Furthermore, Hanna concluded, Hunter did not deserve any sympathy, and neither did his family. Hunter's "squaw is a bad character," Hanna noted, and was willing to "take up with any Indian who wants her." Hunter's children were "pretty much the same."

If a senior bureaucrat held such opinions, it is not surprising that similar ideas permeated the thinking of local officials. In the documentary record, the actions of Constable Frank Edwards, an overzealous Ontario Provincial Police (OPP) officer, stand out. He was the same Edwards who took part in the government-ordered HBC raids in 1913. Complaints against Edwards by the Anishinaabeg became so intense that the Fort William Indian agent, William Brown, eventually took a hand in the matter and wrote to Indian Affairs in Ottawa to obtain some relief for the bands in his agency. From November 1916 to January 1917, Brown received six different complaints from the Anishinaabeg about Constable Edwards, who he believed "disliked the Indians and would prosecute them on every occasion."[18] Samuel Chapleau of the Long Lake Band, for example, informed Brown in November 1916 that Edwards and the local magistrate, O'Conner, had entered his father's hunting cabin without a search warrant to search for "illegal" furs and meat. Several other Anishinaabeg from the Long Lake area also told Brown that Edwards had searched their hunting cabins or knapsacks without a warrant (and never found any "illegal" game or furs).[19] In January 1917, Edwards and game warden George Fanning threatened to arrest an elderly Anishinaabeg, Michael Fox Senior, if he did not provide them with information about Anishinaabeg hunting in the area. Harassment and threats were commonplace. Several months earlier, Fox Senior complained about his son's arrest for having beaver pelts out of season, and about the treatment he received from Edwards and O'Conner.[20] The final incident involved Chief Louis Michano of the Pic River Band and several other men from the same community. On their way to their trapping grounds, they met a local white trapper, George Cook. Cook informed the men that Edwards had given their trap lines to him, and that "he would put some bullets into some of us if we kept on going up the river to set traps." When Michano argued that they had every right to set their traps, Cook stated that he was acting under the authority of Constable Edwards.[21]

Arrest and harassment based on ethnicity, magistrates and court officials colluding with police officers, and threats of imprisonment for failing to cooperate with police seem more likely in the southern United States in the early twentieth century, but First Nations regularly experienced such treatment in Ontario. Brown feared an outbreak of violence if matters continued unchanged. He wrote lengthy letters to J.D. McLean expressing frustration at both the situation and the inability of Indian Affairs to secure any leniency for the Anishinaabeg in his agency. If the situation did not improve, he warned, "the Indians openly state that they will shoot any constables who interfere with them while they shoot game for their own use." Edwards's background and that of George Fanning, the local game officer, did little to endear these two constables to the Anishinaabeg. In addition to his duties as a police officer, Edwards worked for the HBC posts on the Pic River and at Fort William, collecting trappers' outstanding debts for the post managers.[22] One Anishinaabeg hunter told Brown that Edwards would give some confiscated furs to the HBC post he was collecting for and sell the rest to a local fur dealer for personal profit. Another related that Edwards threatened to arrest him if he did not pay a delinquent account at an HBC post. In a separate incident, Edwards purchased "illegal" pelts from an Anishinaabeg hunter at below market value, and sold them to an independent fur trader. Matters were so bad that a local white trapper, Arthur Henry Nichols, took up the cause of Aboriginal trappers and spoke to Brown. Relating a conversation he had with the officers, Nichols said that Edwards believed it was "the Indians [who] were slaughtering so many moose ... and that [he] disliked the Indians and would prosecute them on every occasion."[23] As for Fanning, Brown knew that he had been a trapper before finding employment with the province, and that he was a well-known poacher in the region.[24]

Besides the enforcement officers' dubious backgrounds, there was the broader question of Edwards's treatment of the Anishinaabeg, particularly his searching of their cabins and knapsacks. Although Brown did not consider this element of the arrests in his letter to McLean, an analysis of the 1913 Game Act (the most recent version during these events) reveals that while Edwards was not abusing his powers, he was indeed targeting Anishinaabeg hunters. Sections 42 and 61(4) of the 1913 Game Act gave constables considerable powers of search and seizure. Section 42 allowed an officer to search:

> Every railway and express company and every other common carrier, every person engaged in the business of cold storage, or of purveying or dealing in game or fish, or of lumbering, or in charge of any camp near any fishery or near any place in which game is usually found, every person fishing or in charge of any fishery, and every person holding any lease or license, shall, upon request, permit the Superintendent or any inspector, warden, overseer or other officer to enter and inspect any car, building, premises or enclosure, and to open any receptacle for the purpose of examining all game and fish taken ... and for the purpose of searching for fish or game illegally killed or

procured ... and in case of refusal the officer may, without a search warrant, break such locks and fastenings as may be necessary in order to make such examination.[25]

Section 61(4) repeated much of what the previous section stated. It noted that "every overseer, if he has reason to suspect and does suspect that game, peltries or fish have been killed, taken or shipped or are had in possession contrary to the provisions of this Act," could enter and search premises or any storage receptacle for illegal game and pelts.[26] Since nothing was found in any of the six incidents involving Edwards, he was clearly not adept at assessing search-and-seizure situations but was predisposed to follow his own prejudice. There was also the added irregularity of the local magistrate's accompaniment of Edwards during these searches. Although only a magistrate, O'Conner was still required to adopt a position of neutrality during any legal proceedings.

J.D. McLean was doubtful about pressuring either the OPP or the Game Commission into modifying its treatment of Anishinaabeg hunters, but he forwarded Brown's concerns to Joseph Rogers, OPP superintendent for northwestern Ontario. Rogers stood firmly behind his subordinate. His response and Brown's rebuttal provides an interesting contrast between these two competing perceptions of treaty rights. Rogers firmly believed that Anishinaabeg hunters were decimating the local moose and fur-bearing population of the region. At "nearly every watertank [on the Canadian National Railway] between Nepigon and Folleyette [sic]," Rogers claimed that Anishinaabeg hunters were selling illegally hunted meat and pelts.[27] Selling meat to CNR work crews, Rogers stated, was a common activity among the Anishinaabeg and the leading cause of moose scarcity in northwestern Ontario. As proof, Rogers claimed that one Anishinaabeg hunter shot fourteen moose at one time to sell to railway crews, logging camps, and other locals. Brown's opinions were quite different. He told McLean that Edwards was a zealot who levied fines against everyone on the CNR line for even minor infractions in order to burnish his image as a conscientious constable in the eyes of his superiors.[28] By way of example, Brown recounted how Edwards had fined a local shopkeeper $135 for failing to put the proper labels on bottles of insect repellant.[29] It would also seem that Edwards was prone to exaggeration: according to Brown, the story of an Anishinaabeg hunter shooting fourteen moose was false. Although Superintendent Rogers ended his letter by stating that Edwards was a friend of the Indians and could secure their aid at any time, Brown noted that the local Anishinaabeg would aid Edwards only if he needed someone to dig his grave. Such events may seem parochial and picayune at first glance, but they formed the substance of the broader issues regarding treaty rights and the state's impact on First Nations harvesting rights. How these issues played out on the ground was at the core of the problem, and this became increasingly apparent during the interwar years.

While McLean dealt with complaints about Edwards, Scott turned to outside experts for direction and advice. He was actively considering a legal challenge, and he asked a constitutional lawyer from McGill University, Professor Martin, for aid. Why Scott turned to an outside expert and not the Department of Justice is uncertain. Perhaps he realized that Justice officials would offer the standard response, i.e., that challenging Ontario's game laws in court was a bad political decision. Scott made available to Martin numerous documents that no one outside Indian Affairs had ever seen, and asked Martin to formulate an opinion.

Martin, in return, offered direct and, for that time, radical counsel. He noted in his eight-page memorandum that "under the Robinson Treaties no Indian privilege can be withheld except by deliberately breaking the terms of the treaties."[30] Ontario's game laws were breaking the treaties, and the province had no constitutional right to do so. HBC lawyers had advanced this argument before, but Martin took it a step further, interpreting the Robinson Treaties (indeed, any Aboriginal treaty) as agreements between an "alien people" and the Crown. Martin did not use the term "nation," but the implication was clear: the Robinson Treaties were an agreement between sovereign nations. In 1850, he argued, the Anishinaabeg of Lakes Huron and Superior constituted an alien people because they had not signed a treaty with the Crown; the Anishinaabeg were therefore not British subjects but constituted an independent nation.

In this context, Martin's conclusions placed treaties beyond any provincial interference. Since the British North America Act transferred all authority over "Indians and Lands Reserved for Indians" to the Dominion government, no provincial government could abrogate those treaties unless they were prepared to assume all the obligations that went with the treaties (such as annuity payments). Ontario could no more ignore and violate the dictates of the Robinson Treaties, Martin concluded, than New Brunswick could ignore the provisions of the Webster-Ashburton Treaty with the United States.[31]

Negotiations, Martin noted, were not a productive course of action for Indian Affairs. Ontario's Office of the Attorney General and Department of Game had adopted an "antagonistic attitude," and Indian Affairs should not look for "future concessions from that source." Senior provincial officials were, he said, "uncompromising and flippant" in their handling of this matter. He pointed out that the provincial government had amended its conservation laws to remove any reference to treaty rights. Whereas the 1908 Game Act specifically exempted treaty Indians, the 1913 act contained no such exemption. Martin believed that such legal and political manoeuvring was irrelevant as rights could not be recognized and affirmed and then taken away, but it revealed the provincial government's intransigence on this issue.[32] Local officials took their cue from the province in their "arrogant and unreasonably severe" application of game laws to treaty Indians. Having said this, Martin advised Scott to drop the old policy of leniency and adopt a more aggressive strategy: bring a stated case before the courts to finally settle the issue, and pressure the minister of Indian Affairs to accept this option. Indian Affairs could either wait for a First Nations person to be arrested for hunting moose or deer out of season (an all-too-common event), or agree upon a set of facts with Ontario's attorney general and submit them to a court. Even if Indian Affairs was unsuccessful in this endeavour, it would score a moral victory because the Ontario government would finally admit that it has "no respect for a solemn agreement and written pledge" made between the Crown and the Anishinaabeg. From a legal perspective, even a failed case would be on record and open the possibility of an appeal.

Scott's reaction to this advice, the most radical received by Indian Affairs regarding hunting rights, is unknown, but his actions show that he supported Martin's position and decided to act upon it. Shortly after the memorandum, two Fort William Band members, Chief Alex McCoy and Band Councillor Frank Peltier, complained of their band's treatment at the hands of Constable Edwards. Failing to obtain satisfaction from their Indian agent or Indian Affairs, McCoy and Peltier addressed a petition to King George V. Considering that the Robinson-Superior Treaty was an agreement between the Anishinaabeg and the Crown, their appeal to the monarch, while clearly an overly literal interpretation of the word "Crown," did possess some logic.[33] Both men stated that they could not find justice with either the Ontario government or Indian Affairs regarding their treaty rights. They referred to the numerous arrests in the region over the last two years and to the death of Pierre Hunter. McCoy and Peltier also called attention to the arrest of Joe Martin of the Fort William Reserve for having moose meat in his possession to feed his daughter. It was wrong that "the older people of our Tribe should be unfairly dealt with and deprived of their only means of livelihood" by not being allowed to hunt to support themselves. Joe Martin was in a particularly difficult situation. Both of his sons had enlisted in the Canadian Expeditionary Force to fight in France: one had already been killed and the other wounded. Their father was at home without any support. Two other Fort William men, McCoy and Peltier noted, were also fighting in France. In consideration of their treaty promises, and their reserve's commitment to helping England in its war with Germany, they asked for the Crown's assistance.[34] Indian Affairs' annual report for 1920 noted that of the Anishinaabeg bands in Ontario, Fort William made the most significant contribution of men to the Canadian Expeditionary Force: more than 100 men out of a total adult male population of 282 volunteered.[35] When conscription was introduced, there was only one first-class (i.e., ideally suited for combat) adult male left on the Fort William Reserve. Many of these men were in the 52nd Battalion. Their commanding officer noted that it was a testament to the bravery "of every Indian in this unit" when they "appeared on the casualty list."

McCoy and Peltier's petition never reached the King, as the governor-general's office directed it to Indian Affairs. Scott saw potential in the petition, and although McCoy and Peltier received no satisfaction from Indian Affairs, their situation convinced him of the need to bring a test case before the courts. His efforts ran up against substantial bureaucratic inertia from other government departments, however, specifically the Department of Justice. It was also apparent that Scott's own officials, notably J.D. McLean, resisted his efforts. Scott wrote to E.L. Newcombe, deputy minister of justice, and outlined Professor Martin's legal opinions regarding hunting rights. He concluded that it was now time to determine "the legality of the Indians' claims," and recommended that in the event of another arrest and prosecution of an Anishinaabeg hunter, the Department of Justice and Indian Affairs undertake an appeal on behalf of the accused. Newcombe and his assistant, William Edwards, were of a different opinion. Believing that a court case would prove injurious to Dominion/Ontario relations, Edwards recommended that Indian Affairs review all the treaties that covered Ontario, open negotiations with provincial officials, and press for leniency in the application of game laws against the Anishinaabeg.

Newcombe's perception of this issue was the same as that of his predecessor in the 1890s. Although Scott could not have been surprised by this, Newcombe's intransigence certainly did not help matters. Scott took a genuine interest in McCoy and Peltier's petition. He personally wrote the two men (no other deputy superintendent general had corresponded directly with any other Anishinaabeg petitioner to that point), advising them that their concerns were being considered.[36] J.D. McLean disapproved of Scott's approach. When McCoy and Peltier wrote again to

Indian Affairs in January 1918 to inquire about their hunting rights, McLean responded to their letter, writing to Brown rather than to the chief and the councillor. His advice: the prosecution of the war in France was the government's main concern, and the Fort William Band should try to adhere to existing game laws.

Despite resistance from both the Department of Justice and his own department, Scott continued to press for legal action. He wrote next to Arthur Meighen, the minister responsible for Indian Affairs, in March 1918. Once again, he set a new precedent: there are no records of any Indian Affairs official writing to the minister responsible (or any minister) up to this point, let alone recommending a constitutional challenge to provincial legislation. In a detailed eight-page memorandum, Scott outlined the explicit hunting promises of the Robinson Treaties, the increasingly stringent enforcement of the Game Act by provincial officers, the legal arguments he had received from Professor Martin, and his dissatisfaction with the legal advice he had received from the Department of Justice.[37] He referred to a recent conviction of two Nipissing Anishinaabeg hunters by a Sudbury judge, Frank Latchford. Despite finding the two men guilty of breaking the law, Latchford noted in his decision that Ontario's game laws infringed the treaty rights of the Anishinaabeg. Whether this stemmed from legal reasoning or from political considerations is unclear. Latchford was a longtime Liberal and a thorn in the side of Premier William Hearst's Conservative government and his minister of lands, forests, and mines, George Ferguson.[38] Regardless of his motivation, Latchford's statement supported Scott's belief that Indian Affairs' failure to act left the Dominion government open to "the charge of breach of faith with the Indians." Scott advised Meighen that the government should either introduce a bill in Parliament to establish a national set of game laws (overriding all provincial laws), or open negotiations with the provincial government.

Scott was taking a chance by writing to Meighen, thereby elevating the matter to the political level. He was a bureaucrat, however, and did not seem to understand the broader political landscape affecting the Dominion government. He failed to assess the forces at play in Prime Minister Robert Borden's cabinet. Although a capable minister, Meighen was not the right person for Scott's task. Borden had ample confidence in Meighen's abilities, making him point man on several contentious issues, such as the Naval Bill issue in 1912, the furor over Regulation 17 in Ontario in 1916, and the conscription election of 1917.[39] Meighen may have been the minister of mines (with Indian Affairs as part of his portfolio), but he was not in cabinet to fulfill any real ministerial duties. As Meighen's biographer,

Roger Graham, notes, Borden did not give him "charge of any departments which were vitally important in a wartime [cabinet]" so that Meighen could be directed to those issues that Borden wanted handled quickly and efficiently. Meighen was a minister whose energies were everywhere but with his portfolio. His official position in cabinet also reflected the incredibly low priority Borden placed on Indian Affairs.

Six months passed before Meighen replied to Scott, and he completely adopted the Department of Justice's position: that the matter was a policy issue and not something for the courts to consider.[40] His advice to Scott reflected his lack of interest. He agreed that the treaty rights of the Anishinaabeg required protection, but directed Scott to work towards "modifying" Ontario's game laws in deference to the treaties while at the same time instructing Indian agents to urge bands in their agencies to "comply with Provincial law."

Meighen's instructions ended Scott's efforts for several years. He could not ignore the wishes of his minister, and a constitutional challenge required political support. Undertaking a stated case was a bold move, and lay beyond the purview of any civil servant. He did continue, however, to press provincial officials across Canada to relax their game laws when applied to treaty Indians. In 1919, at a Dominion-Provincial Wildlife Conference, Scott adopted an aggressive position in his defence of treaty hunting rights, and singled out foreign (i.e., American) sport hunters as the chief cause of game depletion in Canada.[41] In a paper titled "The Relation of Indians to Wildlife Conservation," he expressed empathy for the state of First Nations who relied on hunting, fishing, and trapping for their livelihood. The paper provoked the British Columbia and Saskatchewan representatives at the conference to accuse First Nations in their provinces of the unwarranted slaughter of big game animals. The Saskatchewan representative claimed that Scott wanted the provinces to show greater leniency to Aboriginal hunters so Indian Affairs could reduce the amount of food it distributed on reserves. Scott responded that Indian Affairs only wished to "preserve the game; at the same time, we wish to have our Indians well fed, but we do not wish the hunters to feed themselves entirely on the game of the country."[42]

Scholar Frank Tough criticizes Scott for not adopting a stronger stance at this conference, but if one considers the broader context of Scott's situation, his position was understandable.[43] Scott was a conflicted individual. His desire to acculturate Native peoples across Canada was sincere (albeit odious to modern sensibilities). Civilization of First Nations lay at the root of almost all Indian Affairs' policies. At the same time, he realized that this process would not happen quickly. Offering treaty Indians some protection of their hunting and trapping was both necessary and practical until they abandoned these activities in favour of some other occupation or livelihood. He was not opposed to wildlife conservation, nor did he wish to infringe upon provincial jurisdiction in this matter. However, he appreciated the promises made in 1850 by William Robinson, with whom he shared the experience of negotiating a treaty. While Scott's goal was still acculturation, his unique experiences and perspective led him to become the most proactive deputy superintendent general, at least on the issue of hunting rights, Indian Affairs had seen to date. Scott did not want to place First Nations entirely outside of the liberal order; however, he did want to nudge them into a different position relative to the state when it came to hunting.

6
R. v. Padjena:
Local Pressure and Treaty Hunting Rights in Ontario, 1925–31

If any of you gentlemen had a contract with Her Majesty, the Queen, you would think you had some rights.
– T.R.L. MacInnes, Indian Affairs Secretary

In 1928, two Pic Reserve men, Joe Padjena and Paul Quesawa, appeared before Magistrate Depew in the town of White River. Depew found both men guilty of contravening Ontario's game laws by trapping beaver outside the established seasons. Padjena and Quesawa were fined $600 each.[1] The men retained Port Arthur lawyer Arthur McComber and appealed their conviction. They were no doubt surprised when Justice McKay of the District Court in Fort William rendered his verdict in April 1930. McKay overturned the earlier conviction based on the hunting promises contained in the Robinson-Superior Treaty, and ruled that Ontario's game laws could not override those guarantees. The Ontario government appealed, and *R. v. Padjena and Quesawa* (hereafter called *R. v. Padjena*) moved forward. What initially promised to be an important legal decision regarding Anishinaabeg treaty hunting rights eventually foundered because the accused trapped the beaver just outside the northern boundary of the Robinson-Superior Treaty. Since they were outside of their treaty area, Indian Affairs concluded that their treaty rights did not apply.

Shortly after this case, the Ontario government instituted a trapline system. This new approach emerged from the recommendations of the 1931 Black Committee (named after its chairman, W.D. Black, Member of the Provincial Parliament for Addington). The proposal grew from the committee's conclusion that existing laws regarding the trapping of furbearing animals were not working. To solve this problem, the government divided the province into various sections. Within each section, trappers applied for a licence and were allocated a specific piece of land on which to hunt for one season. The provincial Game and Fisheries Department invited Indian Affairs, through its agents, to record where the Anishinaabeg of northern Ontario trapped so this information could be used in the allocation of traplines. Agents were interested in this approach as it offered some chance of relief for bands in their agencies; presciently, the Anishinaabeg were less enthusiastic. The system failed to protect their access to land because trappers received different land each season and there was no guarantee that Anishinaabeg trappers would receive their traditional territory. Anishinaabeg trappers did not use the land in the manner prescribed by the government trapline system. They kept and maintained their traplines throughout their lives, and would pass them on when they became too old to trap or they passed away. Annually altering ownership of traplines ran counter to traditional Anishinaabeg land use.

R. v Padjena and the creation of a trapline system by the Ontario government highlight several important elements in the political dispute regarding treaty hunting rights in Ontario. First, they show that the application of state power with regard to Indian Affairs was not monolithic in nature. As argued in the previous chapter, D.C. Scott was something of an (albeit limited) ally of First Nations when it came to harvesting rights. Although Scott was certainly not interested in having treaties assume meaningful legal status within Canada, he recognized the hardship that Ontario's game laws imposed on the Anishinaabeg. He was willing to take actions that contradicted the orders of his minister, and was also willing to act in a manner that excluded other departments with an interest in the matter, specifically the Department of Justice. Indian agents, often an object of derision in Aboriginal history, also emerge as unlikely allies. Several agents attempted to secure the best relief they could for First Nations in their agency. They worked with them to fight legal battles, secure counsel, and protect traditional trapping territories. As Ontario became even more ruthless in its application of game laws against First Nations, agents could not ignore what they saw in their local area: provincial officials targeting First Nations for arrest and harassment while overlooking the illegal acts of non-Aboriginal hunters and trappers. Where this altruism fell short was in Scott's limited interpretation of the treaties. He was willing to push for protection of hunting rights within treaty boundaries, but legal thinking and concepts were too limited at that time to embrace traditional Anishinaabeg land use and management.

Second, they demonstrate that the provincial government was monolithic in its approach to the issue of treaty rights and hunting. Whereas Indian Affairs slowly changed its approach, the Game and Fisheries Department (as the Game Commission was rebranded) stagnated. Before considering traplines, it is important to consider the Black Committee. It is unique because transcripts and documents pertaining to Indian Affairs' presentations to the Committee still exist. These records highlight the degree of racism and stereotyping that continued to infuse the conservationist thinking of the provincial government almost forty years after the Game Commission was first formed. There is no change in how game officials approached the issue of Indigenous hunting. They were unwilling to listen to any testimony or evidence that highlighted the difficult circumstances First Nations lived in due to the province's game laws, and they disregarded any evidence about Anishinaabeg hunting and trapping practices.

Both events also highlight a further difficulty that emerged concerning the issue of treaty hunting rights: traditional Anishinaabeg land management in the form of the family hunting territory.[2] Both the Game Commission and Indian Affairs understood the hunting promise in the Robinson Treaties to relate only to the physical act of hunting. However, the Anishinaabeg would have understood that their continued right to hunt extended to how they managed the land and wildlife in family hunting territories.[3] It is quite likely that either Padjena or Quesawa had a territory that extended into Treaty 9.[4] It is ironic that although family hunting territories were a core issue in *R. v. Padjena*, because of the limitations of legal thinking at the time it remained unexplored by the lawyers and became the reason why the case fell apart.

When the province initiated its trapline system in the 1930s, its failure to consider how the Anishinaabeg perceived land use and management meant that the trapline not only failed to address Anishinaabeg concerns but further displaced them from their family hunting territories.[5] A poorly thought out system, based on both a limited reading of the Robinson Treaties and their historical context and a provincial bureaucracy too infused with racist stereotyping, meant that the Anishinaabeg lost access to land under the trapline system.

Within this context, the extension of the state's power over wildlife had a dual impact on First Nations. Clearly it affected their treaty rights to engage in the acts of hunting and trapping. In addition, it represented displacement: the loss or restricted use of traditional harvesting territories.

Displacement was already occurring because of wildlife conservation. The creation of national and provincial parks removed land from First Nations who hunted and trapped on such territories. Beginning in the 1920s, the Ontario government began creating game preserves in northern Ontario, such as the Chapleau Game Preserve, to protect animal populations.[6] This resulted in further displacement.

R. v. PADJENA

Padjena and Quesawa were arrested in the spring of 1928 under the provisions of an Ontario Order-in-Council that made it "unlawful for any Indian residing outside of the territory lying north of the main line of the Canadian National Railway ... to have raw pelts of beaver and otter or any part thereof in possession at any time except under special license or permit issued by the Department of Game and Fisheries."[7] Chief Ellis Desmoulin of the Pic Band wired Indian agent J.G. Burke to complain about the arrest. He argued that the accused, indeed all Pic Band members, were "quite within [their] ... treaty rights in trapping beaver." The Pic Reserve had poor soil for farming, Desmoulin explained, and a lack of employment in local logging camps forced Pic men to hunt and trap. Further exacerbating the problem was the fact that all the lumber camps had shut down for the winter. This forced more non-Aboriginal men into the bush to hunt and trap, pushing Anishinaabeg hunters off their traplines. Indian agents, Desmoulin argued, were obligated to protect treaty rights because "at the time our Treaty was made it was stated ... that our full trapping and hunting privileges would be protected for all time."[8]

Chief Desmoulin's broader complaints about local unemployment and white trappers and hunters encroaching on Anishinaabeg territory were not unfounded. Falling pulpwood prices had closed a number of northern logging camps and pulp mills; rising unemployment drove the non-Aboriginal populace into the bush in search of pelts to sell and food to eat.[9] With fur prices fluctuating considerably during the 1920s, trapping provided some respite for unemployed forest workers.[10] An expanded railway system exacerbated the problem by facilitating the arrival of independent fur traders and trappers in the north. Archie Belaney, better known as the "Indian" conservationist Grey Owl, noted that the area around Biscotasing on the CPR line was overrun by "get-rich quick transient hunters [who] depleted the fur bearing animals almost to the point of extinction."[11] In a 1926 survey of the area around Cochrane, Dr. J.J. Wall noted that white trappers were aggressively pushing First Nations off their family territories.[12]

Instead of dismissing Desmoulin's complaint, Agent Burke supported the chief's concerns in a letter to Indian Affairs. Desmoulin, Burke explained, was not the only chief complaining about the dual problem of increasingly restrictive game laws and encroachment of white hunters on Anishinaabeg hunting grounds. Burke informed Scott that he had warned the Anishinaabeg in his agency that they possessed no special privileges when trapping beaver, but argued that it was impossible for the Anishinaabeg to earn a living in any other manner. They were not, he stated, natural offenders of the game laws but merely trying to support themselves.

Scott raised the matter with the deputy minister of Ontario's Department of Game without success.[13] In January 1929, Padjena and Quesawa were brought before Magistrate Depew in the town of White River to answer the charges against them. Burke was stunned. Recent arrests of Anishinaabeg hunters in his agency usually resulted in confiscated furs but no formal charges against the hunter. He believed that the trial was meant to make an example of the two men, and asked Scott to provide a lawyer. Scott refused, believing that, regardless of Indian Affairs' efforts, the men would be found guilty. He advised Burke to attend the trial and ask the magistrate for leniency on compassionate grounds when sentencing the two hunters.[14]

When the trial began, Harold Harrison, the arresting game warden, gave his testimony first; it was short and concise.[15] He and Wilfred Foubert, another game warden from the Lake Nipigon region, intercepted Padjena and Quesawa at White Lake. They searched their toboggan and found thirty "green" (untanned) beaver pelts. When it was time for Padjena and Quesawa to present their defence, they received more support from Burke than just a plea for leniency. Acting as counsel for the accused, Burke did his best to establish a case for leniency while at the same time expounding on the promises in the Robinson-Superior Treaty. He began by cross-examining warden Foubert, clearly attempting to establish the difficulty the Pic Anishinaabeg endured as they tried to support themselves. He led Foubert to admit that he saw no rabbits near the Pic Reserve. Rabbits were an important source of food for the Anishinaabeg. A lack of rabbits drove Padjena and Quesawa to trap beaver as an alternative. Beaver pelts at this time of year were worth very little because the animals were caught at the beginning of winter, before their fur thickened; an adult beaver, however, yielded a considerable amount of food.

Padjena's testimony reinforced what Burke had tried to accomplish with Foubert. Questioned by Burke, he related that he supported a wife, two children, an uncle, and an aunt. He was hunting for moose, caribou, and even rabbit when he eventually settled for beaver because no other game could be found. Chief Desmoulin testified regarding the lack of game for his community to hunt. He also addressed the court regarding the Robinson-Superior Treaty and the Crown's promise to protect Anishinaabeg harvesting rights "so long as the sun moves, the water runs, and the green grass grows." The Crown, Desmoulin said, was breaking this promise. Furthermore, he maintained, white hunters overhunted the animals. In desperation, Anishinaabeg hunters hunted whatever they could whenever they could simply to have enough food to eat. In his statement to Magistrate Depew, Burke said that the closing of logging camps had forced whites to hunt more than usual. They were the ones breaking the game laws, not the Anishinaabeg. Burke asked Depew to take this and the financial situation of the accused into consideration and show them leniency in his decision.

Depew adopted a contractualist interpretation of the treaties: they were the equivalent of a contract between two parties. From this perspective, treaty rights are no different from a clause in a standard contract, and no contract can usurp the legislative authority of the state.[16] By placing the Robinson Treaties in this legal context, Depew further strengthened the state's control over the Anishinaabeg. Their treaties ceased to be unique. They became a legal contract between two parties, subject to state regulation and the requirement of case law. Drawing upon the 1921 decision in *Sero v. Gault*, Depew ruled that the Ontario government could "make regulations affecting Game and Fisheries, and ... include Indians in said Regulations."[17] *Sero v. Gault* concerned a woman from the Tyendinaga Reserve in Hastings County on the Bay of Quinte. The woman, Sero, had her four-hundred-foot fishing seine confiscated by Thomas Gault, a Dominion fishery inspector, and John Fleming, an Ontario game and fisheries warden. Sero argued that the Haudenosaunee, as an independent people and former allies of the British Crown, never submitted themselves to Crown rule when they relocated to the Bay of Quinte in the late eighteenth century. Therefore, neither Gault nor Fleming had the right to confiscate her seine. Justice Riddell of the Supreme Court of Ontario sided with Ottawa and the province. Without a valid fishing licence, Sero was in violation of Ontario's and Canada's fishing regulations. Riddell drew upon pre-Confederation precedents regarding Mohawk sovereignty in Upper Canada. First, he referred to an earlier case in which a Mohawk charged with murder was found guilty and sentenced. He also noted that under English common law, those born within the dominions of the Crown were subjects of the Crown. Based on this, Riddell ruled that the Mohawk were subject to any laws enacted in Canada.[18]

Regarding Padjena and Quesawa, Depew was "lenient" in sentencing. Ontario's Game Act provided for a fine of between $20 and $100 per skin. Depew acknowledged "the hardships which at present the Indians are enduring owing to the scarcity of Game" and set the fine at $20 per skin for a total of $600, or thirty days' hard labour in the Port Arthur Jail.[19] This was a severe burden.

Arthur McComber, a Port Arthur lawyer, filed an appeal on behalf of the convicted. Burke, sympathetic to the plight of the Anishinaabeg, supported the appeal. J.D. McLean, however, refused to back this effort. Indeed, he wrote to the Department of Game to assure provincial officials that Indian Affairs was not behind this effort to overturn the conviction. McLean insisted that Indian Affairs had tried to convince the Anishinaabeg to adhere to provincial conservation laws.[20] McLean's assurances to Game officials were clearly at odds with the sentiments of several of the Indian agents in northern Ontario as well as D.C. Scott. The agents were aware of McLean's unbending policy towards treaty hunting rights and he was quickly left "outside the loop" regarding the *Padjena* appeal. Henceforth, Burke wrote to Scott directly.

Justice McKay of the Ontario Divisional Court in Port Arthur heard the appeal in late April 1929. McComber's arguments rested on several grounds: the contract between the Anishinaabeg and the Crown, the constitutional division of powers under the British North America Act, and existing case law.[21] It was a sophisticated argument. McComber made only one claim that was picayune in nature, that Magistrate Depew had heard a case that lay outside his territorial jurisdiction. This was a technical argument on McComber's part, one he could not ignore on the off chance it led to an acquittal.

When the Crown entered into the Robinson Treaties, McComber argued, it freely made promises to the Anishinaabeg to secure those land cessions. Furthermore, the Crown made no effort to restrict Anishinaabeg harvesting activity after signing the treaties. Anishinaabeg hunters exercised their rights freely and without restraint from the colonial government of Canada or, for some time after 1867, the governments of Ontario and Canada. McComber also stated that the Crown fully understood its promises to the Anishinaabeg. There was no ambiguity in the treaties regarding hunting and trapping.

Only the Dominion government, McComber reasoned, could potentially restrict Anishinaabeg harvesting. First, matters concerning Indians and lands reserved for Indians were given to the Dominion government under section 91(24) of the Constitution. McComber took the constitutional interpretation of treaty rights a step further, arguing that First Nations' treaty rights constituted an interest other than that of Ontario in the land and its wildlife. Section 109 of the British North America Act established that provincial land was "subject to any Trusts existing in respect thereof, and to any Interest other than that of the Province in the same." McComber connected the dots between sections 109 and 91(24): First Nations had an interest in the land, that interest was confirmed in a treaty, and Indians and lands reserved for Indians were a Dominion responsibility; therefore, constitutional jurisdiction over treaty harvesting rights lay with the Dominion government. Overall, McComber concluded, Ontario's Game Act, when applied to treaty Indians, was *ultra vires* of the Ontario legislature.

McComber reserved special criticism for Depew's interpretation of the *Sero v. Gault* decision because there were no similarities between the two incidents. First, the Haudenosaunee on the Bay of Quinte settled there in 1783 because they lost their traditional lands in Upper New York State following the American Revolution. They obtained the Bay of Quinte lands when the Mississauga surrendered a portion of their territory to the Crown (which then deeded it to the Haudenosaunee). Padjena and Quesawa, McComber noted, were descendants of the Pic River Anishinaabeg who inhabited and used the land north of Lake Superior prior to 1850. When their ancestors surrendered their land to the Crown, the treaty protected their harvesting rights. Furthermore, Sero did not claim a treaty right but argued a continued right to fish because the Haudenosaunee had never surrendered their sovereignty to the Crown. Finally, colonial game laws existed in 1850 but the Crown chose to exempt the Anishinaabeg from them in both the Robinson Treaties and the existing game legislation.

By comparison, Crown attorney W.F. Langworthy's arguments were disingenuous and feeble.[22] Langworthy concerned himself with the least important component of McComber's argument: that Depew ruled on a matter outside of his territorial jurisdiction. He spent two pages dissecting this argument to prove that Depew had sufficient authority to try the case. When he addressed McComber's other arguments, he either ignored key elements (such as the constitutional arguments) or was dishonest in his presentation of the facts. First, he attempted to recast the provincial

Order-in-Council that made beaver trapping south of the National Transcontinental Railway illegal as a law of general application. Laws of general application affect everyone. Criminal law, for example, applies to First Nations as much as to any other Canadian. Langworthy wanted Justice McKay to consider this Order-in-Council no differently, and ignore the fact that the order referred specifically to Indians.

Langworthy also questioned the legitimacy of the Robinson-Superior Treaty. Referring to it as the "so called Treaty," he said no evidence existed to prove that the treaty had not been "cancelled or modified, if ever it was effective." Langworthy's use of the phrase "so called" was an allusion to Justice Riddell's decision in *Sero v. Gault,* as Riddell used the same phrase to describe the agreement between the Haudenosaunee that settled on the Bay of Quinte and the Crown.[23] It was not an argument likely to sway McKay. Earlier decisions, including those of the Judicial Committee of the Privy Council, accepted that treaties existed between the Crown and First Nations. What was at issue was the legal weight these treaties carried.

Only at the end of his polemic did Langworthy's real goals become apparent: he wanted the case removed from the court of appeal and sent to the Office of the Attorney General so that it could become a stated case and the constitutional issues could be addressed. Given the outcome of the Hudson's Bay Company's earlier stated case, it is possible that the Attorney General's Office hoped to engage in the same political manipulation of the courts. It would at least allow the provincial government to stall the matter.

Langworthy's arguments proved futile. On 10 April 1930, Justice McKay overturned Padjena and Quesawa's conviction and delivered a stinging indictment of both Ontario's game laws and the province's treatment of the Anishinaabeg. McKay's ruling is interesting for its departure from the contractual interpretation of treaties and the court precedents established in *Sero* (previously mentioned) and the more recent *R. v. Syliboy.*[24] McKay noted that the Robinson-Superior Treaty was binding on both the Ontario and the Dominion governments. Drawing upon McComber's argument, McKay stated that treaties constituted a "supreme law of the land."[25] Furthermore, he concluded that Anishinaabeg hunting rights could not be restricted to reserve lands. Instead, he interpreted the concept of land reserved for Indians in section 91(24) within the broader context of the treaty. Since the Robinson-Superior Treaty promised the Anishinaabeg the right to harvest unimpeded over all unoccupied Crown land, this meant that "reserves and lands reserved for Indians" under section

91(24) included unoccupied Crown land. The Anishinaabeg therefore constituted a competing interest on such land as outlined in section 109 of the Constitution. That interest, furthermore, lay solely within the constitutional purview of the Dominion government.

McKay dealt quickly with Langworthy's argument that the Order-in-Council was a law of general application, saying that it expressly legislated in respect of First Nations. Furthermore, he declared both the Order-in-Council and the Game Act to be *ultra vires*. McKay referenced an earlier Manitoba Court of Appeal ruling, *R. v. Rodgers* (1923) to support his ruling. In that instance, a treaty Indian trapped a mink on reserve and sold the pelt off reserve. Chief Justice Perdue ruled that Manitoba's Game Act was *ultra vires* when applied to treaty Indians hunting on their reserves. Perdue also wrote, in a broader context, that laws of general application cannot apply to those parts of the province over which the government has no jurisdiction.[26] Following that logic, McKay ruled that the provincial government had no jurisdiction when it came to affecting Anishinaabeg treaty rights in Ontario.

McKay's ruling caught Langworthy by surprise. He reserved the right to file notice of appeal after consulting with Ontario's attorney general. Meanwhile, McComber and agents Burke and Frank Edwards (the Indian agent from Kenora who allied with Burke on this issue) contacted Scott and pleaded that Indian Affairs not lose this opportunity to "continue the fight for these Indians."[27] Scott must have been pleased. He could support Padjena and Quesawa without appearing to challenge the Ontario government or its game laws. Now that McKay's verdict was moving forward to a higher court, Scott could argue to provincial officials (and his own minister, who opposed legal challenges) that Indian Affairs had little choice but to become involved in the legal proceedings since it affected Indian Affairs directly.

In this effort, Scott decided to sidestep his own department and the Department of Justice and secure the services of M.H. Ludwig of the Toronto firm of Ludwig, Schuyler and Fisher. Retaining outside legal assistance allowed Scott to direct the appeal since Ludwig would be answerable to him. Scott would not have to contend with opposition from lawyers in the Department of Justice. He controlled all elements of the forthcoming appeal. He corresponded directly with Ludwig, and he did not keep the Department of Justice updated or apprised of the evolving situation.

Other events in the north further convinced Scott that there was little chance of reaching a political settlement with Ontario without the benefit of a court ruling. Within a few days of McKay's ruling, Walter Soulier of the Michipicoten Reserve and his Indian agent, T.J. Godfrey, wrote letters to Scott and A.F. Mackenzie, Indian Affairs' new deputy and secretary (J.D. McLean had finally retired). Godfrey outlined the desperate straits of the Anishinaabeg in his agency, warning that Indian Affairs was responsible for supplying them with relief if they could not secure enough food through hunting. He corroborated everything Soulier said about game wardens' harassment of Anishinaabeg hunters. Further compounding this problem, Godfrey noted, was the most recent and largest example of the Department of Game's indifferent attitude towards treaty rights: the Chapleau Game Preserve, which denied twenty-five to thirty families in his agency access to their traplines.[28]

Scott recognized that the *Padjena* appeal represented another opportunity to settle the issue of treaty hunting rights in Ontario. However, it was an opportunity that could founder if the Ontario government acted as it did in the earlier HBC case, when it stalled for years. Scott wrote to Charles McCrea, Ontario's minister of mines (and minister responsible for game and fish) to prevent a similar occurrence. First, he lied to McCrea, stating that his department was unaware that Padjena and Quesawa had appealed their initial conviction but was now obligated to support both men as they requested Indian Affairs' aid. Scott sought to place the appeal in a positive light, as the best way to settle an issue that was "an embarrassment to both our departments," and said that it was not being undertaken by Indian Affairs in a "hostile spirit."[29]

Compared with the HBC case, the *Padjena* appeal moved forward quickly. In October 1930, Ludwig faced Ontario's counsel, Charles Garvey. Hearing the case was Justice Hodgins, the same Hodgins who had heard the HBC's stated case. During this first meeting, Hodgins informed both lawyers of what happened during that case. Ludwig interpreted this declaration positively, believing that Hodgins considered Ontario's game laws overly restrictive when applied to treaty Indians.[30]

It was a sentiment shared by Garvey, who sought to stall the case. Just before the appeal was to begin in January 1931, Garvey asked Ludwig for a postponement so that the Ontario government could "go fully into the question of Game and Fisheries ... and settle a policy in regard thereto."[31] When the two lawyers appeared back in court, Garvey again asked for time so that the Ontario government could "[lay] down some future policy regarding Indians ... which will be satisfactory to the Department of Indian Affairs."[32] Scott had already advised Ludwig to oppose this motion, noting that he had received no indication that the provincial government was considering new policies. Ludwig duly did so, and the court granted Garvey only one additional month.

It is a cliché to note that a week is a long time in politics. In this case, it took less than two weeks for Ludwig's appeal to fall to pieces. Only two days before the appeal hearing, Ludwig notified Scott that the Crown was including an additional argument in its appeal, specifically that Padjena and Quesawa had trapped their pelts outside the northern boundary of the Robinson Treaties.[33] Ludwig received two weeks to consider this new evidence. He asked Scott for information regarding Treaty 9 and whether it contained hunting promises similar to those found in the Robinson Treaties. A.S. Williams, assistant deputy superintendent general of Indian Affairs, responded that Treaty 9 provided for the regulation of Aboriginal harvesting activity but, regardless, Padjena and Quesawa could not seek protection under a treaty other than the Robinson-Superior Treaty.[34] With this, the *Padjena* appeal ended.

The appeal collapsed over the issue of family hunting territories rather than Treaty 9 and whether it allowed for government regulation of Indigenous hunting. While the official version of Treaty 9 states that Indigenous hunting was subject to regulation, Scott was aware that the Mushkegowuk and Anishinaabeg of Treaty 9 had received oral assurances that their harvesting practices would not be limited by the treaty.[35] Instead, Scott's and Williams's interpretation of the Robinson-Superior Treaty was, by today's standards, limited. It was an issue of treaty right portability: can a First Nation's treaty rights extend beyond its treaty boundaries? This question is generally predicated on whether First Nations made use of a given area prior to the creation of a treaty. In this case, the issue hinged on whether either Padjena or Quesawa was trapping in an area traditionally used by the Pic River Anishinaabeg. The answer is yes.

Scott, however, wanted an ideal case to push the issue of treaty rights. Going forward with an appeal on an issue that was not legally well defined at that time was not something he could risk. It probably never occurred to him that treaty right portability and traditional land use and boundaries were a potential route for the appeal. He could appreciate that a ruling against the Anishinaabeg made the possibility of provincial concessions almost impossible. A clear legal ruling upholding the treaties and the right to hunt and trap for subsistence was the most Indian Affairs was willing to achieve, and it would not push for more. An unfavourable ruling would only strengthen the Department of Game and scupper Scott's chances of negotiating with the Ontario government and those provincial governments across Canada that had enacted similar game laws. As a test case, which is what *R. v. Padjena* was, Scott needed greater assurance of a favourable ruling.

THE BLACK COMMITTEE

Scott's insistence on finding an ideal test case was not irrational. Provincial thinking on the issue of treaty hunting rights had not improved since the first Game Commission in 1892. Indeed, provincial animosity towards the idea of treaty hunting rights and First Nations hunting in general had become more pronounced. Several years before the *Padjena* trial, the Ontario government formed a standing committee to investigate the state of wildlife in the province.[36] Based on the evidence it collected, the standing committee recommended that the Ontario government create another committee to conduct a thorough overview of the state of wildlife in Ontario. Formed in 1931, the Black Committee visited numerous communities throughout the province and took testimony from numerous witnesses.[37] As with previous game committees, it devoted considerable time to the issue of First Nations hunting and treaty rights.

Three separate meetings were held in which both Indian Affairs (represented by Dr. E.L. Stone and T.R.L. MacInnes) and the Hudson's Bay Company (represented by Frank McCarthy, son of Leighton McCarthy, and J.B. Matthews) made presentations to the Black Committee: in Toronto, Fort William, and Chapleau. Despite the best efforts of these men, and others such as local missionaries and RCMP officers, the committee refused to consider First Nations as anything other than a serious detriment to wildlife conservation. The bigotry of the committee members was evident, but Indian Affairs and the HBC also ran up against the prejudice of local conservationists who provided the committee with anecdotal evidence of First Nations depredation. It became clear to Stone, MacInnes, and the others that wildlife conservation policy, whether informed from the bottom up or the top down, was infused with anti-First Nations bias.

Economics underlay much of the committee's desire to regulate wildlife regardless of treaty rights. First Nations hunting threatened a valuable provincial resource that benefited both government revenue and local businesses. By 1930, the Department of Game was reaping approximately $775,000 annually from hunting and fishing licences and other fees. The department actually had a surplus of $88,000.[38] Fines and the sale of confiscated equipment brought in over $20,000, and the provincial government provided food to hospitals and relief agencies by butchering the confiscated game and fish.[39] Far greater than this was the economic value of hunting and trapping. In 1930, the Department of Game estimated the total value of all the pelts trapped in Ontario at $2.5 million dollars.[40] It estimated the total economic value of hunting, trapping, and fishing (involving outfitters, guides, and hotel and tourist operators that catered to this clientele) at between $50 million and $80 million a year.[41] Wildlife was big business.

Indian Affairs' representatives could do little except relate the facts as best they could, and try to embarrass the committee members into acknowledging that First Nations were not the cause of game depletion. MacInnes argued this point strenuously. During the Fort William and Chapleau meetings, local officials such as Indian agents, missionaries, RCMP officers, and others made even stronger representations. Chairman Black remained unmoved by their testimony, however. He even began one Fort William meeting by noting that First Nations were the chief culprits in overhunting. Previous representations by local hunters and provincial officers contained stories of Indigenous peoples wantonly slaughtering animals, and Black wanted to know what steps Indian Affairs took to curb these abuses and discipline its wards.[42]

Other members of the committee were similarly antagonistic. One of them was Jack Miner, better known as "Wild Goose Jack."[43] His work with geese made him a prominent conservationist in Ontario, a legacy that continues to this day. He was, however, as much a product of his time as anyone. Just as the Department of Game sought to control pests (wolves, foxes, weasels, and any other predatory animal), so too did Miner: hawks, falcons, and any other animal that preyed on his beloved geese were destroyed by him and those who supported his conservation plans. Like many conservationists at that time, he did not seek to conserve all wildlife – only those species he liked and believed had value. Just as the early 1892 Game Commission had equated First Nations with wolves, Miner considered First Nations hunters to be pests. Referring to his goose-tagging program, he related how the northern Mushkegowuk slaughtered geese on James Bay. He paid five dollars to anyone who returned the tags to him so he could determine the territory covered by the geese during their migrations. He stated that he sent the money "to Indians who sent down the tags, but the time came when they were sending down so many tags that I had to stop sending up the money."[44]

Miner did not understand (nor did he wish to learn about) the annual goose hunt upon which the northern Mushkegowuk depended. Instead, like other conservationists, he wanted First Nations to abandon traditional practices and integrate themselves into white Canada's tradition and conception of sport hunting. He argued that First Nations were incapable of conservation because this required them to consider their future well-being. First Nations, he maintained, could not see the great business opportunities the tourist trade offered them to work as guides for sport hunters. From his perspective, traditional Aboriginal skills were valuable only insofar as they fit into the burgeoning tourist industry. The tourist trade, he said, was like "ripened wheat ready for the harvest of the people of Northern Ontario." Threatening this harvest were the treaty rights of the Anishinaabeg and Mushkegowuk.

MacInnes was placed in the position of defending treaty rights in Ontario, more specifically those outlined in the Robinson Treaties, as many of the arrests up to this point had occurred in that part of the province. Questions by Black and other committee members reflected their ignorance of not only the treaty promises made by the Crown in 1850 but also other issues. Black asked what rights the Robinson Treaties conferred on the Anishinaabeg. Other members wanted to know whether the Anishinaabeg had exclusive rights to hunt and trap. Could they do so in Algonquin Park? What constituted unoccupied Crown land in Indian Affairs' estimation? Could the Robinson Treaties be renegotiated to remove the hunting clause (an odd question since the Department of Game already considered the treaties inconsequential)? Unaware of differences in climate and soil condition, one committee member asked why the Anishinaabeg of northern Ontario didn't farm like the people of Six Nations Reserve?[45]

Clearly frustrated by the questioning, MacInnes was blunt in his responses. Anishinaabeg within the Robinson Treaties, he stated, possessed the right to hunt, trap, and fish as they pleased on unoccupied Crown land. Aware, no doubt, of the controversy surrounding the Chapleau Game Preserve, MacInnes criticized Ontario's policy of setting aside large tracts of land as game preserves and declaring the land occupied. Regarding farming, MacInnes replied that most of the land in northern Ontario (not to mention the climate) was unsuitable for intensive agriculture. Exasperated, he finally told committee members that "if any of you gentlemen had a contract with Her Majesty, the Queen, you would think you had some rights." MacInnes recommended that all the land north of the Canadian National Railway be set aside as an exclusive First

Nations trapping territory, and that large portions of unoccupied Crown land south of the CNR be reserved for similar use.

Support for Anishinaabeg harvesting rights continued when the committee moved from Toronto to Chapleau and Fort William. G.B. Nicholson, Member of Parliament for Algoma East, Father Couture (a Catholic missionary stationed near Lake Nipigon), Corporal Bibbs of the Royal Canadian Mounted Police, Indian agent Frank Edwards from Fort Frances, Indian agent Albert Spencer from Fort William, and Indian agent Godfrey from Chapleau appeared before the committee to argue in favour of protection for Anishinaabeg hunting. Nicholson's testimony is not recorded, but he submitted a memorandum that detailed his opinions and those of the other presenters. Although he believed in the need to acculturate Indigenous peoples, he recognized "the rights of Native races."[46] He questioned the policy being followed by the province when its game laws impoverished the Anishinaabeg instead of enriching them. White trappers and hunters were to blame for the state of wildlife in Ontario, he argued. They despoiled the wildlife the Anishinaabeg had carefully preserved for generations. Nicholson depicted the Anishinaabeg as natural conservationists, taking only what they required when hunting and trapping, and always preserving a sufficient number of mature animals to repopulate an area. He proposed that all the lands north of the Upper Lakes be set aside as an exclusive First Nations trapping and hunting territory, and that the government restrict the issuance of further licences to white trappers. Existing non-First Nations trappers who already had traplines, Nicholson said, should be granted sufficient time to liquidate their equipment and find a new source of income before the province revoked their licences.[47]

The others' testimony was very similar. They were blunt in their assessment of the province's game laws, and took exception to many of the statements made by committee members that reflected both their ignorance of northern Ontario and their lack of knowledge about the Anishinaabeg and the Robinson Treaties. Chairman Black, for example, did not realize that the Anishinaabeg (and Mushkegowuk) regularly fed their dogs fish in the winter. In an exchange with Edwards, Black said that First Nations were wasting fish by throwing them to their dogs.[48] Edwards asked Black how a First Nations hunter, on his trapline in the winter, was supposed to feed his dogs if not with fish. Others outlined the horrible living conditions of the Anishinaabeg. Godfrey reported that of the 250 families in the Chapleau Indian Agency, none could now make a living solely from trapping due to competition from white trappers. Edwards and Spencer said that the situations in the Fort Frances and Fort William agencies were equally desperate.

Bibbs and Edwards challenged Jack Miner directly during one of the meetings. Miner related the testimony of white trappers that First Nations near Cartier (just west of the town of Sudbury) tore open beaver lodges to slaughter the animals for their pelts. Edwards countered that such evidence was suspect, and that stories of First Nations slaughtering game were grossly exaggerated. He knew two of the white hunters who had appeared before the committee, and said they were both well-known poachers who implicated the Anishinaabeg in order to protect their own livelihood. Bibbs invited committee members to visit some of the reservations to see first-hand how the Anishinaabeg families lived, and why they required large amounts of game to feed themselves. He stated that stories of Aboriginal hunters leaving deer and moose meat to rot in the bush were patently false; the families were too desperate for food to allow such waste.

Bibbs related first-hand accounts of white trappers who forcibly expelled several Anishinaabeg hunters from the Pic Mobert Reserve from their traplines. Paul Kwisiwa (likely the same Paul "Quesawa" from the *Padjena* case) and Joe Tokeney, Edwards said, had animals stolen from their traplines during the past winter. During his investigation, he had found written warnings to the Anishinaabeg to stay off these traplines because they belonged to white trappers. Bibbs noted in his report that another Pic trapper, Nicholas Whiskayjack, faced a similar situation when checking his traps near the reserve. An entire bear was taken from him, and a note was left stating that Whiskayjack was trespassing. Bibbs suspected several local trappers, but game authorities did nothing when presented with the information and evidence.

Ontario's Trapline System

Of the Black Committee's recommendations relating to wildlife conservation, the one that had the greatest impact on the Anishinaabeg was the creation of a provincially regulated trapline system. Northern Ontario was divided into three sections: East, Central, and North.[49] Indian Affairs attempted to work within this system on the understanding that Anishinaabeg trappers would receive preferential treatment so they could retain their familial trapping grounds. This was not the case, however, and the system worked to strengthen provincial control at the expense of Anishinaabeg treaty rights. The government system required that trappers first request a specific piece of land for their trapline (each area was approximately eight square miles in size). If a hunter received a trapline, the licence for that specific territory was valid for one year. Hunters had to renew their licences each year, and there was no guarantee that they would receive the same territory from year to year. Built into the system, therefore, was a disincentive to conserve animals to help ensure a trapline's long-term viability. Trappers took as many as they could each year because the next year they might get a new trapline that had been badly maintained.

Imposed upon the Anishinaabeg, the trapline system became another example of state regulation that disparaged alternate forms of land organization. Deputy Minister McDonald informed MacInnes of the new system in early September 1933, and stated that First Nations trappers required a permit so that the Department of Game could properly locate their trapping grounds. McDonald requested Indian agents to aid the three district game superintendents by recording the location of Anishinaabeg trapping territories in their agencies. Such work was ultimately pointless for several reasons. First, government-issued traplines corresponded roughly to the location of townships, whereas traditional Anishinaabeg hunting/trapping territories did not conform to provincially imposed township lines. Natural boundaries such as a lake or clump of trees were more likely to determine such boundaries.[50] A hunter's family territory could conceivably cross several township lines. Second, the system operated on a first-come, first-served basis. Anishinaabeg trappers received no special privileges to access their traditional lands. Furthermore, it was common for Anishinaabeg trappers to leave their traplines unused for one or two years to give local animal populations an opportunity to breed and repopulate. This was no longer possible under the new system. Finally, as the system was implemented it became apparent that local game officials were often remiss in notifying Anishinaabeg trappers or Indian agents of deadlines for acquiring traplines, depriving them of the opportunity to apply.

Despite these difficulties, MacInnes optimistically instructed Indian agents in March 1937 to gather information from their bands regarding trapping territories in their agencies. He noted that the system would soon take effect, and he wanted the Anishinaabeg to have the best possible trapping grounds and, if possible, "to have the old trapping grounds frequently used by [them]."[51] A report from the Nipissing Agency perhaps convinced MacInnes that an imperfect system was better than the existing chaos. Michael Christianson, general superintendent of Indian agencies, and Thomas McGookin, district superintendent for northeastern Ontario, toured the Nipissing, Temagami, and Matachewan bands in February

1937. Both men noted the growing number of white trappers in the north, which forced Anishinaabeg trappers to travel further to find good trapping grounds. Christianson related that some Nipissing Anishinaabeg used the CPR to go as far as Chapleau.[52] McGookin said that summer guiding employed large numbers of men from the reserves, but this money did not sustain them through the winter. Only hunting and trapping provided them with consistent income and food. McGookin, who oversaw a number of agencies, thought that the trapline system gave the Anishinaabeg an opportunity to prove to game officials that they were conscientious trappers who knew how to manage their traplines.[53]

While Indian Affairs was willing to work within this system, the Anishinaabeg were skeptical. George Prewar provided some insight into Anishinaabeg opinion. Specifically, they did not understand why they should agree to a regulated, restricted system when their treaties promised them continued harvesting rights over all unoccupied Crown land.[54] After forty years of arrests, harassment, and loss of treaty rights, it is not surprising that the bands did not want to take part in the Department of Game's latest conservation scheme. One also cannot overlook the Anishinaabeg perception of Indian Affairs, which had not been able to protect their hunting rights for forty years (and actively worked to undermine other treaty rights). When it sent its Indian agents to the various reserves to gather information for Ontario's proposed trapline system, the Anishinaabeg refused to participate. For example, John Daly of the Nipissing Agency related that when he took the trapline matter to the bands in his agency, the band members "shut up and wont [sic] say anything."[55] It was not a unique response. Fort Frances Indian agent Albert Spencer said that only a minority of the trappers in his agency expressed any interest in the system. Regardless, Spencer set aside land in his agency.[56]

Despite the difficulties faced by some of the agents, all of them requested that fairly large areas of land be set aside for their bands.[57] Agent G.H. Sims in Sault Ste. Marie wanted 550 square miles set aside. Agent Rothera in Thessalon requested 850 square miles for the Thessalon and Mississauga bands, and a separate parcel of 1,000 square miles for the Serpent River and Spanish River bands. Godfrey asked for 2,450 square miles for the Michipicoten Anishinaabeg who hunted in the area of Chapleau, and an additional 1,500 square miles around Missinaibi Lake.

Despite MacInnes's optimism, the trapline system failed almost immediately. Godfrey's annual reports for the Chapleau Agency provide good examples of the problems that arose during the first two winters that the system was in operation. He reported in January 1938 that regulations regarding trapping quotas continued to prevent the Anishinaabeg from getting enough beaver, and when they worked their traplines they could not hunt out-of-season animals such as moose or deer. Beaver quotas were so low, Godfrey stated, that the Anishinaabeg could no longer hunt in such a manner to support their families. All they could do was wait for the March muskrat season.[58] A lack of employment in the agency only exacerbated the problem. Not only did it make trapping and hunting more important to the Anishinaabeg (who could not find work) but it also drove more whites to apply for traplines.[59] Consequently, the bands relied heavily on relief. In his March and April report, Godfrey noted that he distributed extra supplies to many of the families so that they could travel further to find muskrat, moose, and deer.[60] Godfrey, hopeful about the trapline system only a year earlier, now thought it was a policy designed to push Anishinaabeg trappers off the land.

Further Department of Game policies only reinforced this opinion. Godfrey noted in his March 1939 report that the department created an additional short beaver season that spring, but that it was done quickly and quietly. Only a few Anishinaabeg trappers in his agency secured licences because the department specified only a two-day window to purchase licences.[61] On another occasion, Godfrey reported that the department changed some regulations in mid-season, resulting in the arrest of several Anishinaabeg. Once on their lines, Godfrey stated, few families returned to town until the spring melt. They had no way of learning about the new regulations. Lastly, Godfrey said the system was not properly policed by game wardens or provincial officers to prevent poaching. Instead, white trappers trapped "all over the Indians [sic] territory where he has conserved beaver for years." Fort Frances agent J.F. Lockhart agreed. His November 1939 report relates that trappers in his agency still lost ground to white trappers. Lockhart referred to an Anishinaabeg trapper who had used a certain area for ten years only to have a white trapper receive a trapping permit for the same territory.[62]

Anishinaabeg understanding of the treaties was irrelevant to the Department of Game. Racist attitudes towards the Anishinaabeg, so common in the Game Commission's founding 1892 report, continued unchanged and unchallenged forty years later. State interest in the regulation of game grew unabated as the economic value of the province's wildlife increased. Although Indian Affairs took an increasing interest in securing some leniency for Anishinaabeg hunters, the limited nature of case law and legal concepts during this period prevented it from pushing the issue through the courts. *R. v. Padjena* was a failure on the part of Indian Affairs, but it also represented the broader inability of non-Indigenous people to appreciate both the treaties and hunting/trapping from the Anishinaabeg perspective. Until the courts, Indian Affairs, and provincial officials were willing to consider the Anishinaabeg understanding of the treaties, little could be done.

Indian Affairs was slowly coming around to the Anishinaabeg perspective, albeit in a limited fashion. Although still focused on acculturation as the end goal, D.C. Scott and like-minded officials recognized that the Anishinaabeg interpretation that the treaties protected their hunting and trapping was historically and legally correct. Scott could not comprehend the concept of inter-treaty harvesting rights and treaty rights portability based on family hunting territories, but it is clear that senior officials who came after him (including Indian agents) saw that denying the Anishinaabeg access to familial hunting grounds was inherently unfair. Frustrating any effort to reach an accommodation were provincial game officials, who continued to blame the Anishinaabeg for any problems with game management in the province. Unwilling to come to any power-sharing arrangement with Indian Affairs (and certainly not with the Anishinaabeg), the Department of Game extended its control and regulation of wildlife in the province. Short of a legal decision establishing the validity of treaty hunting rights, little could be done to protect Anishinaabeg hunting in the Robinson Treaties.

7
R. v. Commanda, 1937–39

If this isn't discrimination what is?
— Hugh Conn

At the end of the 1930s, Ontario defined and controlled First Nations harvesting rights in Ontario. First Nations efforts to protect their treaty rights in the courts had failed. Indian Affairs was willing to help the Anishinaabeg, but only to a limited extent. It wanted to use the question of treaty rights as a political lever to pry concessions from the Department of Game, but was unwilling to risk a full constitutional confrontation with Ontario over this issue. Further hampering Indian Affairs was its own paternalism: it wanted to recognize treaty rights to secure First Nations some leniency when hunting, but not at the expense of losing its own control over the lives of Indigenous peoples.

The opinions of two scholars concerning this period help explain the conflicting ideas that characterized Indian Affairs at this time. Anthropologist Harold Hawthorn, in his 1966 study *A Survey of Contemporary Indians of Canada,* (often called the Hawthorn report) observed that historically treaties "are relatively unimportant as determinants of government policy."[1] Treaties were useful to Indian Affairs insofar as they advanced a departmental goal, in this case securing some leniency for subsistence hunting. Treaties were not important for their own sake. However, historian John Leslie notes that during the 1930s and 1940s, a slow shift began to occur at Indian Affairs, which began to work towards cooperating with some of the emerging First Nations political organizations.[2] Leslie's research is born out in this study as Indian Affairs was increasingly willing to take the advice of its northern Indian agents, who reported on the difficult condition the Anishinaabeg found themselves in, at least with regard to hunting. The opinions of Leslie and Hawthorn, seemingly irreconcilable, accurately reflect what was happening at Indian Affairs regarding the issue of hunting rights. An older approach (outlined by Hawthorn) reflected the old pattern of paternalism and acculturation that still affected and directed much of what Indian Affairs did; Leslie, however, reveals that Indian Affairs bureaucrats slowly began to understand that older methods of interacting with First Nations did not work. This desire to challenge old approaches was nascent and weak, but suggested an emerging, more modern approach to treaties and treaty rights.

It was a tension reflected in the careers of D.C. Scott and J.D. McLean. During his tenure as department secretary, McLean consistently opposed the extension of any consideration to Aboriginal treaty rights. Scott, albeit in a limited fashion, appreciated the need to offer the Anishinaabeg some protection of their treaty rights. Following his retirement in 1932, it became clear that his approach was the new paradigm for Indian Affairs. This manifested in the 1930s when Secretary MacInnes appeared before the Black Committee and defended Anishinaabeg subsistence hunting in a manner that would have been impossible before Scott became deputy superintendent general. Scott's successor, Dr. Harold McGill, continued his predecessor's approach. As the failure of the trapline system became obvious, both McGill and MacInnes actively sought a test case to bring the question of hunting rights before the courts and force the province to make legal concessions. Until such time, Indian Affairs could not avoid cooperating with the Department of Game. Regardless of any objections made by Indian Affairs, the province would implement its trapline system; it was better to work with the province and attempt to ameliorate the Anishinaabegs' situation as events unfolded. Protesting was futile. Therefore, as the trapline system developed, MacInnes and McGill (now with the new title of Director of Indian Affairs) formulated their strategy to test the constitutionality of Ontario's conservation laws.[3]

McGill did not seek to protect treaty harvesting rights as a matter of principle. It was clear that Ontario's callous application of its game laws unduly affected the Anishinaabeg and was causing a serious hardship. McGill, like Scott before him, wanted to use a legal victory to extract concessions from Ontario. He outlined his goal in a memorandum to his new minister, Thomas Crerar, in September 1937,[4] explaining his intention to appeal a future conviction of an Anishinaabeg hunter arrested within the Robinson Treaties area. McGill said that the hunting matter needed to be settled, but assured the minister that the policy was not meant to provide the Anishinaabeg with unrestricted hunting and trapping rights. There was no interest among anyone at Indian Affairs to set such a precedent. McGill conceded that this policy entailed legal expenses but was necessary considering the years Indian Affairs had devoted to futile negotiations with game officials.

McGill and MacInnes were very particular about the conditions required to initiate a test case. Well aware of why the *Padjena* case failed, both men wanted any future test case to be as legally perfect as possible. For example, when two men from the Fort William Reserve were convicted for possessing moose meat out of season in July 1937, MacInnes refused to support the local Indian agent's request for legal assistance because the men had killed the moose in a provincial game preserve. Despite MacInnes's earlier statements to the Black Committee regarding the province's predilection for creating preserves, he was not convinced that a court would consider a game preserve unoccupied Crown land.[5]

A year passed before Indian Affairs found its "ideal" test case: the arrest of Joseph Commanda, John O'Jeek, Louis Shabogesic, and Angus Shabogesic of the Nipissing Reserve for hunting moose and deer out of season. These men killed the deer near Tomiko Lake, approximately twelve kilometres north of the reserve. This area was unoccupied Crown land and it was an unorganized township. All four men were status Indians covered by the Robinson-Huron Treaty, and the deer was killed for subsistence purposes well within the boundaries of the treaty.

On 17 February 1938, Joseph Commanda appeared before Magistrate McCurry in Sturgeon Falls. Police released John O'Jeek, Louis Shabogesic, and Angus Shabogesic earlier as they had not killed the deer; they only helped carry some of the meat out of the bush. Commanda, however, did not stand alone. John Fisher, also of the Nipissing Reserve, killed a deer and moose shortly after Commanda's ill-fated hunting trip. Arrested by the police, his case was similar enough to Commanda's that the magistrate heard both at the same time. Fisher's and Commanda's circumstances met the conditions Indian Affairs required for a test case. It paid a local lawyer, Marleau, to represent the accused. E.A. Tilley, North Bay's Crown attorney, prosecuted. Trial transcripts reveal a clear difference between how Marleau and Tilley approached their examinations and cross-examinations.[6] They also provide insight into how game wardens operated.

Tilley began with an examination of the two arresting game wardens, William St. Pierre and David Gauthier. He focused on the quantity of moose and deer killed (three moose were killed by Fisher) and the killing of a calf moose less than one year old (one of the three killed by Fisher). When Marleau cross-examined the wardens, he focused on treaty rights and the fact that the animals in question were killed for food, not for trade.

Marleau's strategy was to show the court that the wardens not only disregarded the treaty in this instance, but regularly operated with no concern for the Robinson-Huron Treaty. For example, he had the wardens testify in court that both Commanda and Fisher stated that they had a treaty right to hunt when arrested. Marleau also established that neither warden received any instruction from their superiors to "be lenient with the Indians of Nipissing on account of they had no hunting grounds." He also asked whether either official received information regarding the Robinson Treaties or the hunting promises contained therein. In each instance, both St. Pierre and Gauthier responded, "No." Marleau also established that Commanda and Fisher were within the boundaries of the treaty, that Commanda had no means of making a living apart from hunting, and that he had eight children to support. Magistrate McCurry asked whether the area in which Commanda shot the moose was an unorganized territory, to which Commanda responded, "Yes, sir."

The trial of Commanda and Fisher was only the first step in what MacInnes hoped would be a series of appeals. Marleau wrote MacInnes during the trial to advise him of the particulars of the case and its suitability as a test case.[7] Within several days, MacInnes referred the case to a Department of Mines attorney, Mr. Cory.[8] Cory reported that under the Robinson-Huron Treaty, the Anishinaabeg retained the right to hunt and trap as they had prior to 1850 over all unoccupied Crown land; the *Commanda* case, Cory concluded, provided an ideal test case for Indian Affairs.[9] Acting on this information, Marleau asked Magistrate McCurry that the Ontario Supreme Court adjudicate the matter as a stated case.[10] McCurry refused, convicted Commanda and Fisher of possessing moose meat out of season, and fined each man twenty-five dollars.[11] Indian Affairs paid the fines out of Nipissing's band fund.[12] MacInnes forwarded all files pertaining to *R. v. Padjena* and the *Commanda* appeal to Cory. Deputy minister of mines Charles Carswell requested the deputy minister of justice to both assess and prepare the appeal.[13] Indian Affairs retained J.H. Macdonald, a North Bay lawyer, to represent Commanda and the other hunters.

R. v. Commanda grabbed the attention of senior Ontario bureaucrats and politicians. Harry Nixon, Ontario's provincial secretary and registrar, took a personal interest in the case.[14] In a memorandum to Nixon, an anonymous aide or bureaucrat noted in the margins that during the initial trial, Magistrate McCurry wrote "here for advise [sic] [regarding the trial]."[15] It suggests that the Attorney General's Office was working in conjunction with the magistrate to get a particular ruling. In the case of

Commanda, one of Nixon's advisors wrote to C.L. Snyder, a senior lawyer in the Attorney General's Office, and directed him to follow the case closely. He impressed upon Snyder that "[we] do not want to leave any stone unturned to hold our position in this matter [of treaty rights]." Furthermore, Snyder was to keep the registrar updated on the issue at all times. Snyder directed C.R. Magone, a department lawyer, to take over the case.

Magone put together a detailed legal memorandum by the end of March 1938, and outlined the arguments he would make before the court.[16] His arguments need to be considered in context as they reflect the impact of an earlier 1932 Alberta Court of Appeal decision, *R. v. Wesley.* William Wesley was a Treaty 7 Nakoda man who killed a deer out of season for food on unoccupied Crown land.[17] The local magistrate refused to listen to Wesley's arguments about how the Treaty 7 people interpreted the hunting promise in the treaty, ruling that Wesley's treaty right could be limited by the Natural Resources Transfer Agreement (1930) that regulated hunting in the province.

Wesley's appeal was heard by Justices McGillivray, Clarke, and Mitchell of the Alberta Court of Appeal. All three justices concurred in their ruling: that the signatories to Treaty 7 and the later creators of the Natural Resources Transfer Agreement would not have sought to restrict Aboriginal hunting for food on unoccupied Crown land. In its ruling, the court stated that "the Indian should be placed in a very different position from the white man who generally speaking does not hunt for food and was by the proviso of s.12 [of the Natural Resources Transfer Agreement] reassured of the continued enjoyment of a right which he has enjoyed from time immemorial."[18] The court reached its conclusion by examining the historical context of treaty creation in Canada. Specifically, it considered Article 40 of the Articles of Capitulation of Montreal (1760), the 1763 Treaty of Paris, and the Royal Proclamation. Justice McGillivray, writing on behalf of the court, even referred to the Royal Proclamation as the "Charter of Indian Rights."[19]

Magone must have been aware of this decision as his memorandum outlined arguments based on an analysis of Article 40 of the Articles of Capitulation (1760), the Royal Proclamation, and instructions to Governor James Murray of Quebec in the 1760s. Article 40 promised that the "savages or Indian allies" of France were to be maintained in their lands and not suffer any punishment for having allied with France. Magone noted that the Royal Proclamation of 1763 made the creation of land agreements between First Nations and the Crown a necessity. Lastly, he drew attention to the instructions given to Governor James Murray of Quebec in the

1760s that "upon no account [was he to] ... molest or disturb them [Indians] in the possession of such parts of the said province as they at present occupy and possess." A modern reading of the documents would interpret them as recognizing Aboriginal ownership of land, as Justice McGillivray did in the *Wesley* decision. However, Magone tried a different interpretation: all three documents cast Aboriginal ownership as existing in a particular moment (i.e., "they at present occupy and possess"), First Nations never constituted nations, and future "treaties" alienated First Nations from the land.

Magone interpreted the Articles of Capitulation as establishing that the First Nations did not constitute nations but were "savages or ... allies" of France. If they were not referred to as nations, and not considered such, then a land treaty could not be considered a formal treaty since First Nations are not foreign or independent powers in the classic diplomatic sense. Treaties are only agreements that can be altered. Magone made this argument in an interview with the Toronto *Daily Star*.[20] He also referred to it when he noted that the government of Canada West did not consider its agreement with the Six Nations of the Grand River to be a treaty because the Haudenosaunee did not constitute a nation.[21] Finally, Magone referred to the magistrate's ruling in *R. v. Wesley,* which stated that "our Treaties with the Indians are on no higher plane than another formal agreement." Magone ignored the more important ruling by the Alberta Court of Appeal.

To counter the argument that the Anishinaabeg retained harvesting rights on unoccupied Crown land, Magone drew upon *St. Catherine's Milling and Lumber Company v. R.* He quoted Lord Watson several times to establish that First Nations title to the land was only a "personal and usufructuary right, dependent upon the good will of the Sovereign," and that the Crown had "a substantial and paramount estate underlying the Indian title." He skillfully dissected *St. Catherine's Milling* to neuter that part of the decision in which Lord Watson said that First Nations title was intrinsically tied to their hunting, fishing, and trapping. He noted that Watson made no specific pronouncement regarding hunting, trapping, and fishing since these were not a crucial element of the *St. Catherine's* decision.

Magone referenced *Attorney-General of Canada v. Attorney-General of Ontario* to establish provincial control over the lands in the Robinson Treaties. This decision revolved around whether Ontario was responsible for making increased annuity payments to bands within the Robinson Treaties because of an annuity escalation clause in the treaties.[22] Ultimately the case ended up before the Privy Council. Lord Watson's ruling strengthened the position of the Ontario government in relation to surrendered First Nations lands. Watson noted that the Robinson Treaties vested both the title to the land and all "beneficial interest" in the land with the Province of Ontario. Accordingly, he found the Ontario government liable for making all treaty annuity payments under the terms of the Robinson Treaties. However, he also noted that the Anishinaabeg obtained "no right to their annuity ... beyond a promise and agreement which was nothing more than a personal obligation by the Governor [of the Province of Canada]; [and] that the Indians obtained no rights which gave them any interest in the territory which they surrendered other than that of the Province." Watson's 1896 ruling had no immediate impact as the Dominion and Ontario governments reached a political solution on the annuity question. Forty-one years later, however, it strengthened Magone's argument that the Robinson Treaties were agreements not treaties, and that these agreements nullified any existing First Nations title or rights to the land when those rights passed to Ontario in 1867.

Finally, Magone argued that Ontario's Game Act was a law of general application and did not conflict with the Dominion government's constitutional jurisdiction over First Nations. Magone cited *Sero v. Gault,* which held that "the provisions of the Ontario Game and Fisheries Act and the Dominion Fisheries Regulations applied to Indians." He also referenced *R. v. Martin* and *R. v. Hill,* in which it was ruled that the Ontario Temperance Act and Ontario's Medical Act, respectively, applied to First Nations. Justice Osler stated in *R. v. Hill* that a First Nations person "is no more free to infringe an Act of the Legislature than to disregard a municipal by-law." Magone referred also to *R. v. Rodgers,* in which Justice Prendergast ruled that once First Nations left their reserve, they were subject to provincial legislation. He did not dwell at length upon *R. v. Padjena.* He could not ignore it, but he was selective in his use of it. Instead of citing Justice McKay's ruling, he noted Justice Hodgins's observation about the Hudson's Bay Company's 1914 case that the Court of Appeal "expressed the opinion that it was unwise to judicially determine the rights of the Indians under the so-called Treaty."

Despite this analysis, Magone advised against treating the Anishinaabeg in an offhand and contemptuous manner, believing that sincere negotiation with Indian Affairs was in the province's best interest. Accordingly, he provided Nixon with a political option. Magone believed that Ontario had the lawful authority to regulate game and fish within the province; however, it could not ignore treaty rights to meet its conservation goals.

To this end, Magone recommended two possible courses of action. Either the province could stop prosecuting the Anishinaabeg (or any First Nations with explicit treaty promises to harvest) under the game laws, or "a sum of money should be paid to [the Anishinaabeg] ... by agreement before their rights are taken away."

Nixon's exact reaction to Magone's suggestion is unknown, but he clearly did not agree. *R. v. Commanda* moved forward in the courts, and Magone made a final submission to Justice Greene in April 1938. Magone's arguments and evidence in his submission remained unchanged from his memorandum to Nixon.

Commanda's lawyer, J.H. Macdonald, also submitted arguments to the court. Although his brief is not as well written as Magone's, his arguments demonstrate a level of sophistication.[23] First, he sought to establish the fiduciary relationship between the Crown and First Nations in relation to Aboriginal lands. Macdonald drew upon the Articles of Capitulation, the Royal Proclamation, and Governor Murray's 1763 instructions – the same documents Magone used to argue that First Nations had no legal rights. All three of these documents, Macdonald argued, show that the Crown, from its first occupation of Canada, recognized Aboriginal interest in the land and the importance of hunting to First Nations. He noted that Aboriginal interests were embedded with the Crown, as represented by the Dominion government, and that this relationship received constitutional recognition with section 91(24) of the British North America Act. Continued First Nations interest in the land was further recognized in section 109 of the BNA Act as an "interest other than of the province in the [land and resources]." Macdonald also contended that section 109 reflected promises made in the Robinson Treaties; Anishinaabeg interest in the land remained until it was occupied in such a manner as to prevent hunting. Ontario, therefore, could affect Anishinaabeg hunting rights within the Robinson Treaties only by leasing or selling land within the treaties to "individuals or companies of individuals" who used the land in such a way that hunting and trapping was not possible.

Macdonald was careful not to imply that laws of general application did not affect First Nations. Treaty promises protected First Nations in a specific manner and context. Only the Dominion government could limit a treaty right, Macdonald argued. He referred to *Sero v. Gault* since Sero's conviction in that instance was based on Dominion fishery regulations, not Ontario's. Macdonald also offered a different interpretation of *R. v. Hill*. He quoted from Justice Osler's decision that the "[Dominion] Parliament may, I suppose, remove him [an Indian] from their [jurisdictional] scope, but, to the extent to which it has not done so, he [an Indian] must in his dealings outside the Reserve govern himself by the general law which applies there." Since Parliament had not removed either Fisher or Commanda from their constitutional jurisdiction, the Ontario government could not affect the treaty rights of either man to hunt.

Five months passed before Justice Greene rendered his decision.[24] His ruling hinged on two interpretations: that the Anishinaabeg surrendered their interest in the land in 1850, and that Ontario's game laws constituted laws of general application. Greene referred specifically to *St. Catherine's Milling*, and offered an interesting but flawed interpretation of what happened to Aboriginal interest in the land after the creation of both the Robinson-Huron Treaty and the Constitution. Greene used Treaty 3, signed in 1873, as a point of reference. Treaty 3 was created after Confederation, whereas the Robinson-Huron Treaty was a pre-Confederation treaty. As such, the 1850 surrender was made "to the Crown in the right of the Province of Canada and passed in 1867 to the Province of Ontario without the Dominion of Canada ever having any beneficial interest therein."[25] Furthermore, Anishinaabeg interest in the land could not exist independent of the Dominion government. Since the Dominion government never had an interest in the land, neither could the Anishinaabeg. Greene referred to *Attorney-General for the Dominion of Canada v. Attorney-General for Ontario* to support his interpretation. In this instance, Lord Watson ruled that the First Nations obtained "no right [after the treaties] which gave them any interest in the territory ... other than that of the province."[26] Lastly, Greene ruled that Ontario's Game Act was a law of general application and did not infringe upon Dominion jurisdiction under section 91(24) of the British North America Act. Ontario's primary objective through its legislation, Greene noted, was to conserve wildlife, and it could do so by virtue of sections 92(12) and 92(16) of the British North America Act.[27]

Regardless of who won, an appeal was certain. Neither MacInnes nor McGill thought Greene dealt substantively with the issues raised by Macdonald. First, Greene ignored the hunting promises contained in the Robinson-Huron Treaty. In their opinion, he also misapplied *St. Catherine's Milling:* that decision revolved around which level of government could grant timber licences within the Treaty 3 area, not whether a province could affect specific promises made to First Nations in a treaty. Both men also thought that Greene did not address a pressing issue: What are treaties? Are treaties only land sale agreements or are they proper treaties between nations?

Nixon's opinion of Greene's decision is unknown, but he was certainly interested in preventing any further appeals in light of the province's victory. Nixon tried to shift the issue from the courtroom to the political backroom, writing letters to both Crerar and Prime Minister Mackenzie King to quash the possibility of an appeal by Indian Affairs.[28] Nixon's letter is an odd mix of lies and hyperbole. First, he feigned ignorance about Indian Affairs' motives behind the appeal when the Department of Game was willing to negotiate. In his letter to Crerar, he complained that if Indian Affairs succeeded in its appeal, the Department of Game would "throw up [its] ... hands in any attempt to conserve wildlife."[29] A ready market for fresh deer and moose meat existed in the north, and the Anishinaabeg, Nixon contended, met this demand at the cost of conservation. He also repeated the Department of Game's mantra: legal recognition of First Nations hunting rights would only lead to the wholesale slaughter of game animals. He went so far as to inform King that a legal ruling in the First Nations' favour would be a catastrophe. Already emboldened by their treaty promises, the First Nations in northern Ontario would become uncontrollable if Indian Affairs succeeded in its appeal. Ontario's deer and moose population, Nixon warned, would be decimated over the winter as the First Nations inflicted an "indiscriminate slaughter." Regardless, he concluded, an appeal was unnecessary as the Anishinaabeg were "well pleased with the treatment they receive from the Department of Game."

Nixon's letter had its intended affect. King sent him a short message stating that Indian Affairs would consider the matter.[30] Crerar directed the matter to McGill, who wrote a detailed reply to Nixon.[31] Despite some bluster at the beginning of his letter, McGill agreed to drop the appeal in return for substantive negotiations with Ontario's attorney general and Department of Game officials. McGill's uncooperative comments at the beginning were likely a political manoeuvre on his part, a warning to Nixon that Indian Affairs would take up another case at some point in the future if negotiation failed. Referring specifically to ongoing problems with the trapline system in northern Ontario, McGill suggested that officials from his department and the Department of Game meet to reach a compromise solution.

McGill clearly yielded to political pressure from his minister. As with Scott in 1917, he found himself overtaken by world and national events. In September 1939, King wanted smooth relations between Ottawa and Queen's Park. Nazi forces had invaded and conquered Poland only a few days before Nixon's letter to King. Canada was at war. Ensuring good provincial relations was foremost in the prime minister's mind. Given

King's already rancorous dealings with Ontario premier Mitchell Hepburn, no further reasons were required for the relationship to sour.[32] McGill was well aware of the broader context within which the appeal existed. In a draft letter that he never sent to Nixon, he chided the minister for appealing to King at a time "when, for reasons which you fully appreciate, his [King's] time and that of his staff, is fully occupied with matters of great national urgency."[33] This statement is missing from McGill's final letter to Nixon, perhaps removed at Crerar's insistence or as a result of his own better judgment. Crerar had a cozier political relationship with Hepburn than King, and McGill perhaps erred on the side of caution before criticizing the Ontario government. During the 1937 General Motors Strike, Crerar broke ranks with King (who refused to support Hepburn's strike-breaking actions) and supported the Ontario government. Perhaps Crerar once again chose the premier over the prime minister, and McGill had no choice but to follow.

McGill was not opposed to negotiation; he always intended the *Commanda* appeal to accomplish this. However, without the advantage of a favourable court ruling, Indian Affairs' position in any talks was weak. Secretary MacInnes and D.J. Allan, superintendent of Indian Affairs' Reserves and Trusts Division, met with provincial officials in Toronto in November 1939. They wanted a small committee struck, composed of Indian Affairs and Department of Game officials, to analyze the problem and arrive at a compromise.[34]

This never happened. Over the next five years, the Department of Game continued to implement its trapline system as it saw fit, and Indian Affairs was as impotent as ever in its efforts to secure leniency for the Anishinaabeg. It led a new official at Indian Affairs, Hugh Conn, to write a detailed memorandum in 1944 outlining what had transpired between 1939 and 1944.[35] Conn brought to this task a detailed knowledge of northern hunting, trapping, and First Nations as he had worked for the Hudson's Bay Company for some time before moving on to Indian Affairs. This gave him an appreciation of Mushkegowuk and Anishinaabeg lives in the north, and by the early 1940s, he was Indian Affairs' point man on the hunting issue. Political interference, Conn stated bluntly, ended Indian Affairs' plans for an appeal in 1939. Directives from both the Prime Minister's Office and Crerar instructed McGill to drop the matter and find a settlement. As a result, Conn argued, Indian Affairs lost its best opportunity to finally settle the hunting issue. Nixon had feared that the appeal would succeed, and any provincial statement about "Indian welfare" was a ruse. By dropping the appeal, Conn argued, McGill lost the leverage needed to extract concessions from the Department of Game. Any effort by Indian Affairs to negotiate was therefore futile because Game officials rejected all compromise. Conn cited the most recent effort by senior officials to open a dialogue only to have the offer refused by Deputy Minister Taylor at the Department of Game. Conn concluded that even a limited knowledge of Indian Affairs' files on this issue made it apparent that negotiating with the Department of Game was an utter waste of time.

Conn painted Taylor as a duplicitous figure who openly lied to Indian Affairs. Taylor presented a face of conciliation to the public while privately stonewalling all efforts at appeasement. Conn noted comments made by Taylor in several interviews with the *Toronto Star* in 1939. In these statements, Taylor said that his department would form a special commission to investigate the trapline situation and the rights of Anishinaabeg south of the CNR line.[36] He made a similar announcement on 16 February 1940, noting that his department was "trying to adhere to the spirit of the treaties, having in mind the changed conditions and the value of fur and game."[37] In the margins of his memorandum, Conn pencilled in a series of question marks beside the quotation, reflecting both his incredulity and his frustration. Conn highlighted a recent dealing with Taylor in which he tried to arrange discussions about First Nations traplines north of the CNR line. Taylor refused to discuss the matter until the legislature had made changes to the Game Act. Conn noted in his memorandum that once the legislation was changed, the Department of Game quickly registered thirty-nine townships to white trappers and effectively locked out a large number of Indigenous trappers. He noted that Part I, section 2 of the new Game Act defined a "person," for the purposes of the legislation, as "any individual, including Indians, firm or body corporate." Clearly, in practice, First Nations were not being treated as "persons." Conn asked: "If this isn't discrimination, what is?" Taylor, he said, applied the Game Act as he pleased to suit the larger goal of discriminating against First Nations.

Treaties, Conn argued, constituted solemn promises that could not be ignored by either Indian Affairs or the federal government. Since negotiations with the Department of Game had proved fruitless historically, Conn suggested a more radical approach to force the issue: Indian Affairs, through its agents, should encourage the Anishinaabeg and Mushkegowuk to hunt and trap regardless of whether or not the land was leased to a white trapper. Once arrests took place, Indian Affairs could force the matter by providing lawyers and money to fund all necessary appeals. Conn conceded that such litigation would prove costly, but felt that "the benefits that would be derived by the Indians from a favourable decision warrant taking the risk involved."

Such action was not forthcoming, but Conn's memorandum reflected the willingness of a new generation of Indian Affairs bureaucrats to be both blunt in their assessment of the Department of Game and willing to put forth radical advice to resolve the issue. Conn's frustration would not find an outlet, however, and, more importantly, the Anishinaabeg found no opportunity for redress. Almost one hundred years after entering into a treaty with William Robinson, they still lacked the treaty rights the Crown promised them. Despite Conn's protestations that Taylor and the Department of Game were to blame for this state of affairs, he failed to consider how Indian Affairs' own policies and attitudes towards First Nations facilitated this travesty. McGill and others before him recognized that promises were made to the Anishinaabeg at Sault Ste. Marie in 1850. This recognition extended back to the first arrest of Barnaby Commanda and Wilson Ottawaska in 1898, but Indian Affairs refused to live up to its fiduciary obligation. Despite this acknowledgment of the special nature of treaties, senior Indian Affairs officials were consistently willing to sacrifice those promises and the Anishinaabeg on the altar of political opportunism. If the Anishinaabeg wanted protection, it would not come from Indian Affairs.

Epilogue

Indian Affairs offered little respite to First Nations in the period following the Second World War. Historian John Leslie notes that after 1945 Indian Affairs was bereft of new ideas. Acculturation, the long-desired Holy Grail of Indian policy, proved illusory but officials could not conceive of a different approach to the "Indian problem." Change did occur, however, and the tone of Indian policy slowly, often imperceptibly, shifted between 1943 and 1963. For example, federal officials gradually began to listen to First Nations concerns, although they rarely acted on what they learned. Indigenous peoples remained the recipients of policy, not active participants in its formulation, but officials at least opened their ears. As Leslie writes: "These two decades constitute a historical bridge when an entrenched philosophy and government program directed at Indian assimilation was questioned."[1]

Indian Affairs was capable of change – slow, grudging, and glacial change but change nevertheless. Some officials began to question the effectiveness of acculturation and saw that some of the government's policies affected First Nations adversely. Once this realization occurred, a transformation took place as acculturation lost some of its force in policy and was rebranded as "integration." Positive change also occurred under two different administrations: the government of Louis St. Laurent amended the Indian Act in 1951 and allowed First Nations to retain lawyers to file land claims, and the government of John Diefenbaker gave First Nations the right to vote federally in 1960.

It was the 1969 White Paper of Prime Minister Pierre Trudeau's government, entitled Statement of the Government of Canada on Indian Policy, that pushed matters forward regarding government Indian policy and acculturation. The way in which the White Paper was unveiled and its prescriptions proved what First Nations leaders had long believed: they could not trust the federal government to work cooperatively and constructively with them. Despite extensive consultation with First Nations leaders through the 1960s and a growing body of academic research about treaty rights, including the Hawthorn Report, the Trudeau government chose to issue a policy statement completely at odds with everything Aboriginal leaders proposed. Restating all of the White Paper's recommendations here is unnecessary.[2] Regarding treaty hunting rights, the White Paper reflected outdated policies and thinking:

> The right to hunt and fish for food is extended unevenly across the country ... Although game and fish will become less and less important for survival as the pattern of Indian life continues to change, there are those who, at this time, still live in the traditional manner that their forefathers lived in when they entered into treaty with the government. The Government is prepared to allow such persons transitional free hunting of migratory birds under the Migratory Birds Convention Act and Regulations.[3]

It is an interesting contrast. While the White paper recognizes the right to hunt, it assumes that this right is transitory as First Nations make the "transition" to the dominant Euro-Canadian society. It is a perfect liberal statement: true equality for First Nations requires them to acculturate and give up rights protected by treaty. Once that happens, they will be equal and have full access to all the benefits of the Canadian state. While the writers of the White Paper may have had the best of intentions, they ignored the fact that First Nations' experience of Canada might lead them to have a different conception of what a just society looks like.

First Nations' reaction to the White Paper caught the Trudeau government off-guard. Within a year, the government withdrew it. More importantly, First Nations leaders recognized that working with Indian Affairs was simply not an option. Just as earlier Indian Affairs bureaucrats realized that only a legal victory would enable them to extract concessions from Ontario's Department of Game, First Nations leaders learned that Indian Affairs, provincial bureaucrats, and politicians were the same. First Nations needed a legal victory to force change.

Unshackled in 1951 from the legislative prohibition that prevented them from hiring lawyers to protect their treaty rights, First Nations turned to sympathetic lawyers and began to redraw the boundaries of the state's authority over them. It was a slow process. Early legal victories were ambiguous because the courts had no clear jurisprudence to draw upon. There were occasional triumphs, but there were also defeats.[4]

Despite this legal uncertainty, First Nations found new allies in their struggle to have their rights recognized. In order to convince the courts, they needed a body of scholarship and writing to support their claims. In the 1960s, a small group of legal scholars and academics began taking an interest in First Nations. Kenneth Lysyk, Douglas Sanders, and Gérald La Forest, as well as former civil servants such as Hugh Conn, began to research and advocate on behalf of First Nations across Canada. All of these men (except La Forest) worked with the Indian-Eskimo Association of Canada in 1966 to produce a small publication called *Native Rights in Canada*.[5] Written to "clarify basic legal problems pertinent to [Indians'] future progress," this book argued that First Nations were in a unique constitutional and legal position compared with other Canadians by virtue of their treaties and special relationship with the Crown. It was an idea that Lysyk expanded upon a year later in his article "The Unique Constitutional Position of the Canadian Indian." This early example of activist scholarship found further expression in the federally commissioned Hawthorn-Tremblay Report, which advanced the concept of First Nations as "citizen-plus": possessed of the normal rights and responsibilities of Canadian citizens but also additional rights by virtue of their treaties and history.[6]

As the scholarship increased, so did the court victories. Of seminal importance was the 1973 Supreme Court of Canada decision *Calder v. Attorney-General of British Columbia*.[7] It fundamentally altered the legal landscape and forced the federal and provincial governments to take Aboriginal land and resource claims seriously. It also marked a turning point in the courts. From then on, the Supreme Court has slowly and (somewhat) consistently upheld treaty rights and the concept of Aboriginal rights. The inclusion of Aboriginal and treaty rights in section 35 of the Canadian Charter of Rights and Freedoms further entrenched these concepts in Canada's legal framework and altered the relationship between First Nations and the state.[8] Governments must now deal with First Nations in a more equitable manner.

Problems and conflict still occur, but Barnaby Commanda and Wilson Ottawaska would find the amount of change, at least with regard to hunting and trapping rights, difficult to believe. Today's First Nations possess greater legal recognition of their rights than at any point in the last one hundred years. What they could never achieve through negotiations with politicians and bureaucrats, they have achieved through the courts. At each step along the way, different levels of government (regardless of party affiliation) have fought, and often continue to fight, against this recognition. Even in late twentieth- and early twenty-first-century Canada, the state is unwilling to accommodate new perspectives and approaches.[9]

This book began with Hugh Conn's description of a hypothetical hunter, standing on the shores of a lake, wondering whether he should shoot a moose, shoot a duck, or catch a fish, and which was least likely to get him arrested. That hunter's grandson or granddaughter could well be standing on the same lakeshore today and facing the same dilemma: should he or she shoot a moose or a duck, or catch a fish? In many ways, their rights are better protected than their grandfather's. They have better control of the hunt, but to what extent? New questions about Aboriginal hunting have emerged since Conn posed his question. How will modern state authorities respond to First Nations demands that traditional knowledge and beliefs about wildlife be incorporated into twenty-first-century wildlife policies? What will environmental groups do if a First Nation decides to hunt in a manner that conflicts with their ideas about the environment and conservation?[10] The question of who controls the hunt has not been entirely answered.

Appendices

Appendix 1:
Ontario's Wildlife Conservation Legislation, 1877–1937

1877	An Act for the Protection of Game and Fur-bearing Animals, R.S.O. 1877, c. 200.
1887	An Act for the Protection of Game and Fur-bearing Animals, R.S.O. 1887, c. 221.
1892	An Act to Amend the Act for the Protection of Game and Fur-bearing Animals, S.O. 1892, c. 58. Royal assent, April 14, 1892. https://archive.org/stream/statutesofprovin1892onta#page/662/mode/2up/
1893	An Act to Amend and Consolidate the Laws for the Protection of Game and Fur-bearing Animals, S.O. 1893, c. 49. Short title: The Ontario Game Protection Act, 1893. Royal assent, May 27, 1893. https://archive.org/stream/statutesofprovin1893onta#page/194/mode/2up/
1896	An Act to Make Further Provisions for the Protection of Game, S.O. 1896, c. 68. Royal assent April 7, 1896. https://archive.org/stream/statutesofprovin1896onta#page/228/mode/2up/
1897	The Ontario Game Protection Act, R.S.O. 187, c. 287.
1900	An Act to Amend and Consolidate the Ontario Game Protection Act, S.O. 1900, c. 49. Short title: The Ontario Game Protection Act. Royal assent, April 30, 1900. https://archive.org/stream/statutesofprovin1900onta#page/146/mode/2up/
1902	An Act to Amend the Ontario Game Protection Act, S.O. 1902, c. 39. Royal assent, March 17, 1902. https://archive.org/stream/statutesofprovin1902onta#page/204/mode/2up/

1904 An Act to Amend the Ontario Game Protection Act, S.O. 1904, c. 28. Royal assent, April 26, 1904.
https://archive.org/stream/statutesofprovin1904onta#page/224/mode/2up/

1905 An Act to Amend the Ontario Game Protection Act, S.O. 1905, c. 33. Royal assent, May 25, 1905.
https://archive.org/stream/statutesofprovin1905onta#page/90/mode/2up/

1907 An Act respecting the Game, Fur-bearing Animals and Fisheries of Ontario, S.O. 1907, c. 49. Short title: The Ontario Game and Fisheries Act. Royal assent, April 20, 1907.
https://archive.org/stream/statutesofprovin1907onta#page/336/mode/2up/

1908 An Act to Amend the Ontario Game and Fisheries Act, S.O. 1908, c. 65. Royal assent, April 14, 1908.
https://archive.org/stream/statutesofprovin1908onta#page/456/mode/2up/

1910 An Act to Amend the Ontario Game and Fisheries Act, S.O. 1910, c. 101. Royal assent, March 19, 1910.
https://archive.org/stream/statutesofprovin1910onta#page/772/mode/2up/

1911 An Act to Amend the Ontario Game and Fisheries Act, S.O. 1911, c. 76. Royal assent, March 24, 1911.
https://archive.org/stream/statutesofprovin1911onta#page/518/mode/2up/

1912 An Act to Amend the Ontario Game and Fisheries Act, S.O. 1912, c. 75. Royal assent, April 16, 1912.
https://archive.org/stream/statutesofprovin1912onta#page/720/mode/2up/

1913 An Act respecting the Game, Fur-bearing Animals and Fisheries of Ontario, S.O. 1913, c. 69. Short title: The Ontario Game and Fisheries Act. Royal assent, May 6, 1913.
https://archive.org/stream/statutesofprovin1913onta#page/954/mode/2up/

1914 The Ontario Game and Fisheries Act, R.S.O. 1914, c. 262.
http://digitalcommons.osgoode.yorku.ca/cgi/viewcontent.cgi?article=5138&context=rso

1927 The Game and Fisheries Act, R.S.O. 1927, c. 318.
http://digitalcommons.osgoode.yorku.ca/cgi/viewcontent.cgi?article=4655&context=rso

1937 The Game and Fisheries Act, R.S.O. 1937, c. 353.
http://digitalcommons.osgoode.yorku.ca/cgi/viewcontent.cgi?article=3912&context=rso

APPENDIX 2: CHART FROM THE REPORT OF THE VIDAL-ANDERSON COMMISSION, 1849

Designation or locality of bands	Chief's name	Residence	Total number of individuals in band	Boundaries and remarks
Fort William	Joseph Peau de Chat	Fort William	175	From Pigeon River (the boundary between Canada and the United States) along the Lake eastward
Lake Nepigon	Mishemuskquaw	Lake Nepigon	357	To Puckuswawsebe in which the Nepigon and Pic Bands are included; the division between the bands not known, and extending Northward & westward to the Height of Land, the Province boundary
Pic	Shong Shong Louison (or Mistoche)	The Pic River	165	" "
Long Lake	Unknown	South side of Height of Land	40	Part of a large band adjoining the Pic band on the North
Michipicoton	Totomoneh Chickenass	Michipicoton River	160	From Puckuswawsebe eastward in common with the Batchewawnung and St. Marie bands, and back to the Height of Land
Batchewawnung	No chief	Batchewawnung Bay	50	" "
Sault Ste. Marie	Nabanagoghing Shinguakouse	Sault Ste. Marie Garden River	204 [in total]	The east boundary claimed by the Sault Ste. Marie band is Squash Point at the east of Lake George but it interferes with the next

St. Joseph's	Kewokouse	St. Joseph's Island	25	From Echo River (Lake George) to Grand Batture, Lake Huron
Mississaga	Pawtossewag	Near the Mississaga River	74	From Grand Batture to Isle aux Rosses
Inland Indians	Unknown	About Green Lake	40	Lands South of the Height & in rear of the 2 land and next Bands
Serpents	Waytauntegowenene Mainwaywaybenaise	Serpent River	35	From Isle aux Rosses to Nid d'aigle (4 miles west of Spanish River) From Nid d'aigle to La Cloche R. & back to the Inland Band
La Cloche & Spanish River	Penaiseseh	About La Cloche River	250	Between the Lake bands and the height about White Fish Lake
White Fish Lake	Shawwenawyezhik	White Fish Lake	74	[no entry]
Mebawwenawning	Shawwawnosseway	Manitowaning	50	From La Cloche to Grumbling Point
French River	Waygenawkaingh Mishshquongay Payneequenaishcum	Beau Soleil Island near Penetanguishene & Isle aux Sable	4,075	From Saugeen Bay to the surveyed lands and back to the sources of the Rivers running into the lake
			Total 1,918	

Source: Archives of Ontario, Sir Aemilius Irving Papers, MU 1464, file 26/31/4, "Report of Commissioners Vidal and Anderson," 1849, Appendix B.

Notes

Foreword

1. There is of course a library of writing on Locke; recognizing that this Foreword is an ideas piece intended to provoke reflection on the book, referencing is kept to a basic minimum. The most useful starting points for further exploration of the issues discussed here are the *Stanford Encyclopedia of Philosophy,* "John Locke," https://plato.stanford.edu/entries/locke/ and "Locke's Political Philosophy," https://plato.stanford.edu/entries/locke-political/#StaNat; and Barbara Arneil, *John Locke and America: The Defence of English Colonialism* (Oxford: Clarendon Press, 1996). The validation phrase is adapted from Herman Lebovics, "The Uses of America in John Locke's *Second Treatise of Government,*" *Journal of the History of Ideas* 47, 4 (1986), 577.
2. John Locke, *Two Treatises of Government*, ed. Peter Laslett (Cambridge: Cambridge University Press, 1960), and available at https://en.wikisource.org/wiki/Two_Treatises_of_Government. The quotations immediately following are drawn from this source.
3. *Stanford Encyclopedia,* "John Locke" and "Locke's Political Philosophy"; John Locke, *Second Treatise of Government,* Chap. IX, "Of the Ends of Political Society and Government," sections 123–26.
4. The phrase "dangerous belief" is from the *Second Treatise* and is quoted in *Stanford Encyclopedia,* "John Locke."
5. John Locke, *Second Treatise of Government*, Chap. V, "Of Property," section 26.
6. The block and other quotes are from Locke, *Second Treatise,* "Of Property," sections 31 and 51. For interpretation of these parts of Locke, see Lebovics, "The Uses of America in Locke's Second Treatise of Government," 567–81; E.J. Hundert, "The Making of Homo Faber: John Locke between Ideology and History," *Journal of the History of Ideas* 33 (1972): 3–22.
7. Locke, *Second Treatise,* "Of Property," section 37.
8. Adam Smith, *An Inquiry into the Nature and Causes of the Wealth of Nations* (London: W. Strahan and T. Cadell, 1776) and also the edition edited by Edwin Cannan (New York:

Modern Library, 2000); Karl Marx, *Capital: A Critique of Political Economy* [1867], transl. B. Fowkes (London: Penguin Books, 1981).
9 Arneil, *John Locke and America*.
10 John Dunn, *The Political Thought of John Locke: An Historical Account of the Argument of the 'Two Treatises of Government'* (Cambridge: Cambridge University Press, 1969), 97, 101, 103, quoted by Arneil, *John Locke and America*, 21. Arneil also points out (24) that most of the 195 volumes classed as "Voyages and Travels" in John R. Harrison and Peter Laslett, eds., *The Library of John Locke* (Oxford: Clarendon Press 1965), were accounts of trips to the Americas by European travellers. "Selectively," because as Arneil demonstrates, Locke, the empiricist of renown, proceeded from theory to evidence in his use of these sources and ignored reports that did not fit with his conceptualization of Indigenous peoples as living in a state of nature.
11 As demonstrated in Arneil, *John Locke and America;* with the final quote from 190 (see also 193–94 on this point).
12 Locke, *Second Treatise,* "Of Property," section 33.
13 See Arneil, *John Locke and America*, 194.
14 James Morrison, *The Robinson Treaties of 1850: A Case Study,* prepared for the Royal Commission on Aboriginal Peoples, Treaty and Land Research Section (1996), 39-40, http://publications.gc.ca/collections/collection_2017/bcp-pco/Z1-1991-1-41-160-eng.pdf.
15 See Arneil, *John Locke and America*, 194–97.
16 R.W. Rawson, J. Davidson, and J. Hepburn, *Report on the Affairs of the Indians in Canada: Laid before the Legislative Assembly, 20th March, 1845*. In making this argument the commissioners referred to Swiss philosopher Emer de Vattel, *The Law of Nations*, published in translation in 1797 from which these quotations come; the work (with translations of three earlier essays) is most readily available as Emer de Vattel, *The Law of Nations, Or, Principles of the Law of Nature, Applied to the Conduct and Affairs of Nations and Sovereigns, with Three Early Essays on the Origin and Nature of Natural Law and on Luxury*, edited and with an Introduction by Béla Kapossy and Richard Whitmore (Indianapolis: Liberty Fund, 2008). For an assessment of the Rawson report, see John Leslie, "The Bagot Commission: Developing a Corporate Memory for the Indian Department," *CHA Historical Papers* 171 (1982): 31–52.
17 Rawson et al., *Report on the Affairs of the Indians in Canada.*
18 The modern beginnings of a substantial literature on this topic may be in Thomas L. Haskell, "Capitalism and the Origins of the Humanitarian Sensibility, Part 1," *American Historical Review* 90, 2 (1985): 339–61, and "Capitalism and the Origins of the Humanitarian Sensibility, Part 2," *American Historical Review* 90, 3 (1985): 547–66, together with Felix Driver, "Moral Geographies: Social Science and the Urban Environment in Mid-Nineteenth Century England," *Transactions of the Institute of British Geographers*, New Series 13, 3 (1988): 275–87. See also Alan Lester, "Obtaining the 'Due Observance of Justice': The Geographies of Colonial Humanitarianism," *Environment and Planning D: Society and Space* 20, 3 (2002): 277–93, and Alan Lester and Fae Dussart, *Colonization and the Origins of Humanitarian Governance: Protecting Aborigines across the Nineteenth-Century British Empire* (Cambridge: Cambridge University Press, 2014), as well as Elaine Hadley, *Living Liberalism: Practical Citizenship in Mid-Victorian Britain* (Chicago and London: University of Chicago Press, 2010). Claire McLisky offers a useful commentary on the challenges of labelling in "'Due Observance of Justice, and the Protection of their Rights': Philanthropy,

Humanitarianism and Moral Purpose in the Aborigines Protection Society circa 1837 and Its portrayal in Australian Historiography, 1883-2003," *Limina* 11 (2005): 57-66.

19 Morrison, *The Robinson Treaties of 1850*, 67. In 1839, the Act for the Protection of the Lands of the Crown in this Province from Trespass and Injury declared it a penal offence for anyone to acquire land in Upper Canada "for the cession of which to Her Majesty no agreement hath been made with the Indian tribes occupying the same, and who may claim title thereto" (2 Victoria, Chap. 15, U.C.).

20 L.F.S. Upton, "The Origins of Canadian Indian Policy," *Journal of Canadian Studies* 8, 4 (1973), 57.

21 Sir George Murray to Sir James Kempt, 25 January 1830, LAC, RG 10, Vol. 116, cited by R.J. Surtees, "The Development of an Indian Reserve Policy in Canada," *Ontario History* 61, 2 (1969), 90.

22 The phrase "desolating effects" is from *Report of the Parliamentary Select Committee on Aboriginal Tribes (British Settlements)*, reprinted with comments by the "Aborigines Protection Society" (London: William Ball, 1837), 59; other quotes are from *Information Respecting the Aborigines in the British Colonies, Circulated by Direction of the Meeting for Sufferings, Being Principally Extracts from the Report Presented to the House of Commons, by the Select Committee Appointed on that Subject* (London: Darton and Harvey, 1838), https://ia600300.us.archive.org/24/items/cihm_21680/cihm_21680.pdf.

23 Cited by Lester and Dussart, *Colonization and the Origins of Humanitarian Governance*, 95.

24 Donald B. Smith, *Sacred Feathers: The Reverend Peter Jones (Kahkewaquonaby) & the Mississauga Indians* (Toronto: University of Toronto Press, 1987). For a description of the River Credit Mission, see *Information Respecting the Aborigines in the British Colonies*, 36 and 37.

25 Lord Glenelg to the Earl of Durham, 22 August 1838, British Parliamentary Papers (1839), 233, cited by Leslie, "The Bagot Commission," 37.

26 Herman Merivale, *Introduction to a Course of Lectures on Colonization and Colonies* (London: Longman, Orme, Brown, Green, and Longmans, 1839), and *Lectures on Colonization and Colonies, Delivered before the University of Oxford in 1839, 1840 and 1841* (Longman, Orme, Brown, Green, and Longmans, 1841; new edition 1861).

27 For discussion of Merivale's position, see David T. McNab, "Herman Merivale and the Native Question, 1837-1861," *Albion: A Quarterly Journal Concerned with British Studies* 9, 4 (1977): 359–84.

28 Leslie, "The Bagot Commission," 39; Rawson et al., *Report on the Affairs of the Indians in Canada*.

29 Leslie, "The Bagot Commission," 40.

30 Here lay a key question for the British Empire as a whole: How might the humanitarian impetus of the 1830s and early 1840s be continued as settler societies moved toward self-government? On this point see Lester and Dussart, *Colonization and the Origins of Humanitarian Governance*, 228–39. As David McNab summarized the resolution of this issue: "From 1855 to 1860 the Colonial Office debated the feasibility of giving the government of the Province of Canada the power to control Indian affairs and the methods to be adopted to facilitate this change. A commission was appointed in 1858 to inquire into these problems ... After reading the commission's report of 1858 and Head's suggestions, Merivale concluded that it would be advantageous to 'get rid of the responsibility of the

Home Government' in Indian Affairs, and his view prevailed in the Colonial Office. He prepared the dispatch, which gave effective control over Indian affairs in the Canadas to the local government as long as its actions were 'consistent ... with the full preservation of the faith of the Imperial Government so far as it may be pledged to the natives.'" David T. McNab, "Herman Merivale and the Colonial Office Indian Policy in the Mid-Nineteenth Century," *Canadian Journal of Native Studies* 1, 2 (1981), 286.

31 For some introduction to mining in northern Ontario, see W. Robert Wightman and Nancy M. Wightman, *The Land Between: Northwestern Ontario Resource Development, 1800 to the 1990s* (Toronto: University of Toronto Press, 1997).

32 Alexander Morris, lieutenant governor of Manitoba, described the Robinson treaties as precursors of the "numbered treaties" – eleven treaties encompassing most of western Canada east of the Rocky Mountains signed between 1871 and 1921, with the first seven concluded by 1877. Alexander Morris, *The Treaties of Canada with the Indians of Canada and The North-West Territories* (Toronto: Willing and Williamson, 1880), 16, cited by Morrison, *The Robinson Treaties of 1850*, 2.

33 Morrison, *The Robinson Treaties of 1850*, 5.

34 Ibid., 6

35 Ibid.

36 See Elizabeth Raymer, "Robinson Treaties First Nations Launch Court Actions over Annuity Augmentations," *Canadian Lawyer*, 5 October 2017, http://www.canadianlawyermag.com/author/elizabeth-raymer/robinson-treaties-first-nations-launch-court-actions-over-annuity-augmentations-14754/; Ashifa Kassam, "First Nations Seek to Raise Canada's Rent after 150 Years of $4 Payments," *The Guardian*, 15 October 2017, https://www.theguardian.com/world/2017/oct/15/canada-first-nations-treaty-annuity-lawsuit?CMP=share_btn_link.

37 McNab, "Herman Merivale and the Native Question," 366.

38 The phrase "authoritarian vice" is from Steven Friedman, "The Ambiguous Legacy of Liberalism: Less a Theory of Society, More a State of Mind," in *Intellectual Traditions in South Africa: Ideas, Individuals and Institutions,* ed. Peter C. J. Vale, Lawrence Hamilton, and Estelle H. Prinsloo, 29-50 (Scottsville: University of KwaZulu-Natal Press, 2014), which did much to influence my thinking in this foreword. Several commentators have noted that liberalism stands foremost, albeit uncertain, among political philosophies in the world today. This point is made in several places, including Michael P. Zuckert, *Launching Liberalism: On Lockean Political Philosophy* (Lawrence: University Press of Kansas, 2002).

39 Ian McKay, "The Liberal Order Framework: A Prospectus for a Reconnaissance of Canadian History," *The Canadian Historical Review* 81, 4 (2000): 616–45, quotes from 621 and 623.

40 C.B. Macpherson, *The Political Theory of Possessive Individualism: Hobbes to Locke* (Oxford; Clarendon Press, 1962); C.B. Macpherson, *The Real World of Democracy* (Oxford: Clarendon Press, 1966), 79, cited by Ian McKay, "A Half-Century of Possessive Individualism: C.B. Macpherson and the Twenty-First-Century Prospects of Liberalism," *Journal of the Canadian Historical Association* 25, 1 (2014): 307–40, quotes from 308–9.

41 Ian McKay, "A Half-Century"; see also Gal Gerson, *Margins of Disorder: New Liberalism and the Crisis of European Consciousness* (Albany: State University of New York, 2004).

42 C.B. Macpherson, *The Life and Times of Liberal Democracy* (Oxford: Oxford University Press, 1977), 1; Friedman, "Ambiguous Legacy of Liberalism," 34.

43 McKay, "Liberal Order Framework," 637.

44 Jean Chrétien, Minister of Indian Affairs and Northern Development, *Statement of the Government of Canada on Indian Policy*, 1969 (The White Paper, 1969), available in *Aboriginal Policy Studies* 1, 1 (2011): 192–215, and at https://www.aadnc-aandc.gc.ca/eng/1100100010189/1100100010191.

45 Ken Coates, "The Indian Act and the Future of Aboriginal Governance in Canada," Research Paper for the National Centre for First Nations Governance, May 2008, http://fngovernance.org/ncfng_research/coates.pdf.

46 Harold Cardinal, *The Unjust Society: The Tragedy of Canada's Indians* (Edmonton: M.G. Hurtig, 1969) and 2nd ed. (Vancouver: Douglas & MacIntyre, 1999), 140.

47 The term "citizens plus" derives from Harry Hawthorn, ed., *A Survey of Contemporary Indians of Canada: Economic, Political Educational Needs and Policies* (Ottawa: Indian Affairs Branch, 1966). It was adopted in the response to the 1969 White Paper; see Indian Association of Alberta, *Citizens Plus* ["The Red Paper"] (Edmonton: Indian Association of Alberta, 1970), available in *Aboriginal Policy Studies* 1, 2 (2011): 188–281, and used as the title of Alan Cairns's book, *Citizens Plus: Aboriginal People and the Canadian State* (Vancouver: UBC Press, 2000)

48 The phrasing, which echoes Taylor's position, is from one of interviewer Chris Bloor's questions to Taylor in Chris Bloor, "Interview: Charles Taylor," *Philosophy Now* 74 (July/August 2009), https://philosophynow.org/issues/74/Charles_Taylor. For further discussion of communitarianism, the label attached to the arguments of Taylor, Alasdair MacIntyre, and others by their critics, see *Stanford Encyclopedia of Philosophy*, "Communitarianism," https://plato.stanford.edu/entries/communitarianism/.

49 *Stanford Encyclopedia*, "Communitarianism," and for fuller comparative discussion of Kymlicka and Taylor, *Stanford Encyclopedia of Philosophy*, "Multiculturalism," https://plato.stanford.edu/entries/multiculturalism/.

50 For a succinct summary, see Hamar Foster, "Canada: 'Indian Administration' from the Royal Proclamation of 1763 to Constitutionally Entrenched Aboriginal Rights," in *Indigenous Peoples' Rights in Australia, Canada, and New Zealand* 351–77, ed. Paul Havemann (Auckland: Oxford University Press, 1999).

51 This was written in October 2017 in the wake of the Quebec legislature's enactment of Bill 62, which denied government services to individuals wearing the niqab or other face-covering attire. Canadians are not alone in this and, as Steven Friedman, "Ambiguous Legacy of Liberalism," concludes: "Understanding what is required to preserve liberalism's commitment to freedom while transcending its limits is the core challenge facing South African democratic theory," 47.

Introduction

1 *Joint Committee of the Senate and House of Commons on Indian Affairs: Minutes of Proceeding and Evidence*, no. 11, 11 May 1961 (Ottawa: Queen's Printer, 1961): 417. I want to thank Dr. John Leslie for bringing this document to my attention.

2 Kenneth Lysyk, "The Unique Constitutional Position of the Canadian Indian," *Canadian Bar Review* 45 (1967): 513.

3 See Robert J. Surtees, "Indian Land Cessions in Ontario, 1763–1862: The Evolution of a System" (PhD dissertation, Carleton University, 1982); Douglas Leighton, "The Development

Notes to pages 4–10

of Federal Indian Policy in Canada, 1840–1890" (PhD dissertation, University of Western Ontario, 1975); David McNab, "Herman Merivale and the British Empire, 1806–1874, with Special Reference to British North America, Southern Africa, and India" (PhD dissertation, University of Lancaster, 1978); John Milloy, "The Era of Civilization: British Policy for the Indians of Canada, 1830–1860" (PhD dissertation, Oxford University, 1978); Donald B. Smith, "The Mississauga, Peter Jones and the White Man: The Algonquians' Adjustment to the Europeans on the North Shore of Lake Ontario to 1860" (PhD dissertation, University of Toronto, 1975). A smaller unpublished study of the Robinson Treaties is Douglas Leighton, "The Historical Importance of the Robinson Treaties of 1850," paper presented to the Annual Meeting of the Canadian Historical Association, 9 June 1982.

4 Patrick Macklem, *Indigenous Difference and the Constitution of Canada* (Toronto: University of Toronto Press, 2001), 21. See in particular ch. 5 for a treatment of treaties in relation to the Canadian state.
5 See Sidney Harring, *The White Man's Law: Native People in Nineteenth Century Canadian Jurisprudence* (Toronto: University of Toronto Press, 1998), for an overview of how the power of the Canadian state extended over First Nations in the court system.
6 Macklem, *Indigenous Difference and the Constitution of Canada*, 8.
7 Ian McKay, "The Liberal Order Framework: A Prospectus for a Reconnaissance of Canadian History," *Canadian Historical Review* 81, 4 (2004): 624.
8 This argument is developed in more detail in David Calverley, "The Dispossession of the Northern Ojibwa and Cree: The Case of the Chapleau Game Preserve," *Ontario History* 101, 1 (2009): 83–103. A similar argument is advanced by Calverley in "The Impact of the Hudson's Bay Company on the Creation of Treaty Number Nine," *Ontario History* 98, 1 (2006): 30–51. In the latter case, the Mushkegowuk and other nations chose their reserves based on the location of HBC posts. The posts themselves were located in relation to where the Mushkegowuk traditionally harvested.
9 "Acculturation" is the most accurate characterization of Indian Affairs policy. "Assimilation" implies intermarriage between First Nations and different ethnic groups. Indian Affairs never advanced a policy of this nature. It did want First Nations to abandon their traditional beliefs and practices and assume those of the dominant (Anglo-British) culture. This is more properly referred to as acculturation.
10 See Karl Jacoby, *Crimes against Nature: Squatters, Poachers, Thieves, and the Hidden History of American Conservation* (Los Angeles: University of California Press, 2001), 197–98.
11 The standard biography of Mowat is Margaret Evans, *Sir Oliver Mowat* (Toronto: University of Toronto Press, 1992).
12 Christopher Armstrong, *The Politics of Federalism: Ontario's Relations with the Federal Government, 1867–1942* (Toronto: University of Toronto Press, 1981).
13 Peter Kulchyski and Frank Tester, *Kiumajut (Talking Back): Game Management and Inuit Rights, 1900–70* (Vancouver: UBC Press, 2007).
14 Ibid., 7.
15 Within this approach, Kulchyski and Tester are also adopting a Marxist approach as the state works alongside private interests for "the accumulation of capital and the expansion of the commodity form" (ibid., 8).
16 J. Alexander Burnett, *A Passion for Wildlife: The History of the Canadian Wildlife Service* (Vancouver: UBC Press, 2003).
17 Gerald Killam, *Protected Places: A History of Ontario's Provincial Parks System* (Toronto: Dundurn Press, 1993); George Warecki, *Protecting Ontario's Wilderness: A History of Changing*

Ideas and Preservation Politics, 1927–1973 (New York: Peter Lang, 2000). This is a trend that goes back to the 1960s with Robert Craig Brown's "The Doctrine of Usefulness: Natural Resources and National Park Policy in Canada, 1887–1914," in *Canadian Parks in Perspective*, ed. J.G. Nelson (Montreal: Harvest House, 1970). It is important to note, however, that Killam's book was written at a time when there was limited scholarly interest in conservation laws and their impact on First Nations.

18 Mark David Spence, *Dispossessing the Wilderness: Indian Removal and the Making of the National Parks* (New York: Oxford University Press, 1999), 5. Spence focuses on Yosemite, Yellowstone, and Glacier National Parks. Karl Jacoby explores the concept of dispossession (in a broader sense, not specifically related to Aboriginal peoples) in *Crimes against Nature*. See also Robert H. Keller and Michael F. Turek, *American Indians and National Parks* (Tucson: University of Arizona Press, 1998). Their book differs from Spence's as they are more interested in analyzing the relationship between various First Nations and the Parks Service. Their point is that First Nations are actors in this relationship; they are not simply being acted upon.

19 The most direct, and perhaps the best, response I had to my query regarding what to call the people of Treaty 9 was this: "Not just Cree people are Treaty 9 – everyone is Treaty 9" (private correspondence in possession of the author). There is another argument – that the historian should be true to the sources and use the terminology found in the documents. Language in documents should be treated with great care; however, there is often language in documents that historians will not use when writing their narratives.

20 A recent example of this issue in Ontario is *R. v. Powley*, [2003] 2 SCR 207, 2003 SCC 43. See also Lori Sterling and Peter Lemmond, "*R. v. Powley:* Building a Foundation for the Constitutional Recognition of Métis and Aboriginal Rights," *Supreme Court Law Review* 24 (2004): 243–67.

21 Examples of some studies are Peggy Blair, "Take for 'Granted': Aboriginal Title and Public Fishing Rights in Upper Canada," *Ontario History* 62, 2 (2000): 31–55; Edwin Koenig, "Fisheries Conflict on the Saugeen Peninsula: Toward a Historical Ecology," in *Papers of the Twenty-Eighth Algonquian Conference*, ed. David Pentland (Winnipeg: University of Manitoba Press, 1997); Victor P. Lytwyn, "Ojibwa and Ottawa Fisheries around Manitoulin Island: Historical and Geographical Perspectives on Aboriginal and Treaty Fishing Rights," *Native Studies Review* 6, 1 (1990): 1–30; D.E. Sanders, "Indian Hunting and Fishing Rights," *Saskatchewan Law Review* 38, 1 (1973–74): 45–62; Roland Wright, "The Public Right of Fishing, Government Fishing Policy and Indian Fishing Rights in Upper Canada," *Ontario History* 86 (1994): 337–62.

CHAPTER 1: HUNTING ACTIVITY AND THE ROBINSON TREATIES, 1783–1850

1 Archives of Ontario (AO), Sir Aemilius Irving Papers, MU 1464, file 26/13/4, Typescript copy of Report of Commissioners Vidal and Anderson, 1849 (hereafter Vidal-Anderson Report).

2 See T.R. Millman, "Anderson, Thomas Gummersall," in *Dictionary of Canadian Biography*, vol. 10 (Toronto/Laval: University of Toronto/Université Laval, 2003), http://www.biographi.ca/en/bio/anderson_thomas_gummersall_10E.html.

3 Sidney Harring makes this argument about the nature and intent of treaties. See Harring, *White Man's Law*, 11. Rhonda Telford's PhD dissertation is the most detailed study of the Robinson Treaties in relation to mineral development in the north. In ch. 2, she outlines

the process whereby the government sought to protect existing (and illegal) mining operations in the regions. See Telford, "'The Sound of the Rustling of the Gold Is under My Feet Where I Stand.'"

4 See Jack Stagg, *Anglo-Indian Relations in North America to 1763, and an Analysis of the Royal Proclamation of 7 October, 1763* (Ottawa: Department of Indian Affairs and Northern Development, Treaties and Historical Research Centre, 1981).

5 Several studies examine this period. See Colin Calloway, *Crown and Calumet: British-Indian Relations, 1783–1815* (Norman: University of Oklahoma Press, 1987). See also Robert Allen, *His Majesty's Indian Allies: British Indian Policy in the Defence of Canada, 1774–1815* (Toronto: Dundurn Press, 1992).

6 This doesn't mean that early treaties were perfect. There are examples of sloppy recordkeeping. In one instance, the land being treated for was not written into the treaty. A standard reference for this early treaty period is Robert J. Surtees, "Indian Land Cessions in Ontario, 1763–1862." See also Surtees, *Indian Land Surrenders in Ontario, 1763–1867* (Ottawa: Department of Indian Affairs and Northern Development, Treaties and Historical Research Centre, 1984) (hereafter DIAND and T&HRC), and "Canadian Indian Treaties," in *Handbook of North American Indians*, vol. 4, *History of Indian-White Relations*, ed. Wilcomb E. Washburn (Washington, DC: Smithsonian Institution, 1988), 202–10.

7 Monetary payments and the inclusion of annuity payments (as part of the treaty process) were not implemented by the Indian Department until the 1840s.

8 The Haudenosaunee leadership was divided. Some people followed Joseph Brant to the Grand River while others followed John Deserontyon to the Bay of Quinte. Two short studies of Joseph Brant (or Thayendanega in Mohawk) and John Deserontyon, respectively, are Barbara Graymont, "Thayendanega," in *Dictionary of Canadian Biography*, vol. 5, *1801–1820* (Toronto: University of Toronto Press, 1983), and Charles M. Johnston, "Deserontyon, John," in *Dictionary of Canadian Biography*, vol. 5, *1801–1820* (Toronto: University of Toronto Press, 1983). See also M. Eleanor Herrington, "Captain John Deserontyon and the Mohawk Settlement at Desoronto," *Queen's Quarterly* 29 (1921): 165–80. The split between Brant and Deserontyon is explored in William N. Fenton and Elisabeth Tooker, "Mohawk," in *Handbook of North American Indians*, vol. 15, *The Northeast*, ed. Bruce Trigger (Washington, DC: Smithsonian Institution, 1978), 476.

9 Cited in Surtees, *Indian Land Surrenders in Ontario*, 22.

10 The 1805 treaties with the Anishinaabeg of the Credit River included the provision of ball and shot, gunpowder, and fishing hooks. See Canada, *Indian Treaties and Surrenders from 1680 to 1902, Treaty Numbers 281–482*, vol. 3 (Ottawa: Brown and Chamberlain, 1891), 40. Peggy Blair addresses Aboriginal concerns about continued harvesting rights in *Lament for a First Nation: The Williams Treaties of Southern Ontario* (Vancouver: UBC Press, 2008). See in particular ch. 2.

11 During negotiations for land along the Credit River in 1805, Chief Quinipeno told Crown representative William Claus that white settlers were causing problems for the Anishinaabeg. Quinipeno stated that "when we encamp on the Land [the settlers] drove us off and shoot our dogs and never give us any assistance." Cited in Smith, "The Mississauga, Peter Jones and the White Man," 67. See also Leo A. Johnson, "The Mississauga–Lake Ontario Surrender of 1805" *Ontario History* 83, 3: (1990): 233–53. The Anishinaabeg secured access to two fishing locations in the 1805 treaty because of their concerns. Claus negotiated another treaty with the Anishinaabeg of Rice Lake in 1818. Chief Buckaquet requested that "his people be allowed to continue hunting and fishing where they could still find fish and

game." Claus replied that the rivers and forests were open to all people. Later that year, Claus negotiated another treaty for land between Kempenfelt Bay on Lake Simcoe and Nottawasaga Bay on Georgian Bay. He informed the assembled Chippewa that by selling their land to the King, they could continue to use it "as they always had." See Surtees, *Indian Land Surrenders in Ontario*, 186–88.

12   In 1811, William Claus negotiated with the Chippewa for a tract of land between Lake Simcoe and Georgian Bay. It was an important military supply route that the Crown had first obtained limited access to in 1785; now the Crown wanted to build a road between the two points, and construct fortifications and buildings. These earlier treaties were the Collins Treaty and the "Between the Lakes Purchase" of 1785 and 1792, respectively. See Surtees, "Land Cessions, 1763–1830," *Aboriginal Ontario: Historical Perspectives on First Nations*, ed. Edward S. Rogers and Donald B. Smith (Toronto: Dundurn Press, 1994), 106–7. See also Benjamin Frobisher to Henry Hamilton, 2 May 1785, in *The Valley of the Trent*, ed. E.G. Guillet (Toronto: University of Toronto Press, 1967), 132–36. During the 1811 negotiations, one of the chiefs, Yellowhead, asked that his people receive their annual treaty presents in the early fall "in order to facilitate their moving to winter hunting grounds while the weather was not too cold." Cited in Surtees, "Indian Land Cessions in Ontario, 1763–1862," 177. Yellowhead's reference to "presents" was to the annual distribution of goods by the Indian Department to First Nations in Ontario to maintain their allegiance during times of war. It is likely that the treaty payment would be made at the same time as the annual present distribution. Yellowhead also asked the Indian Department to provide the services of a blacksmith so the Anishinaabeg's guns, traps, and other metal implements could be repaired. John Askin, another Indian Department employee, received a similar request during treaty talks for land along the Thames River in 1818. See Surtees, ibid., 198.

13   See Donald B. Smith, "The Dispossession of the Mississauga Indians: A Missing Chapter in the Early History of Upper Canada," in *Historical Essays on Upper Canada: New Perspectives*, ed. J.K. Johnson and Bruce G. Wilson (Ottawa: Carleton University Press, 1991), 23–51. Smith has continued to write about the Anishinaabeg, or Mississauga, of Upper Canada. While his concern is not harvesting rights, the impact of settlement on the traditional cultures of the Mississauga is expertly outlined. See Smith, *Sacred Feathers: The Reverend Peter Jones (Kahkewaquonaby) and the Mississauga Indians*, 2nd ed. (Toronto: University of Toronto Press, 2013). See also Smith, *Mississauga Portraits: Ojibwe Voices from Nineteenth Century Canada* (Toronto: University of Toronto Press, 2013).

14   See Gerald Craig, *Upper Canada: The Formative Years, 1784–1841* (Toronto: McClelland and Stewart, 1963), 85–144. A good, short outline of anti-American sentiment in Upper Canada is provided in Fred Landon, *Western Ontario and the American Frontier* (Toronto: McClelland and Stewart, 1967), 44–58.

15   Robert Surtees argues that this desire to "civilize" Native peoples grew out of the effect of Evangelical Christian groups on British colonial policy in general. John Milloy argues that this policy emerged as the British Colonial Office sought to reduce expenditures in its Indian Department in Canada: Native peoples who farmed were less likely to require assistance. See Surtees, "Indian Land Cessions in Ontario, 1763–1862." See also Milloy, "The Era of Civilization."

16   It was an idea some First Nations people, such as Peter Jones, an Anishinaabeg convert to Methodism, attempted to adapt to their own ends. For a short summary, see Donald B. Smith, "Jones, Peter," in *Dictionary of Canadian Biography*, vol. 8 (Toronto/Laval: University

of Toronto/Université Laval, 2003), http://www.biographi.ca/en/bio/jones_peter_8E.html. Smith's longer biography of Jones provides greater detail. See also Smith, *Sacred Feathers*. One such settlement was at Manitowaning on Manitoulin Island. See Ruth Bleasdale, "Manitowaning: An Experiment in Indian Settlement," *Ontario History* 66, 3 (1974): 147–57. Robert Surtees considers the Coldwater Narrows settlement in "The Development of an Indian Reserve Policy in Canada," *Ontario History* 61, 2 (1969): 87–98. David McNab explores the connection between Britain's evangelical movement and the creation of missionary movements in England in "Herman Merivale and the British Empire," 183–215. A more general treatment of the shift in Indian Department policy and its impact on Native peoples is offered in Edward S. Rogers, "The Algonquian Farmers of Southern Ontario, 1830–1945," in *Aboriginal Ontario: Historical Perspectives on the First Nations*, ed. Edward S. Rogers and Donald B. Smith (Toronto: Dundurn Press, 1994), 122–40. Rogers notes that the Anishinaabeg and other Native peoples along the Lower Great Lakes (present-day southern Ontario) continued to rely heavily on hunting and fishing after 1830 even as farming became a more widespread practice on the reserves.

17 See S.F. Wise, "Head, Sir Francis Bond," in Dictionary of Canadian Biography, vol. 10 (Toronto/Laval: University of Toronto/Université Laval, 2003), http://www.biographi.ca/en/bio/head_francis_bond_10E.html. A short summary of Bond Head's opinions are offered in Robert J. Surtees, *Treaty Research Report: Manitoulin Island Treaties* (Ottawa: DIAND, T&HRC, 1986), 6. It is also considered in Surtees, "Indian Land Cessions in Ontario, 1763–1862." See also Peter Schmalz, *The Ojibwa of Southern Ontario* (Toronto: University of Toronto Press, 1991); and Peter Schmalz, *The History of the Saugeen Indians* (Toronto: Ontario Historical Research Publication No. 5, 1977). Both treaties are also considered in Milloy, "The Era of Civilization." The Manitoulin Island Treaty is also analyzed in W.R. Wightman, *Forever on the Fringe: Six Studies in the Development of Manitoulin Island* (Toronto: University of Toronto Press, 1982). The official texts of these treaties are provided in Canada, *Indian Treaties and Surrenders from 1680 to 1890, Treaty Numbers 1-138*, vol. 1 (Ottawa: Brown Chamberlin, 1891): 112.

18 See Robert J. Surtees, "Indian Reserve Policy in Upper Canada" (MA thesis, Carleton University, 1966).

19 Robert J. Surtees, *Treaty Research Report: The Robinson Treaties* (Ottawa: DIAND, T&HRC, 1984), 5. Telford notes that by the late 1840s there were thirty-seven mining leases on Lake Superior and twenty-seven on Lake Huron. The total value of these leases, to the government, was $400,000 over five years. That means each lease, on average, provided the government with $1,250 per year. See Telford, "The Sound of the Rustling," 127. Unfortunately, the Bank of Canada's online inflation calculator does not allow for calculations prior to 1914; $400,000 in 1914 dollars is equivalent to approximately $8.6 million in 2017 dollars. It would be worth substantially more in 1849 currency.

20 Telford, ibid., 148–54.

21 Ibid., 122. The petition came from Chief Shingwaukonse of Garden River.

22 Library and Archives Canada (LAC), RG 10, vol. 151, Report of Lieutenant Harper, RN, 1 September 1845. Harper's comments were directed more towards Métis claims in the Sault. He wrote in his report that no one "on the British side (with the exception of the Hudson's Bay Company) owns one foot of soil or land – their [Métis] Houses are built and their little gardens planted under the fear that they may be ordered off at any moment and lose all – no title deed can be got as the Natives here claim the land." Regarding the

Anishinaabeg claims, Harper thought they were preventing a solution to Métis claims at the Sault. See Janet Chute, *The Legacy of Shingwaukonse: A Century of Native Leadership* (Toronto: University of Toronto Press, 1998), 103. Anishinaabeg leaders such as Shingwaukonse had more complicated attitudes towards natural resources than Harper realized. See Janet Chute, "Pursuing the Great Spirit's Plan: Nineteenth Century Ojibwa Attitudes towards the future of Logging and Mining on Unsurrendered Indian Lands North of Lakes Huron and Superior," in *Social Relations in Resource Hinterlands – Papers from the 27th Annual Meeting of the Western Association of Sociology and Anthropology*, ed. Thomas W. Dunk (Thunder Bay: Lakehead University, Centre for Northern Studies, 1991), 173–204; and Janet Chute, "A Unifying Vision: Shingwaukonse's Plan for the Future of the Great Lakes Ojibwa," *Journal of the Canadian Historical Association* 7 (1997): 55–80.

23 James Morrison, *The Robinson Treaties: A Case Study*, prepared for the Royal Commission on Aboriginal Peoples (1996), 32, http://publications.gc.ca/collections/collection_2017/bcp-pco/Z1-1991-1-41-160-eng.pdf.

24 Ibid., 45.

25 Ibid., 78.

26 Anishinaabeg who allied themselves to the British during the War of 1812 and resided in the Michigan Territory were relocated to Upper Canada following the war at the direction of the Indian Department. See Chute, *The Legacy of Shingwaukonse*, 29. See also AO, RG 1, Series A-I-6, vol. 25, no. 4, Alexander Vidal to Denis Benjamin Papineau, 27 April 1846. Papineau must have been unaware of the Indian Department's official position regarding resettled First Nations: their land was subject to the Royal Proclamation. Issues surrounding the Grand River lands hinged on this interpretation. However, it was easier to deny First Nations claims in the north so the government could continue to sell private mining and timber leases unhindered, and reap the rewards. Regarding the Grand River, Joseph Brant disagreed with the Crown's position. Brant came into conflict with colonial officials on many occasions as he sold Grand River lands to settlers. Officials argued that these lands were subject to the dictates of the Royal Proclamation, whereas Brant claimed that this land was given to the Six Nations and that they could do with it as they wished. An extensive literature exists on this topic. Smaller works include Sally Weaver, "The Iroquois: The Grand River Reserve in the Late Nineteenth and Early Twentieth Centuries, 1875–1945," in Rogers and Smith, *Aboriginal Ontario*, 213–58. See also Weaver, "Six Nations of the Grand River, Ontario," in *Handbook of North American Indians*, vol. 15, *Northeast*, ed. Bruce Trigger (Washington, DC: Smithsonian Institution, 1987), 525–37. Work specific to the Haudenosaunee of the Bay of Quinte includes Charles Hamori-Torok, "The Iroquois of Akwesasne (St. Regis), Mohawks of the Bay of Quinte (Tyendinaga), Onyota'a (the Oneida of the Thames), and Wahta Mohawk (Gibson), 1750–1945," in Rogers and Smith, *Aboriginal Ontario*, 258–72. George Ironside, the Indian agent at Manitowaning, received instructions that Shingwaukonse and his band should be relocated to Manitoulin Island, "where they might enjoy the same advantages that others who already reside there have so much profited by." Cited in Chute, *The Legacy of Shingwaukonse*, 104.

27 AO, RG 1, Series A-I-6, vol. 25, no. 4, Alexander Vidal to Papineau, 27 April 1846.

28 Phil Bellfy notes the cross-border nature of treaty participation in "Cross-Border Treaty Signers: The Anishnaabeg of the Lake Huron Borderlands," in *Lines Drawn upon Water: First Nations and the Great Lakes Borders and Borderlands*, ed. Karl Hele (Waterloo, ON: Wilfrid Laurier University Press, 2008), 21–42. Bellfy's article is particularly valuable for its appendices and lists of chiefs and headmen who took part in various treaty signings.

Karl Hele, in "The Anishinabeg and Métis in the Sault Ste. Marie Borderlands: Confronting a Line Drawn upon the Water," notes that the Canada/US border in the area needs to be understood "in terms of territories defined in terms of alliances, kinship, and ties of ethnicity." Hele notes how some chiefs and bands accepted treaty annuities from both governments. See Hele's article in Hele, *Lines Drawn upon Water*, 65–84. The quotation is on page 68.

29 LAC, RG 10, vol. 123, Chiefs to Governor-General, 5 July 1847.
30 Sir Arthur G. Doughty, ed., *The Elgin-Grey Papers, 1846–1852*, vol. 2 (Ottawa: J.O. Patenaude, 1937), 549, Lord Elgin to Colonial Secretary Earl Grey, 21 November 1849.
31 Ibid., vol. 1, Elgin to Grey, 23 November 1849. See also LAC, RG 10, vol. 173, Anderson to Civil Secretary, 9 October 1848.
32 It was common for the Anishinaabeg to set small, restricted fires to clear an area of heavy forest growth. Such selective burning encouraged the spread of some berry species and facilitated the growth of animal populations, notably deer. See Shephard Krech III, *The Ecological Indian: Myth and History* (New York: W.W. Norton, 1999), 101–22. E. Reginald Good notes that early settlers in Upper Canada benefited from this selective burning as it created fields ideal for cultivation. See Good, "Mississauga-Mennonite Relations in the Upper Grand River Valley," *Ontario History* 87, 2 (1995): 160. See also Good, "Colonizing a People: Mennonite Settlement in Waterloo Township," in *Earth, Water, Air and Fire: Studies in Canadian Ethnohistory*, ed. David T. McNab (Waterloo, ON: Wilfrid Laurier University Press, 1998), 145–80.
33 Doughty, *The Elgin-Grey Papers*, vol. 4, Anderson to Civil Secretary, 26 August 1848.
34 See LAC, RG 10, vol. 718, J.B. Macaulay, "Report on the Indians of Upper Canada." Also Canada, Legislative Assembly, *Report on the Affairs of the Indians in Canada*, Section III, Journals, Legislative Assembly, Canada (1847), Appendix T. To be fair, the Legislative Assembly did not claim jurisdiction over the Sault until 1845.
35 Vidal-Anderson Report. Both Vidal and Anderson kept private diaries of their trip. See University of Western Ontario, Regional Collection, Alexander Vidal Papers, "Journal of Proceedings on my mission to the Indians of Lake Superior and Huron, 1849," transcribed by George Smith. Anderson's diary is located at the Metropolitan Toronto Library, Baldwin Room, T.G. Anderson Papers, "Diary of Thomas Gummersall Anderson, a visiting Supt. of Indian Affairs at this time 1849 at Coburg."
36 This is considered in Macklem, *Indigenous Difference and the Constitution of Canada*, 136–38. See also Jeremy Webber, "Relations of Force and Relations of Justice: The Emergence of Normative Community between Colonists and Aboriginal Peoples," *Osgoode Hall Law Journal* 33: 623–60. Macklem draws upon Webber's argument to argue that early pre-British treaties were nation-to-nation agreements with no expectation that rights contained therein would require court protection. A similar argument can be extended to this element of the Robinson Treaties. They constituted nation-to-nation agreements, and neither the Crown nor the Anishinaabeg could foresee a time when the harvesting clause in the treaties would require legal consideration.
37 Webber, ibid., 627.
38 Vidal-Anderson Report, 2. Both Telford and Chute examine the Vidal-Anderson Report in greater detail. Both note that Vidal hoped to isolate the senior chiefs, such as Shingwaukonse, by getting lesser chiefs (for lack of a better term) to accept the terms offered. Vidal provided an example of this in an American treaty with the Anishinaabeg. He wrote in a private journal that, during negotiations, the "principal chief can be coerced by

inferiors." See Chute, *The Legacy of Shingwaukonse*, 125–26. See also Telford, "The Sound of the Rustling," 146. Telford also notes that Vidal could be quite belligerent with the chiefs, and at times threatened the Anishinaabeg that they would receive no further presents or money if they did not accept the government's terms. See Telford, ibid., 148–149, 154. See also Chute, ibid., 124–130.

39 Vidal-Anderson Report, 9. It seems more likely that the Anishinaabeg had a decent understanding of the value of minerals, ore, and timber in the north.
40 A statement that reveals the government's ignorance of the north and its resource potential.
41 Vidal-Anderson Report, 11. Arthur Ray, Jim Miller, and Frank Tough note that the Anishinaabeg desire to cede all the land was due to the fact that the interior bands wanted treaty monies to offset poor hunts and reduced credit at HBC posts. Ceding only the lakeshore would not aid the interior Anishinaabeg. See Ray et al., *Bounty and Benevolence: A History of Saskatchewan Treaties* (Montreal and Kingston: McGill-Queen's University Press, 2000), 39.
42 See Ray et al., ibid., 39.
43 Vidal-Anderson Report, 12.
44 The Mica Bay incident is covered in both Surtees, *Treaty Research Report: The Robinson Treaties*, and Morrison, *The Robinson Treaties: A Case Study*. See also W. Robert Wightman and Nancy M. Wightman, "The Mica Bay Affair: Conflict on the Upper Lakes Mining Frontier, 1840–1850," *Ontario History* 83, 3 (1991): 161–81. There is some debate over the catalyst for the Mica Bay Incident. The Wightmans consider Alan Macdonell, a lawyer in the area, as the main cause of the incident, while Rhonda Telford and Janet Chute attribute the impetus to the Anishinaabeg leadership. See Telford, "The Sound of the Rustling," 158–62. See also Chute, *The Legacy of Shingwaukonse*, 130–36. Telford rightly notes that Vidal's and Anderson's heavy-handed approach helped cause the Mica Bay incident.
45 LAC, RG 1, E1, vol. 72, Executive Council Minutes, 19 November 1849.
46 Following the incident at Mica Bay, both chiefs surrendered to authorities to face charges. They were brought to Toronto for trial, but then released and allowed to return to their communities to take part in the treaty negotiations. Shingwaukonse's charges resurfaced after the treaty, conveniently when he began to threaten that he would travel to London to petition Queen Victoria directly. See Chute, *The Legacy of Shingwaukonse*, 144. While he was eventually pardoned, the government passed a new law in 1853 that made it illegal for anyone to incite "Indians or half-breeds" in the province to disturb the peace. Shingwaukonse's planned trip to London would likely have constituted a disturbance. Macdonell advised the chief not to travel to England. Shingwaukonse passed away in March 1854. See Chute, ibid., 155–59.
47 Julia Jarvis, "Robinson, William Benjamin," in *Dictionary of Canadian Biography*, vol. 10 (Toronto/Laval: University of Toronto/Université Laval, 2003), http://www.biographi.ca/en/bio/robinson_william_benjamin_10E.html.
48 LAC, RG 1, E1, State Book "J," Executive Council Minutes, 11 January 1850.
49 AO, Sir John Beverly Robinson Papers, "Diary of William B. Robinson on a visit to the Indians to make a treaty, 1850," 1 May 1850 (hereafter Robinson Diary).
50 Robinson Diary, 5 September 1850.
51 Ibid., 6 September 1850. The views of the Lake Superior chiefs are examined in Lise C. Hansen, "The Anishinabek Land Claim and the Participation of the Indian People Living on the North Shore of Lake Superior in the Robinson Superior Treaty of 1850" (Toronto: Ministry of Natural Resources, Office of Indian Resource Policy, 1985). Also Hansen, "Chiefs

and Principal Men: A Question of Leadership in Treaty Negotiations," *Anthropologica* 29, 1 (1987): 39–60.
52 Telford, "The Sound of the Rustling," 151–52.
53 Brief biographies of both men are found in Morrison, *The Robinson Treaties: A Case Study,* 102–3.
54 Robinson Diary, 7 September 1850.
55 Ibid., 7 September 1850.
56 Ibid., 9 September 1850.
57 Robinson likely understood that recognizing Métis land would set a precedent for future treaties in the north. It was a potentially expensive precedent given the sizable Métis population in the region and areas further north.
58 Alexander Morris, *The Treaties of Canada with the Indians of Manitoba and the North-West Territories Including the Negotiations on Which They Were Based* (Saskatoon: Fifth House Publishers, 1991), 303, 305.
59 Ibid.
60 Webber, "Relations of Force and Relations of Justice," 627.

Chapter 2: Ontario's Game Laws and First Nations, 1800–1905

1 "Ontario Game and Fish Commission: Commissioners' Report," *Ontario Sessional Papers* (Toronto: Warwick and Sons, 1893), 5 (hereafter "Commission Report" accompanied by the year of publication and page reference).
2 *Statutes of the Province of Ontario* (Toronto: L.K. Cameron, 1892).
3 The term "bag limit" refers to how many of a particular type of animal a person who possesses a valid, state-issued licence can take within a specified period.
4 Janet Foster addresses the "myth of superabundance" in her study *Working for Wildlife: The Beginning of Preservation in Canada* (Toronto: University of Toronto Press, 1998), 4. This "settler mentality" was not particular to Ontario but was common throughout North America. See James Tober, *Who Owns the Wildlife? The Political Economy of Conservation in Nineteenth-Century America* (Westport, CT: Greenwood Press, 1981). John M. Mackenzie examined this phenomenon within the British Empire in *The Empire of Nature: Hunting, Conservation and British Imperialism* (New York: Manchester University Press, 1988).
5 "Extracts from Mrs. Simcoe's Diary," in *The Town of York, 1793–1815: A Collection of Documents of Early Toronto,* ed. Edith G. Firth (Toronto: University of Toronto Press, 1962), 218.
6 John Riley cites sources that relate how residents of York spent several days shooting pigeons because they were so abundant. See John L. Riley, *The Once and Future Great Lakes Country: An Ecological History* (Montreal and Kingston: McGill-Queen's University Press, 2014), 136. Riley cites a number of sources that relate the abundance of wildlife in the Lower Great Lakes region, and how settlers made use of the wildlife in ch. 5, "Taking the Wildlife, 1500–1900."
7 William Caniff, *The Settlement of Upper Canada* (Toronto: Dudley and Burns, 1869; reprinted by Mika Silk Screening, 1971), 199.
8 Thomas Radcliff, "William Radcliff to Arthur Radcliff, December 1832," *Authentic Letters from Upper Canada: Including an Account of Canadian Field Sports by Thomas William Magrath* (Toronto: Macmillan, 1952), 106. This book was originally published in 1833. The Magrath family settled on the Credit River at Erindale in May 1827.
9 Ibid.

10 W.L. Smith, *The Makers of Canada: The Pioneers of Old Ontario* (Toronto: George N. Morang, 1923), 106. James Tober makes similar observations regarding early settler society in the United States. See Tober, *Who Owns the Wildlife?* 4–5.
11 Elmsley to Richard Cartwright, 5 December 1797, in Firth, *The Town of York*, 224.
12 J.G. Simcoe to Henry Dundas, 28 April 1792, in *The Correspondence of Lieut. Governor John Graves Simcoe with Allied Documents Relating to His Administration of the Government of Upper Canada*, ed. E.A. Cruickshank (Toronto: Champlain Society, 1923), 1: 141. This is also outlined in Blair, *Lament for a First Nation*. Blair quotes Simcoe noting, in 1791, that "the Indians can in no way be deprived of their rights to their Territory and Hunting Grounds ... and any portion of Lands ceded by them held as a Reservation must, and shall be fully protected as well as rights reserved on certain Streams and Lakes for fishing, and hunting privileges or purposes" (15).
13 "A Visit with Joseph Brant on the Grand River, 1792," in *Valley of the Six Nations: A Collection of Documents on the Indian Lands of the Grand River*, ed. Charles Johnston (Toronto: University of Toronto Press, 1964), 60–61.
14 This stands in contrast with England. P.B. Munsche notes that game in eighteenth-century England was narrowly defined to encompass only hares, partridges, pheasants, and moor fowl. These animals could occasionally be found off estates, in which cases they could be hunted in accordance with national laws. Laws for deer were different. Deer "as a result of enclosure ... had become a type of private property and were entitled to legal protection as such." Punishments reflected this. Breaking the game laws meant a five-pound fine or three months in prison. Hunting a privately owned deer meant that you stole it and faced transportation for seven years. See Munsche, *Gentlemen and Poachers: The English Game Laws, 1671–1831* (Cambridge: Cambridge University Press, 1981), 3–4.
15 Richard S. Lambert and Paul Pross, *Renewing Nature's Wealth: A Centennial History of the Public Management of Lands, Forests and Wildlife in Ontario, 1763–1967* (Toronto: Department of Lands and Forests, 1967), 447. Laws regarding salmon fishing are noted in J. David Wood, *Making Ontario: Agricultural Colonization and Landscape Re-creation before the Railway* (Montreal and Kingston: McGill-Queen's University Press, 2000), 18.
16 "An Act to prevent certain Wild Fowl and Snipes from being destroyed at improper seasons of the year, and to prevent the trapping of Grouse and Quail in this Province," in *Provincial Statutes of Canada* (Montreal: Stewart Derbyshire and George Desbarats, 1845) (hereafter *Provincial Statutes of Canada* followed by the year when the legislation was passed).
17 "An Act to prevent the hunting of Deer at improper seasons of the year, and further to amend the laws for the preservation of Game," *Provincial Statutes of Canada*, 1851; "An Act for the better protection of Game in Upper Canada," *Provincial Statutes of Canada*, 1860.
18 Cited in Blair, *Lament for a First Nation*, 29.
19 See Douglas McCalla, *Planting the Province: The Economic History of Upper Canada, 1784–1870* (Toronto: University of Toronto Press, 1993), for an overview of Upper Canada's growing agricultural production in the nineteenth century.
20 "Report on the Affairs of the Indians of Canada laid before the Legislative Assembly, 20th March 1845," *Journals of the Legislative Assembly*, Section III, 24, app. 1.
21 *Report of the Special Commissioners Appointed on the 18th of September, 1856, to Investigate Indian Affairs in Canada* (Toronto: Stewart Derbyshire and George Desbarats, 1858), app. 21.
22 See Peter George, "Ontario's Mining Industry, 1870–1940," in *Progress without Planning: The Economic History of Ontario from Confederation to the Second World War*, ed. Ian Drummond (Toronto: University of Toronto Press, 1987), 52–76. Christopher Armstrong

and H.V. Nelles examine the political and constitutional issues surrounding resource development in Ontario are examined in Christopher Armstrong, *The Politics of Federalism*, and H.V. Nelles, *The Politics of Development: Forest, Mines and Hydro-Electric Development in Ontario, 1849–1941* (Toronto: Macmillan of Canada, 1974).

23 On the St. Catherine's issue see S. Barry Cottam, "An Historical Background of the *St. Catherine's Milling and Lumber Co.* Case" (MA thesis, University of Western Ontario, 1987). See also Cottam, "Indian Title as a 'Celestial Institution': David Mills and the *St. Catherine's Milling* Case," in *Aboriginal Land Use in Canada: Historical and Legal Aspects*, ed. Kerry Abel and Jean Friesen (Winnipeg: University of Manitoba Press, 1991), 247–66. Cottam also considers the case in "Federal/Provincial Disputes, Natural Resources and the Ojibway, 1867-1924" (PhD dissertation, University of Ottawa, 1994). In the same volume, see also Anthony J. Hall "*The St. Catherine's Milling and Lumber Company versus the Queen*: Indian Land Rights as a Factor in Federal-Provincial Relations in Nineteenth Century Canada," 267–86. See also Donald B. Smith, "Aboriginal Rights a Century Ago: Were the Indians Cheated in 1885? An Old Case Re-examined," *The Beaver* 67, 1 (1987): 4–15.

For an analysis of Lord Watson, the JCPC judge who wrote the *St. Catherine's Milling* decision, see John Saywell, *The Lawmakers: Judicial Power and the Shaping of Canadian Federalism* (Toronto: University of Toronto Press, 2002). Historians Donald B. Smith and Barry Cottam disagree on the impact of the *St. Catherine's Milling* decision. Smith maintains that a victory by the Dominion government would have protected Aboriginal resource rights against provincial intrusion in future legal proceedings. Cottam argues that the outcome of the decision is irrelevant, stating that if "Macdonald's conception of Indian title held, the Indians would have lost their lands to a federal, not a provincial, government." Within the context of Ontario's game laws, a Dominion victory would have helped First Nations.

There has been a growing literature examining provincial resource policies in relation to First Nations. Two major works on hydro development are James B. Waldram, *As Long as the Rivers Run: Hydroelectric Development and Native Communities in Western Canada* (Winnipeg: University of Manitoba Press, 1988), and Jean L. Manore, *Cross-Currents: Hydroelectricity and the Engineering of Northern Ontario* (Waterloo: Wilfrid Laurier University Press, 1999). Rhonda Telford's study of mining is another example of the trend towards resource studies. See Telford, "'The Sound of the Rustling of the Gold Is under My Feet Where I Stand; We Have a Rich Country': A History of Aboriginal Mineral Resources in Ontario" (PhD dissertation, University of Toronto, 1996).

24 Cited in Smith, "Aboriginal Rights a Century Ago," 11.

25 Mowat's and Macdonald's conflicting views of Confederation and battles over provincial rights can be seen from varying perspectives in several studies. Macdonald's centralist vision is put forth in Donald Creighton, *John A. Macdonald: The Old Chieftain* (Toronto: Macmillan, 1955), esp. 322–24, and in Creighton, *Canada's First Century* (Toronto: Macmillan, 1970), 45–49. Margaret Evans's study of Mowat provides a different picture of the Mowat-Macdonald feud. See *Mowat*, 141–80. Christopher Armstrong provides an excellent analysis of these battles within the context of competing conceptions of the constitution in *The Politics of Federalism*, 1–32. An older but still useful overview of this debate is G.P Browne's introduction to *Documents on the Confederation of British North America* (Toronto: McClelland and Stewart, 1969).

26 See Sidney L. Harring, "'The Liberal Treatment of Indians': Native People in Nineteenth Century Ontario Law," *Saskatchewan Law Review* 56, 2 (1993): 297–371. See also Harring, *White Man's Law*.

27 The Migratory Birds Convention Act (1917) is the most obvious example of US influence on Canadian wildlife conservation. See Kurk Dorsey, "Scientists, Citizens, and Statesmen: US-Canadian Wildlife Protection Treaties in the Progressive Era," *Diplomatic History* 19, 3 (1995): 407–29. R. Peter Gilles and Thomas R. Roach examine the American influence on forest conservation in "The American Influence on Conservation in Canada, 1899–1911," *Journal of Forest History* (October 1986): 160–74. They consider a similar theme in "The Beginnings of a Movement: The Montreal Congress and Its Aftermath, 1880–1896," in *Consuming Canada: Readings in Environmental History,* ed. Chad Gaffield and Pam Gaffield (Toronto: Copp Clark, 1995), 131–51. Neil S. Forkey examines US-Canadian conflict over fisheries conservation in "Anglers, Fishers, and the St. Croix River: Conflict in a Canadian-American Borderland, 1867–1900," *Forest and Conservation History* 37 (October 1993): 179–87.

28 Approaches to conservation in the United States soon influenced conservation not just in Ontario but also throughout Canada. Historiography surrounding this development is extensive. In general, two themes emerge in the historical literature about the origins of the conservation movement. Some scholars argue that the impetus for wildlife conservation emerged from local hunters (a bottom-up development), while others point to urban elites and intellectuals as the driving force behind this nascent environmentalism (a top-down development). Thomas Dunlap and Richard Judd belong to the former camp, while Henry Clepper, Roderick Nash, Samuel Hayes, and John Reiger argue that conservation began at the top and filtered down to the middle and lower economic classes. Henry Clepper, *Leaders of American Conservation* (New York: Ronald Press, 1966); Roderick Nash, *Wilderness and the American Mind* (New Haven, CT: Yale University Press, 1973). Richard Judd sees a conservationist sentiment beginning with local people: *Common Lands, Common People: The Origins of Conservation in Northern New England* (Cambridge, MA: Harvard University Press, 1997). A similar debate exists in Canada. Janet Foster argues in *Working for Wildlife: The Beginning of Preservation in Canada* (Toronto: University of Toronto Press, 1978) that bureaucratic innovation was the wellspring of conservation. Tina Loo, *States of Nature: Conserving Canada's Wildlife in the Twentieth Century* (Vancouver: UBC Press, 2006), sees a dual origin (and at times a more important role for private citizens) for conservation; however, she also acknowledges that increasing state regulation worked to marginalize local approaches to conservation. Neil Forkey provides an excellent overview of the utilitarian and romantic approaches in Canada in *Canadians and the Natural Environment to the Twenty-First Century* (Toronto: University of Toronto Press, 2012).

29 Philip D. Thomas, "Thoreau, Henry David," in *Biographical Dictionary of American and Canadian Naturalists and Environmentalists,* ed. Keir B. Sterling et al. (Westport, CT: Greenwood Publishing, 1997), 775; Nash, *Wilderness and the American Mind,* 39, 95. Thoreau is best known for this quotation: "I went to the woods because I wished to live deliberately, to front only the essential facts of life, and see if I could not learn what it had to teach, and not, when I came to die, discover that I had not lived." See Henry David Thoreau, *Walden* (Ottawa: Prospero Books, 1999 [reprint]), 75.

30 The camping movement for children is an excellent example of a business based on extolling the transcendental value of spending time in natural settings and "getting back to nature." See Sharon Wall, *The Nurture of Nature: Childhood, Antimodernism, and Ontario Summer Camps, 1920–1955* (Vancouver: UBC Press, 2010). See also Wall, "Totem Poles, Teepees, and Token Traditions: 'Playing Indian' at Ontario Summer Camps, 1920–1955," *Canadian Historical Review* 86, 3 (2005).

31 In the United States, conservationist John Muir (1838–1914) was the first to blend the transcendental with the concrete. As one of the founders of the Sierra Club, and a driving force behind the creation of Yosemite National Park, Muir sought to preserve wilderness areas as a refuge for urbanites. As environmental historian Roderick Nash notes, Muir "camouflaged his radical [conservationist ideas] in more acceptable rhetoric centered on the benefits of nature for people." See Nash, *Wilderness and the American Mind*, 39, 41. See also Paul Cammarate and Keir B. Sterling, "Muir, John," in Sterling et al., *Biographical Dictionary of American and Canadian Naturalists and Environmentalists*, 563–66. Donald Worster makes the same observation in his more recent biography of Muir, noting that Muir was similar in some respects to Thoreau because he saw a oneness between human beings and nature. However, Muir saw the potential of science to explain the natural world and control it. See Donald Worster, *A Passion for Nature: The Life of John Muir* (Oxford: Oxford University Press, 2008). Gifford Pinchot, usually associated with the strictly utilitarian approach to conservation, also blended the two. Char Miller's biography of Pinchot notes that Pinchot's utilitarianism tempered as he aged. He realized that the value of nature "cannot be measured in board feet and cords, in dollars and cents." See Miller, *Gifford Pinchot and the Making of Modern Environmentalism* (Washington DC: Island Press, 2001), 338. Miller's argument is best summarized in his own words, namely, that Pinchot's "legacy lies in his greening, in his deliberate effort to reach an ever more complete understanding of the tangled interactions between the civilized and the wild" (376). See also Michael Osburn, "Pinchot, Gifford," in *Biographical Dictionary of American and Canadian Environmentalists*, ed. Keir B. Sterling, Richard P. Harmond, George A. Cevasco, and Lorne F. Hammond (Westport, CT: Greenwood Publishing, 1997): 630–33.
32 Patricia Jasen examines this in *Wild Things: Nature, Culture and Tourism in Ontario, 1790–1914* (Toronto: University of Toronto Press, 1995), 106–11.
33 To make their trip north complete, the anglers often sought out "real" Indian guides to take them to the best spots. See Mark Chochla, "Victorian Fly Fishers on the Nipigon," *Ontario History* 91, 2 (1999): 151–64. Nipigon, sport fishing, and provincial conservation policies are considered in J. Michael Thoms, "Illegal Conservation: Two Case Studies of Conflict between Indigenous and State Natural Resource Management Paradigms" (MA thesis, Trent University, 1996). Jasen considers the tourist desire to have a "real" Indian guide during their Nipigon excursions to make their trip "authentic" (*Wild Things*, 136–49).
34 Tourism and resource development in the Temagami Region is examined in Bruce Hodgins and Jamie Benidickson, *The Temagami Experience: Recreation, Resources and Aboriginal Rights in the Northern Ontario Wilderness* (Toronto: University of Toronto Press, 1989). Robert Surtees examined the construction of the Temiskaming and Northern Ontario Railway in *The Northern Connection: Ontario Northland since 1902* (Toronto: Captus Press, 1992).
35 Ontario "Report of the Survey and Exploration of Northern Ontario, 1900," *Ontario Sessional Papers* (Toronto: L.K. Cameron, 1901), 94. Nimrod is mentioned in the Book of Genesis, 10: 8–9: "And Cush begat Nimrod: he began to be a mighty one in the earth. / He was a mighty hunter before the Lord: wherefore it is said, Even as Nimrod the mighty hunter before the Lord." See *The Bible: Authorized King James Version* (Oxford: Oxford University Press, 1997). A full study of the use of biblical imagery by survey crews awaits a scholar. Edward Barnes Borron, sent to survey northern Ontario's resources in the 1880s, commented on the north's tourism potential. He also noted the detrimental impact that railways, mining, and logging were having on First Nations. See Ontario, "Report of E.B.

Borron, Stipendiary Magistrate, on that part of the Basin of Hudson's Bay Belonging to the Province of Ontario," *Ontario Sessional Papers* (Toronto: L.K. Cameron, 1885). See also Morris Zaslow, "Edward Barnes Borron, 1820-1915: Northern Pioneer and Public Servant Extraordinary," in *Aspects of Nineteenth-Century Ontario*, ed. F.H. Armstrong et.al. (Toronto: University of Toronto Press, 1974): 297–311.
36 Cited in Hodgins and Benidickson, *The Temagami Experience*, 109.
37 Jamie Benidickson examines the role of canoeing in the recreation movement of the late nineteenth and early twentieth centuries in *Idleness, Water, and a Canoe: Reflections on Paddling for Pleasure* (Toronto: University of Toronto Press, 1997), 65–77.
38 Commission Report 1897, 4. No similar concern was expressed about the women.
39 An earlier study of how the utilitarian approach was applied to national parks policy is Brown, "The Doctrine of Usefulness."
40 Commission Report 1892, 16.
41 Ecological or environmental science at this time was known more commonly as natural history. It reflected the Victorian fascination with science and nature, and the ability of the former to explain the latter. It also sought to exploit natural resources by better understanding their properties. While some of the work done was important, it was largely amateur. Natural history societies soon became a common feature of late-nineteenth-century towns and cities. Local physicians and pharmacists, people who by virtue of their profession received scientific training at university, often formed the backbone of these organizations. Systematically observing and cataloguing Canada's flora and fauna during field trips, some societies published large and comprehensive studies of various species. Thomas McIlwraith, a Hamilton fuel dealer, for example, wrote *The Birds of Ontario* in 1886, and it was the standard reference work for some time. Carl Berger examines this in *Science, God, and Nature in Victorian Canada* (Toronto: University of Toronto Press, 1983). Ontario's Game Commission reflected this convergence of utilitarian conservationism, amateur science, and economic demands. Dr. G.A. MacCallum from Dunnville, Ontario, was the chair of the commission. A trained physician, he came to this position with a strong background in biology and chemistry and a love of science, but had no formal training in wildlife biology (Lambert and Pross, *Renewing Nature's Wealth*, 449). While no information exists about the other permanent members of the commission, none of them is listed as being a university-trained biologist. When the commission required detailed scientific information regarding different species in Ontario, it relied on the few experts that existed. The last portion of its 1892 report, for example, contains illustrated descriptions of the various fauna found in Ontario. Unlike today, with a plethora of researchers and biologists specializing in single animals, the commission had only three individuals to draw upon: Professor Frederick True, curator of the Department of Mammals for the Smithsonian Institution in Washington, DC; Dr. H.M. Smith of the United States Fish Commission; and Professor Ramsay Wright, professor of biology at the University of Toronto. See Commission Report 1892.
42 Commission Report 1892, 11–12.
43 Ibid., 24–31.
44 Ibid., 191.
45 Commission Report 1905, 7; Commission Report 1906, 9.
46 See "An Act to amend and consolidate the Laws for the Protection of Game and Fur-bearing Animals," in *Statutes of the Province of Ontario* (Toronto: L.K. Cameron, 1893), 194. Section 2(3) states: "No one person shall during any one year or season kill or take more in all than

two deer, elk, moose, reindeer or caribou. But this shall not apply in the case of deer which are the private property of any person ..."
47 The price is noted in *Rod and Gun,* April 1900, 218.
48 Commission Report 1896, 5. It is important to note that the report contains no statistics to verify its claim about the number of deer killed.
49 Commission Report 1898, 6.
50 "Deer Shooting in Ontario," *Rod and Gun,* April 1900, 218.
51 The European depiction of wolves is considered briefly in Karen Jones, "*Never Cry Wolf:* Science, Sentiment, and the Literary Rehabilitation of *Canis lupus,*" *Canadian Historical Review* 84, 1 (2003): 66–67.
52 Commission Report 1892, 325.
53 *Rod and Gun,* November 1899, 103. Perhaps the best-known literary rehabilitation of wolves occurred with the publication of Farley Mowat's novel *Never Cry Wolf.*
54 Commission Report 1905, 17.
55 Commission Report 1906, 9.
56 Commission Report 1903, 7.
57 Crust hunting also relies on dogs. Small beagles can run over the snow without breaking the crust. The dogs tire the deer (biting at its hamstrings), while the hunter follows behind.
58 Commission Report 1892, 13–14, 60.
59 Commission Report 1893, 6.
60 Commission Report 1905, 15.
61 Ibid., 17.
62 Commission Report 1895, 9.
63 "An Act to Amend and Consolidate the Laws for the Protection of Game and Fur-Bearing Animals," in *Statutes of the Province of Ontario* (Toronto: L.K. Cameron, 1892), 204.
64 Records for this no longer exist. The finding aid in the Archives of Ontario notes that a helpful bureaucrat purged the attorney general's record of virtually all Aboriginal material in the 1960s when the files were being transferred to the archives. The official considered the material to be of little interest to future historians. Early records for the Ontario Ministry of Natural Resources were similarly redacted when transferred to the archives.
65 Records of Ontario legislature debates are silent on the 1913 amendment.

Chapter 3: First Nations, the Game Commission, and Indian Affairs, 1892–1909

1 It is important to bear in mind that magistrates often did not have any legal training. They are often, even today, volunteers who agree to act in a judicial capacity in their community. Magistrates handle small, minor offences. It is possible that local magistrate Quibell was a North Bay resident with no legal training.
2 The Bank of Canada online inflation calculator does not allow calculations prior to 1914. However, $50 in 1914 is equivalent to $1,080 in 2017 dollars.
3 John Tobias, "Protection, Civilization, Assimilation: An Outline History of Canada's Indian Policy," in *As Long as the Sun Shines and Water Flows: A Reader on Canadian Native Studies,* ed. Ian A.L. Gettey and Antoine S. Lussier, Nakoda Institute Occasional Paper No. 1 (Vancouver: UBC Press, 1981), 39. See also John Leslie and Ron Maguire, eds., *The Historical Development of the Indian Act* (Ottawa: DIAND, T&HRC, 1978), 89–105.

4 Tobias, ibid., 48.
5 Ibid., 48.
6 Douglas Leighton, "A Victorian Civil Servant at Work: Lawrence Vankoughnet and the Canadian Indian Department, 1874–1893," in Gettey and Lussier, *As Long as the Sun Shines and Water Flows,* ed. Ian A.L. Getty and Antoine S. Lussier (Vancouver: UBC Press, 1981), 108.
7 Leslie and Maguire, *Historical Development of the Indian Act,* 98. These branches were more concerned with ensuring that Indian Affairs ran within its budget than with protecting the treaty rights of Mushkegowuk. D.C. Scott, after his ascension to the position of deputy superintendent general, hoped that the Timber Branch would manage reserve timber resources to make bands financially self-sustaining. See Mark Kuhlberg, "'Nothing It Seems Can Be Done about It': Charlie Cox, Indian Affairs' Timber Policy and the Long Lac Reserve, 1924–1940," *Canadian Historical Review* 84, 1 (2003): 33–63.
8 Leslie and Maguire, ibid., 99.
9 D.J. Hall, "Clifford Sifton and Canadian Indian Administration, 1896–1905," in Gettey and Lussier, *As Long as the Sun Shines and Water Flows,* 123.
10 See Paul Romney, "Mowat, Sir Oliver," in *Dictionary of Canadian Biography, 1901–1910,* vol. 13 (Toronto: University of Toronto Press, 2003). See also Joseph Schull, *Laurier* (Toronto: Macmillan, 1965). See also Laurier LaPierre, *Sir Wilfrid Laurier and the Romance of Canada* (Toronto: Stoddart Publishing, 1996).
11 Leighton, "A Victorian Civil Servant at Work," 109.
12 Ibid.
13 Robert J. Surtees, *The Original People* (Toronto: Holt, Rinehart and Winston of Canada, 1971), 44.
14 D.J. Hall, "Clifford Sifton and Canadian Indian Administration, 1896-1905," 122.
15 LAC, RG 10, Series B-8, vol. 11194, file 4, box 50, A. Power to McLean, 20 July 1897.
16 Ibid., Power to McLean, 5 July 1898.
17 Ibid.
18 Ibid. E.L. Newcombe to McLean, 27 August 1898.
19 LAC, RG 10, vol. 2405, file 84.041, pt. 1, Browning and Leask to J.D. McLean, 17 December 1898. See also ibid., Browning and Leask to Clifford Sifton, 17 August 1898.
20 Ibid., McLean to Browning and Leask, 24 August 1898.
21 Ibid., J.D. McLean to Browning and Leask, 23 October 1898.
22 David W. Elliot, "Aboriginal Title," in *Aboriginal Peoples and the Law: Indian, Métis and Inuit Rights in Canada,* ed. Bradford W. Morse (Ottawa: Carleton University Press, 1991), 98–99. Gérard La Forest makes a similar observation in *Natural Resources and Public Property under the Canadian Constitution* (Toronto: University of Toronto Press, 1969), 113.
23 La Forest, ibid., 112.
24 Ibid., 117–18.
25 Jack Woodward, *Native Law* (Toronto: Carswell, 1989), 212.
26 Cited in La Forest, *Natural Resources and Public Property,* 119 (emphasis added).
27 LAC, RG 10, vol. 2405, file 84.041, pt. 1, Memorandum, 31 August 1898.
28 Ibid., McLean to E.J. Davis, 18 September 1898.
29 Ibid., J.M. Gibson to James A. Smart, 23 September 1898.
30 Ibid., Smart to Gibson, 19 October 1898.
31 Ibid., Joseph Rogers to Gibson, 26 April 1899.

32 Ibid.
33 Ibid., Gibson to Smart, 27 April 1899.
34 Ibid., Smart to Gibson, 5 May 1898.
35 In the original rough draft of his letter, Smart argued that "those purchasers [whites] are more guilty than their comparatively ignorant dupes." See ibid., Rough draft of Smart's letter to Gibson, 2 May 1899.
36 "An Act to Amend the Ontario Game Protection Act," in *Statutes of the Province of Ontario* (Toronto: L.K. Cameron, 1905), 90.
37 Ibid.
38 Ibid., 147. The act noted that "no beaver or otter shall be hunted, taken or killed or had in possession by any person before the first day of November, 1905."
39 "An Act to Amend and Consolidate The Ontario Game Protection Act, 1910," in *Statutes of the Province of Ontario* (Toronto: L.K. Cameron, 1910), 134.
40 LAC, RG 10, vol. 6743, file 420-8-1. McLean to George P. Cockburn, 6 December 1906.
41 Ibid.
42 Ibid., McDougall to McLean, 27 December 1909.
43 Ibid., Chief Moses McCoy to McLean, 29 December 1909.
44 Section 29 (1) of the 1907 Game Act states: "Except under the authority of a license, no one shall fish in the waters of Lake Nepigon [sic] in the District of Thunder Bay, in the River Nepigon in the same District, nor in any tributaries of the said Lake or River." Section 29(2) continued: "This section and the conditions applicable to licenses authorizing such fishing shall apply to Indians as well as to all other guides, boatmen, canoemen, camp assistants or helpers of any kind of any fishing party or persons who may hold any such license." See "An Act Respecting the Game, Fur-bearing Animals and Fisheries in Ontario," in *Statutes of the Province of Ontario*. Toronto: L.K. Cameron, 1907), 348. The cost of obtaining a license was $15 for two weeks, $20 for three weeks, and $25 for four weeks. Again, the Bank of Canada inflation calculator does not consider the pre-1914 period. However, the costs of the licences in 2017 dollars would be $324, $432, and $540, respectively. The amount of time allotted to each licence coincided with the fishing season and the period when tourists made fishing trips. The Anishinaabeg, therefore, were capable of guiding fishermen but not fishing themselves, as the price of a licence was unreasonable for those who lived in the area and relied heavily on fish throughout the year. The issues and events surrounding the Nipigon area and fishing are explored in Thoms, "Illegal Conservation." See also Chochla, "Victorian Fly Fishers on the Nipigon," and Jasen, *Wild Things*.
45 LAC, RG 10, vol. 6743, file 420-8-1, McCoy to McLean, 29 December 1909.
46 Ibid., J.G. Ramsden to McLean, 8 March 1910.
47 Ibid., McLean to Ramsden, 11 March 1910.
48 Ibid., McLean to McDougall, 3 January 1910. Also McLean to Langworthy and McComber, 15 February 1910.
49 Ibid., McCoy to McLean, 29 December 1909. The 1900 Game Act states that the law would not affect any treaty rights conferred upon Mushkegowuk "with reference to hunting on their reserves of hunting-grounds or in any territory specially set apart for the purpose." See "An Act to Amend and Consolidate the Ontario Game Protection Act," in *Statutes of the Province of Ontario* (Toronto: L.K. Cameron, 1900), 164. The correspondence implies that Ogima argued that he was hunting on a hunting territory, but the transcripts of the trial could not be located.

Chapter 4: Traders, Trappers, and Bureaucrats, 1892–1916

1 Hudson's Bay Company Archives (HBCA), A.12/FT230/1, C.C. Chipman to William Armit, 20 June 1892.
2 An older but still invaluable study of the intermingling of cultural, political, and economic practices is Arthur J. Ray and Donald Freeman, *Give Us Good Measure: An Economic Analysis of Relations between the Indians and the Hudson's Bay Company* (Toronto: University of Toronto Press, 1978). Ray and Freeman argue that the fur trade, while centred on the HBC (and the North West Company until 1821) had to adapt to regional factors, not least of which were the cultural practices of First Nations. As a result, Ray and Freeman conclude that the fur trade was an amalgamation of European and First Nations practices (236). It is an argument developed fully in Richard White's *The Middle Ground: Indians, Empires, and Republics in the Great Lakes Region, 1650–1815*, 2nd ed. (Cambridge: Cambridge University Press, 2011). While White does not deal with the HBC, his argument that First Nations and Europeans found accommodation in the *pays d'en haut* reflects the idea that Europeans and First Nations could find accommodation.
3 Loo, *Making Law, Order, and Authority in British Columbia*.
4 HBCA, A.12/FT230/1, C.C. Chipman to William Ware, 7 July 1897.
5 There have been two studies of the Temiskaming and Northern Ontario Railway. Albert Tucker's *Steam into Wilderness* (Toronto: Fitzhenry and Whiteside, 1978) is concerned more with the provincial politics that surrounded the railway. Robert J. Surtees's *The Northern Connection* provides a more regionally focused analysis of the railway's growth, and weaves the story of mineral discoveries into the narrative of the railway. S.A. Pain's *The Way North: Men, Mines and Minerals* (Toronto: Ryerson Press, 1964) is a strong local history of mining development in northern Ontario. More academic analysis can be found in H.V. Nelles's *The Politics of Development* and Morris Zaslow's *The Opening of the Canadian North, 1870–1914* (Toronto: McClelland and Stewart, 1971).
6 HBCA, A.12/FT230/1, Chipman to Ware, 21 February 1905.
7 Ibid., Chipman to Ware, 29 January 1906.
8 This firm no longer exists. It splintered into two firms: McCarthy Tétrault and Osler, Hoskin & Harcourt. The author contacted both firms to see whether either had any records pertaining to the HBC case. Both reported that they did not.
9 HBCA, A.12/FT230/1, Chipman to Ware, 28 July 1909. At $60 per pelt, the fine for the beaver pelts was $900, equivalent to $19,455 in 2017 dollars.
10 Ibid., Chipman to Ware, 11 August 1909, and Chipman to Ware, 15 October 1909.
11 Ibid., McCarthy to Chipman, 14 April 1908.
12 Ibid., T. Clouston to Ware, 1 March 1910. The total fine was $6393.35 (approximately $138,202 in 2017 dollars).
13 Sidney Harring examines harvesting issues to some extent in *The White Man's Law*, for example, the case of *Sero v. Gault* and the incident on Manitoulin Island in 1863. Both relate to fishing. The Manitoulin incident is instructive for how the Anishinaabeg on the island perceived the issue: they maintained that they retained sovereignty over the fishery. Harring, however, does not examine the legal arguments put forth by the defendant's lawyer or examine the case in detail. In the *Sero* case no similar examination is offered. Rather, Harring is more concerned with the general trend of cases and how they reflect the attitudes of Canadian lawmakers and courts regarding Aboriginal rights.

14 The height of land was the southern boundary of the Company's land in Ontario. North Bay is significantly south of the height of land.
15 HBCA, A.12/FT230/1, Chipman to Ware, 8 April 1910.
16 Ibid., Chipman to Ware, 8 April 1910.
17 LAC, RG 10, vol. 6743, file 420-8, McCarthy to Frank Pedley, 17 March 1910. Chelmsford is located just west of Sudbury.
18 Ibid.
19 Ibid., J. Mulligan to McLean, 2 April 1910.
20 HBCA, A.39/14, Chipman to Ware, 8 April 1910.
21 LAC, RG 10, vol. 6743, file 420-8, Draft of Stated Case, 28 October 1910.
22 Equivalent to $138,202 in 2017 dollars.
23 LAC, RG 10, vol. 6743, file 420-8, McCarthy to Pedley, 14 June 1910. See also AO, Sir Aemilius Irving Papers, MU 1469, box 31, package 37, "Northwest Angle Treaty: Game and Fisheries."
24 HBCA, A.39/14, Bischoff to Chipman, 26 June 1910.
25 LAC, RG 10, vol. 6743, file 420-8, Newcombe to McLean, 2 September 1910.
26 HBCA, A.12/FT319/1a, McCarthy to Chipman, 22 October 1910.
27 Ibid.
28 LAC, RG 10, vol. 6743, file 420-8, McLean to Edwin Tinsley, 2 December 1910. See also "An Act Respecting Game, Fur-Bearing Animals and Fisheries of Ontario," ch. 49 in *Statutes of the Province of Ontario* (Toronto: L.K. Cameron, 1907), 339–41.
29 LAC, RG 10, vol. 6743, file 420-8, McLean to Cockburn, 10 December 1910.
30 Ibid., McLean to Tinsley, 15 December 1910.
31 Ibid., Kelly Evans to McLean, 14 December 1910. One of Evans's questions pertained to reservations that bordered on lakes, and to what extent reserve boundaries extended into rivers and lakes.
32 HBCA, A.12/FT319/1a, McCarthy to McLean, 3 January 1911.
33 LAC, RG 10, vol. 6743, file 420-8, McLean to Evans, 26 December 1910.
34 Ibid.
35 HBCA, A.12/FT319/1a, McCarthy to Chipman, 22 April 1911.
36 Ibid., N.M.W.J. McKenzie to Hall, 16 June 1912.
37 Ibid., Hall to F.C. Ingrams, 19 June 1912.
38 Ibid., McCarthy to Hall, 26 June 1912.
39 Ibid., Hall to McCarthy, 23 June 1912.
40 Ibid., McCarthy to Hall, 26 June 1912.
41 Ibid. See also ibid., McKenzie to Hall, 22 June 1912.
42 Ibid., John Routledge to Hall, 21 June 1912. The old HBC post at Fort William was closed in 1883 and levelled in 1902, but the Company maintained a small operation in the town.
43 Charles W. Humphries's biography of Whitney makes no mention of the meeting and there is no record in Whitney's papers. See *"Honest Enough to be Bold": The Life and Times of Sir James Pliny Whitney* (Toronto: University of Toronto Press, 1985).
44 HBCA, RG 2/2/8, "Fur Seizures in Ontario and Quebec," 31 July 1912.
45 HBCA, A.39/14, Ontario Game and Fisheries Act, Memorandum of Mr. Younger, K.C., and Mr. F.D. MacKinnon, 28 October 1912. They also drew the directors' attention to section 92(16) of the Constitution, which granted the provinces jurisdiction over "Matters

of a merely local or private nature." Since the HBC's trade was both national and international, Younger and MacKinnon argued that the Ontario government had no right to restrict it. This argument was not used by McCarthy, but is noted here to show the extent to which Company lawyers were willing to argue their case.

46 HBCA, RG 2/2/7, McCarthy to Nanton, 31 July 1912.
47 Ibid., Nanton to McCarthy, 8 August 1912.
48 Armstrong, *The Politics of Federalism*, 124.
49 See Humphries, *"Honest Enough to be Bold."* Christopher Armstrong also analyzes the close relationship between Whitney and Borden in *The Politics of Federalism*, 122–24.
50 HBCA, A.12/FT319/1a, Hall to Ingrams, 28 August 1912.
51 This is noted throughout Humphries, *"Honest Enough to Be Bold,"* particularly 220.
52 HBCA, A.12/FT319/1a, McCarthy to Hall, 16 November 1912.
53 Ibid., Hall to Whitney, 20 January 1913. These furs would be worth approximately $324,250 in 2017 dollars.
54 Ibid., McCarthy to Hall, 11 February 1913.
55 Ibid., McCarthy to Hall, 3 April 1913.
56 Ibid., McKenzie to Hall, 26 May 1913.
57 Ibid., J.S.H.S. Stanger to McKenzie, 23 May 1913.
58 HBCA, RG 2/2/7, Bacon to Nanton, 12 June 1914.
59 Ibid.
60 LAC, RG 10, vol. 6747, file 420-8x, pt. 1, Ludwig to Mackenzie, 15 October 1930.
61 Ibid., Nanton to Ingrams, 25 June 1914.
62 HBCA, RG 3/FT319/1B, McCarthy to Ingrams, 11 November 1914.
63 Ibid., Memorandum regarding 1916 Game Laws, 7 December 1916.
64 Ibid.

Chapter 5: The Transitional Indian, 1914–20

1 E. Brian Titley, *A Narrow Vision: Duncan Campbell Scott and the Administration of Indian Affairs in Canada* (Vancouver: UBC Press, 1986), 25, 34.
2 Ronald Graham Haycock, *The Canadian Indian as a Subject and Concept in a Sampling of the Popular National Magazines Read in Canada, 1900–1970* (Waterloo, ON: Waterloo Lutheran University Press, 1970), 1.
3 See James Morrison, *Treaty Research Report: Treaty No. 9, 1905-1906* (Ottawa: DIAND, T&HRC, 1986). See also John S. Long, *Treaty No. 9: The Negotiations, 1901–1928* (Cobalt, ON: Cobalt Highway Book Shop, 1978), and "'No Basis for Argument?' The Signing of Treaty No. 9 in Northern Ontario, 1905–1906," *Native Studies Review* 5, 2 (1989): 19–54. The new standard scholarly reference for Treaty 9 is John Long, *Treaty No. 9: Making the Agreement to Share the Land in Far Northern Ontario in 1905* (Montreal and Kingston: McGill-Queen's University Press, 2013). The impact of the older fur trade system on the Mushkegowuk/Anishinaabeg and the future structure of Treaty 9 is examined in David Calverley, "The Impact of the Hudson's Bay Company on the Creation of Treaty Number Nine." The main Indian Affairs documentary source for Treaty 9 is LAC, RG 10, vol. 3033, file 235,225, pt. 1. The impact of Treaty 9 on resource development is examined in Patrick Macklem, "The Impact of Treaty 9 on Natural Resource Development in Northern Ontario," in *Aboriginal and Treaty Rights in Canada: Essays on Law, Equality and Respect for Difference*, ed. Michael Asch (Vancouver: UBC Press, 1998), 97–134.

4 Brian Titley argues that Scott's poetry and other literary work provide no insight into his actions as deputy superintendent general of Indian Affairs. As evidence, he notes that literary scholars cannot reach a consensus on the interpretation of Scott's Indian poetry. Lack of agreement, however, is not particular to English scholars and is insufficient reason to dismiss their work. There is a similar lack of consensus among historians about many past events and people, yet Titley doesn't make similar qualifications about the validity of historical scholarship. See Titley, *A Narrow Vision*, 30–32.
5 Stan Dragland, *Floating Voice: Duncan Campbell Scott and the Literature of Treaty 9* (Concord, ON: House of Anansi Press, 1994). See also David Calverley, "The Poet and the Bureaucrat: Reconsidering Duncan Campbell Scott," in *Visions and Voices in Temagami*, ed. A.W. Plumstead (North Bay: Nipissing University, 2000), 63–75.
6 Dragland, ibid., 31.
7 Ibid., 51.
8 Cited in ibid., 48. Scott's article is found in *Scribner's Magazine* 40 (November 1906): 573–83.
9 D.C. Scott, "The Onondaga Madonna," in *Canadian Anthology*, ed. Carl F. Klinck and Reginald E. Watters (Toronto: Gage Educational Publishing, 1974), 149.
10 Scott was also aware of how traditional Aboriginal religious beliefs continued in the north. One of the RCMP officers, Joseph Vanasse, wrote a short article titled "The White Dog Feast." It recounts the commissioners' arrival at Lac Seul. A local shaman was performing the ceremony, and he became indignant when the commissioners had the temerity to tell him to stop. See Joseph L. Vanasse, "The White Dog Feast," *Canadian Magazine* (November 1907): 62–64.
11 Kelly Evans, *Final Report of the Ontario Game and Fisheries Commission, 1909–1911* (Toronto: L.K. Cameron, 1912), 198.
12 Evans's comments regarding Native peoples are on pages 198–201 of his report (ibid.).
13 See Steven High, "Native Wage Labour and Independent Production during the Era of Irrelevance," *Labour/Le Travail* 37 (Spring 1996): 243–64.
14 See Calverley, "The Impact of the Hudson's Bay Company on the Creation of Treaty Number Nine."
15 J.W. Anderson, *Fur Trader's Story* (Toronto: Ryerson Press, 1961), 101–2. It is important to note that the Mushkegowuk (like the northern Anishinaabeg) used fish to feed their dogs. This accounts for the large quantity of fish listed.
16 LAC, RG 10, vol. 2406, file 84.041, pt. 2, Alexander McCoy and Frank Peltier to D.C. Scott, 2 October 1916.
17 Ibid., W.J. Hanna to Scott, 20 October 1916.
18 Ibid., Statement of Arthur Henry Nichols to W.R. Brown, 2 November 1916.
19 Ibid., Statement of Samuel Chapleau to W.R. Brown, 2 November 1916; Brown to J.D. McLean, 7 November 1916.
20 Ibid., Brown to McLean, 5 January 1917. There is no indication that there was any physical mistreatment of Fox Junior, and Brown's letter to McLean does not provide any specifics about the mistreatment. It is likely that Fox Senior was referring to verbal comments made by Edwards and O'Conner to his son.
21 Ibid., Chief Louis Michano to Brown, 7 January 1917.
22 Ibid., Brown to McLean, 7 November 1916.
23 Ibid., Statement of Arthur Henry Nichols to W.R. Brown, 2 November 1916.
24 Ibid., Brown to McLean, 7 November 1916.

25 "An Act Respecting Game, Fur-Bearing Animals and Fisheries of Ontario," in *Statutes of the Province of Ontario* (Toronto: L.K. Cameron, 1913), 970–71 (emphasis added).
26 Ibid., 978–79.
27 LAC, RG 10, vol. 2406, file 84.041, pt. 2, Joseph Rogers to McLean, 15 January 1917.
28 Ibid., Brown to McLean, 22 January 1917.
29 Equivalent to $2,366 in 2017 dollars.
30 LAC, RG 10, vol. 2406, file 84,041, pt. 2. Memorandum from Martin to Scott, 19 December 1916.
31 The Webster-Ashburton Treaty resolved the boundary dispute between New Brunswick and Maine in 1842. See Edelgard E. Mahant and Graeme S. Mount, *An Introduction to Canadian-American Relations,* 2nd ed. (Scarborough: Nelson Canada, 1989), 27–29.
32 LAC, RG 10, vol. 2406, file 84,041, pt. 2, Memorandum from Martin to Scott, 19 December 1916.
33 Ibid., Petition of Ojibwa Indians, 29 June 1917.
34 Barbara M. Wilson, *Ontario and the First World War, 1914–1918: A Collection of Documents* (Toronto: University of Toronto Press, 1977), cx. Wilson notes that the Ontario average for its adult male population was 31 percent. It was ironic that Canada's First Nations made a significant contribution to the war effort for a country that did not even grant them citizenship unless they agreed to give up their treaty rights. Scott estimated that 35 percent of Canada's First Nation male population (of enlistment age) volunteered for overseas service with the Canadian Expeditionary Force.
35 Ibid.
36 LAC, RG 10, vol. 2406, file 84.041, pt. 2, Scott to McCoy and Peltier, 29 August 1917.
37 Ibid., Scott to Arthur Meighen, 6 March 1918.
38 Peter Oliver, *G. Howard Ferguson: Ontario Tory* (Toronto: University of Toronto Press, 1977), 97–100, 172. See also Charles M. Johnston, *E.C. Drury: Agrarian Idealist* (Toronto: University of Toronto Press, 1986), 171–72, 174. Latchford had a deep dislike of Ferguson. For example, he later sat on a provincial Royal Commission set up by Premier Ernest Drury in the early 1920s to investigate ministerial interference in Ontario's Department of Lands and Forests during Ferguson's premiership.
39 Roger Graham outlines Meighen's tenure in the Borden cabinet in *Arthur Meighen,* vol. 1, *The Door of Opportunity* (Toronto: Clark, Irwin, 1960).
40 LAC, RG 10, vol. 2406, file 84.041, pt. 2, Meighen to Scott, 31 October 1918.
41 Scott's position during this conference is analyzed in Bruce Alden Cox, "Whitemen Servants of Greed: Foreigners, Indians and Canada's Northwest Game Act of 1917," in *New Faces of the Fur Trade: Selected Papers of the North American Fur Trade Conference, Halifax, Nova Scotia, 1985,* ed. Jo-Anne Fiske et al. (East Lansing: Michigan State University, 1996), 121–35. See also Frank Tough, "Conservation and the Indian: Clifford Sifton's Commission of Conservation, 1910–1919," *Native Studies Review* 8, 1 (1992): 61–73.
42 Cox, ibid., 123.
43 See Frank Tough, "Ontario Appropriation of Indian Hunting: Provincial Conservation Policies vs. Aboriginal and Treaty Rights, ca. 1892–1930" (prepared for the Ontario Native Affairs Secretariat, January 1991). See also Tough, "Conservation and the Indian."

CHAPTER 6: *R. v. Padjena*, 1925–31

1 $8,445.65 in 2017 dollars.

2   There is a vast literature on family hunting territories. Frank Speck, *Family Hunting Territories and Social Life of the Various Algonquian Bands of the Ottawa Valley*, Memoir 70, no. 8 (Ottawa: Department of Mines, Geological Survey, 1915). See also Speck, "The Family Hunting Band as the Basis of Algonkian Social Organization," *American Anthropologist*, New Series, 17, 2 (1915): 289–305. See also Speck and Loren C. Eiseley, "Significance of Hunting Territory Systems of the Algonkian in Social Theory," *American Anthropologist*, New Series, 41, 2 (1939): 269–80. Charles Bishop and Edward Rogers wrote about the family territorial system as well. Rogers argues that the system was pre-contact in origin (something Speck also believed). Bishop thought the family hunting system emerged because of the fur trade. In any case, it was a pre-treaty phenomenon. See Charles Bishop, *The Northern Ojibwa and the Fur Trade* (Toronto: Holt, Rinehart and Winston, 1974), 8–11; Bishop, "The Emergence of the Northern Ojibwa: Social and Economic Consequences," *American Ethnologist* 3 (1976): 39–54; Bishop and M.E. Smith, "Early Historic Populations in Northwestern Ontario: Archaeological and Ethnohistorical Interpretations," *American Antiquity* 40 (1975): 54–63; Bishop, "The Emergence of Hunting Territories among the Northern Ojibwa," *Ethnology* 9 (1970): 1–15; Bishop, "The Question of Ojibwa Clans," *Actes du Vingtième Congrès des Algonquinistes* (Ottawa: Carleton University Press, 1989): 43–61. See also Edward S. Rogers and J. Garth Taylor, "Northern Ojibwa," in *The Handbook of North American Indians*, vol. 6, *Subarctic,* ed. Helm J. Washington (Washington, DC: Smithsonian Institution, 1981); Rogers, "Changing Settlement Patterns of the Cree-Ojibwa of Northern Ontario," *Southwestern Journal of Anthropology* 19, 1 (1963): 64–88; Rogers, "Band Organization among the Indians of Eastern Subarctic Canada," *Contributions to Anthropology: Band Societies,* ed. David Damas, Anthropological Series 84, Bulletin 228 (Ottawa: National Museum of Canada, 1969), 21–50; Rogers, "Cultural Adaptations: The Northern Ojibway of the Boreal Forest, 1670–1980," *Boreal Forest Adaptations,* ed. A.T. Steegman (New York: Plenum Press, 1983).

3   See David Calverley, "Ojibwa Harvesting Rights and Family Hunting Territories: Rethinking Treaty Boundaries," in *This Is Indian Land: The 1850 Robinson Treaties,* ed. Karl S. Hele (Winnipeg: University of Manitoba Press, 2016), 43–72.

4   Ibid., 50–51, 57.

5   A similar process is outlined in Toby Morantz's *The White Man's Gonna Getcha: The Colonial Challenge to the Crees in Quebec* (Montreal and Kingston: McGill-Queen's University Press, 2002). Morantz outlines how "bureaucratic colonialism" was slowly extended over the Mushkegowuk of northern Quebec. Traplines represented a loss of autonomy as traditional Mushkegowuk systems of land and resource division were replaced by systems designed by Indian Affairs and the Quebec government.

6   On the issue of the Chapleau Game Preserve, see David Calverley, "The Dispossession of the Northern Ojibwa and Cree"; David T. McNab, *Research Report on the Chapleau Game Preserve and New Brunswick House Indian Reserve #76, Treaty #9* (Toronto: Ministry of Natural Resources, 1980), 5. The creation of Quetico Provincial Park and its effect on the Anishinaabeg of that area is examined in Deborah Doxtator and Jean Manore, "Research Report: Administrative History of Access by Native People to Quetico Provincial Park" (Toronto: Ontario Native Affairs Directorate, 1988). There are a number of articles about Canadian parks and the displacement of Aboriginal peoples, e.g., Bruce Hodgins and K. Cannon, "The Aboriginal Presence in Provincial Parks and Other Protected Places," in *Changing Parks: The History, Future, and Cultural Context of Parks and Heritage Landscapes,* ed. Bruce Hodgins and John Marsh (Toronto: Dundurn Press, 1998), 50–76; Theodore

Binnema and Melanie Niemi, "'Let the Line be Drawn Now': Wilderness, Conservation and the Exclusion of Aboriginal Peoples from Banff National Park in Canada," *Environmental History* 11 (2006): 724–50; Jean L. Manore, "Contested Terrains of Space and Place: Hunting and the Landscape Known as Algonquin Park, 1890–1950," in *The Culture of Hunting in Canada*, ed. Jean L. Manore and Dale G. Miner (Vancouver: UBC Press, 2007), 121–47. A more recent study is Brad Martin, "Negotiating a Partnership of Interests: Inuvialuit Land Claims and the Establishment of Northern Yukon (Ivvavik) National Park," in *A Century of Parks Canada, 1911–2011*, ed. Claire Campbell (Calgary: University of Calgary Press, 2011), 273–301. A recent study of Banff National Park is Courtney Mason, *Spirits of the Rockies: Reasserting an Indigenous Presence in Banff National Park* (Toronto: University of Toronto Press, 2014). The United States context is explored in Mark David Spence, *Dispossessing the Wilderness*; Keller and Turek, *American Indians and National Parks*.

7 Cited in *R. v. Padjena and Quesawa*. The legal decision is found in Brian Slatterly et al., *Canadian Native Law Cases with Comprehensive Subject and Statute Indexes* (Saskatoon: University of Saskatchewan Native Law Centre, 1986), 27–34.

8 LAC, RG 10, vol. 6747, file 420-8x, pt. 1, Chief Ellis Desmoulin to Indian Affairs, 19 December 1928.

9 The drop in pulpwood prices in the late 1920s is explored in Morris Zaslow, *The Northward Expansion of Canada, 1914–1967* (Toronto: McClelland and Stewart, 1988), 82–85.

10 Cited in Arthur Ray, *The Canadian Fur Trade in the Industrial Age* (Toronto: University of Toronto Press, 1990), 107–14.

11 Archie Belaney, *Pilgrims of the Wild* (London: Peter Davies, 1935), 8. Grey Owl is examined in Donald B. Smith, *From the Land of Shadows: The Making of Grey Owl* (Saskatoon: Western Producer Prairie Books, 1990).

12 Ray, *The Canadian Fur Trade*, 202–3.

13 LAC, RG 10, vol. 6747, file 420-8x, pt. 1, D. Macdonald to Scott, 31 December 1928.

14 Ibid., Scott to Burke, 24 January 1929.

15 DIAND, T&HRC, Unit Number P.92, *Padjena, Joe and Paul Quesawa v. Rex*/Police Magistrate, District of Thunder Bay, typed transcript of Proceedings of Trial, 25 January 1929.

16 See Macklem, *Indigenous Difference and the Constitution of Canada*, 140–44.

17 DIAND, T&HRC, Unit Number P.92, *Padjena, Joe and Paul Quesawa v. Rex*/Police Magistrate, District of Thunder Bay, typed transcript of Proceedings of Trial, 25 January 1929. *Sero v. Gault* is found in Slatterly et al., *Canadian Native Law Cases*, 27–34. Constance Backhouse considers the racism inherent in the *Sero v. Gault* decision in her work *Colour-Coded: A Legal History of Racism in Canada, 1900–1950* (Toronto: University of Toronto Press, 1999), 103–31.

18 First Nations in relation to criminal law in Upper Canada is examined in Harring, *White Man's Law*, 109–18. Harring's analysis outlines that the law was not applied systematically at first, but that by the 1840s colonial authorities believed that First Nations in Upper Canada were subject to criminal law.

19 DIAND, T&HRC, Unit Number P.92, *Padjena, Joe and Paul Quesawa v. Rex*/Police Magistrate, District of Thunder Bay, Judgment in case of *King vs. Joe Padjena and Paul Quesawa*, 25 January 1929. Six hundred dollars is equivalent to $8,458 in 2017 dollars.

20 LAC, RG 10, vol. 6747, file 420-8x, pt. 1, McDonald to McLean, 28 February 1929; McLean to McDonald, 11 March 1929.

21 DIAND, T&HRC, Unit Number P.92, *Padjena, Joe and Paul Quesawa v. Rex*/Police Magistrate, District of Thunder Bay, Argument of appellants on appeal to Ontario Divisional Court, 10 April 1929.
22 LAC, RG 10, vol. 6747, file 420-8x, pt. 1, W.F. Langworthy to Justice McKay, 1 March 1930.
23 Backhouse, *Colour-Coded*, 126.
24 In *Syliboy*, Justice Patterson stated that the Mi'kmaq, at the time of their 1752 treaty with the Crown, were an "uncivilized" people and therefore not an independent nation capable of entering into a treaty. Patterson also noted that in the treaty, the Mi'kmaq asked for the right to hunt in Nova Scotia. According to Patterson, an independent nation would not ask to assert a right. The wording of the treaty, Patterson concluded, indicates that the Mi'kmaq were seeking a privilege from the Crown not asserting a right. See Macklem, *Indigenous Difference and the Constitution of Canada*, 138–40.
25 Slatterly et al., *Rex v. Padjena and Quesawa*, 10 April 1930, in *Canadian Law Cases*.
26 Ibid.
27 LAC, RG 10, vol. 6747, file 420-8x, pt. 1, Burke to Scott, 12 April 1930. Also Edwards to Scott, 16 April 1930. Agents Burke and Edwards wrote to Scott prior to the *Padjena* case to outline how the Mushkegowuk in their agencies (which combined covered parts of Treaties 3 and 9 and the Robinson-Superior Treaty) were being harassed by local police and game officials. Lacking employment opportunities, they contended, the Anishinaabeg had to hunt and trap to support themselves. Compounding this issue was the fact that local white hunters and visiting sport hunters broke game laws but game officials turned a blind eye to these infractions. The agents also contended that local outfitters knowingly sold domestic hunting licences to foreign tourists. See ibid., Edwards and Burke to Scott, 22 December 1927.
28 Ibid., Walter Soulier to Indian Affairs, 11 April 1930; T.J. Godfrey to A.F. Mackenzie, 3 April 1930; Godfrey to Mackenzie, 23 April 1930. The context surrounding the Chapleau Game Preserve highlights the issues of treaty rights portability that underlay the Padjena/Quesawa case. The Chapleau Game Preserve was inside the Treaty 9 area. The reserve it most affected was the New Brunswick House Reserve, which was located almost at the centre of the preserve, but the Michipicoten Anishinaabeg also lost access to traditional trapping grounds because of the preserve, inside which a number of Michipicoten hunters had territory.
29 Ibid., Scott to Charles McCrea, 16 May 1930.
30 Ibid., Ludwig to Mackenzie, 15 October 1930.
31 Ibid., Ludwig to Mackenzie, 13 December 1930.
32 Ibid., Ludwig to Scott, 14 January 1931.
33 Ibid., Ludwig to Scott, 26 January 1931.
34 Ibid., Williams to Ludwig, 3 February 1931.
35 See John Long, *Treaty No. 9;* Calverley, "The Dispossession of the Northern Ojibwa and Cree." Another important study is John Long, "How the Commissioners Explained Treaty Number Nine to the Ojibwa and Cree in 1905," *Ontario History* 98, 1 (2006): 1–29. An earlier article by Long provides further analysis. "No Basis for Argument," 21–54. Several crucial primary sources provide ample evidence that the First Nations who signed Treaty 9 were promised continued harvesting rights in a manner similar to that of the Robinson Treaties. See the diary of the provincial representative, Daniel McMartin, Queen's University Archives, Misc. Collection, "Dr. MacMartin, Diary of a Journey to the NWT., 1905."

Samuel Stewart's diary is in LAC, RG 10, vol. 11. Duncan Campbell Scott's diary is in LAC, RG 10, vol. 1028. Scott's friend Pelham Edgar went north with the commissioners in 1906. His diary is located at LAC, RG 10, vol. 1028.

36 "Minutes of the Meetings of the Fish and Game Committee," in *Journals of the Legislative Assembly of the Province of Ontario* (Toronto: Kings Printer, 1927).
37 "Twenty-Fourth Annual Report of the Game and Fisheries Department, 1930," *Ontario Sessional Papers,* Sessional Paper No. 9 (Toronto: Kings Printer, 1931), 29 (hereafter Game and Fish Report).
38 Game and Fish Report, 1930, 1. In 2017 dollars, revenue from hunting and fishing licences was equivalent to $10,676,861.70. A profit of $88,000 was equivalent to $1,212,340.43.
39 Equivalent to $275,531.91 in 2017 dollars.
40 Equivalent to $34,441,489.36 in 2017 dollars.
41 Game and Fish Report, 1930, 5. Equivalent to between $688 million and $1.1 billion in 2017 dollars.
42 LAC, RG 10, vol. 6746, file 420-8C, Minutes of Meeting of Special Game Committee, 10 August 1931, 2 (hereafter Special Game Committee).
43 Miner's full name was John Thomas Miner.
44 LAC, RG 10, vol. 6746, file 420-8C, Minutes of Meeting of Special Game Committee, 10 August 1931, 2.15–16.
45 Ibid.
46 Nicholson also prepared a detailed memorandum for the Black Committee. See LAC, RG 10, vol. 6746, file 420-8C, Memorandum Re. Game Conservation, 2 September 1931.
47 See Morantz, *The White Man's Gonna Getcha,* 145.
48 Special Game Committee, Minutes of Port Arthur Meeting, 3 September 1931.
49 LAC, RG 10, vol. 6746, file 420-8E, pt. 7, McDonald to MacInnes, 12 September 1933. The Eastern and Central sections encompassed all the land lying east of the French and Mattawa Rivers and all territory between those rivers, the Canadian National Railway, and the Manitoba border. The northern territory was all the land north of the CNR.
50 Frank Speck noted the use of natural landmarks to demarcate family hunting territories. See *Family Hunting Territories and Social Life of the Various Algonquian Bands of the Ottawa Valley.*
51 LAC, RG 10, vol. 6748, file 420-8-2, pt. 1, MacInnes to agent Godfrey, 15 March 1937. An identical memorandum was sent to the Sault Ste. Marie, Parry Sound, Manitowaning, Thessalon, Sturgeon Falls, Fort William, and Fort Frances agencies.
52 LAC, RG 10, vol. 6746, file 420-8, pt. 8, Michael Christianson to Dr. McGill, 22 February 1937.
53 LAC, RG 10, vol. 6746, file 420-8-2, pt. 1, Godfrey to MacInnes, 12 June 1937. McGookin outlined how Anishinaabeg trappers would rotate their traplines; that is, they would trap in one area of their territory one winter and move on to a different area the following winter.
54 Ibid., Prewar to MacInnes, 12 November 1937.
55 Ibid., John Daly to MacInnes, 2 September 1937. Robin Brownlie's analysis of John Daly's contentious tenure as agent provides some explanation for their uncooperative behaviour, although frustration with the game laws further explains Anishinaabeg actions. See Robin Brownlie, "Man on the Spot: John Daly, Indian Agent for Parry Sound," *Journal of the Canadian Historical Association* 5 (1994): 63–86. Also, Robin Brownlie, *A Fatherly Eye: Indian*

Agents, Government Power, and Aboriginal Resistance in Ontario, 1918–1939 (Don Mills: Oxford University Press, 2003).
56 LAC, RG 10, vol. 6748, file 420-8-2, pt. 1, Albert Spencer to MacInnes, 30 July 1937; John Daly to MacInnes, 2 September 1937.
57 Ibid., Memorandum, 27 September 1937.
58 LAC, RG 10, vol. 10751, series C-V-2, file 484/42-2, Chapleau Agency Report, January 1938.
59 Ibid., Chapleau Agency Report, February 1938.
60 Ibid., Chapleau Agency Report, March and April 1938.
61 Ibid., Chapleau Agency Report, March 1939.
62 LAC, RG 10, vol. 6747, file 420-8x-3, Fort Frances Agency Report, November 1939.

CHAPTER 7: *R. V. COMMANDA*, 1937–39

1 Harold Hawthorn, ed., *A Survey of the Contemporary Indians of Canada: Economic, Political, Educational Needs and Policies,* vol. 1 (Ottawa: Indian Affairs Branch, 1966), 248. See also Robert J. Surtees, *Canadian Indian Policy: A Critical Bibliography* (Bloomington: Indiana University Press, 1982), 54; Olive P. Dickason, *Canada's First Nations: A History of Founding Peoples from Earliest Times,* 3rd ed. (Don Mills, ON: Oxford University Press, 2002), 375–76.
2 This process is outlined in John Leslie, "A Historical Survey of Indian-Government Relations, 1940–1970" (Paper prepared for the Royal Commission on Aboriginal Peoples Liaison Office, Ottawa, 1993), 1–5.
3 When the Department of Indian Affairs was placed under the aegis of the Department of Mines and Resources, the new title of Director was given to the bureaucratic head of Indian Affairs, while another official became deputy minister of the entire department.
4 LAC, RG 10, vol. 6747, file 420-8x, pt. 2, C.W. Jackson, Secretary to the Minister, to Dr. H.W. McGill, 11 September 1937; Memorandum, 25 September 1937.
5 Ibid., MacInnes to Burke, 8 July 1937.
6 AO, RG 4-32, file 797, year 1939, Transcript of trial, *Rex v. Joe Commanda, Rex v. John Fisher,* 17 February 1938.
7 LAC, RG 10, vol. 6746, file 420-8, J.A. Marleau to MacInnes, 17 February 1938.
8 LAC, RG 10, vol. 6747, file 420-8x, pt. 2, MacInnes to Cory, 22 February 1938.
9 Ibid., Cory to MacInnes, 24 February 1938.
10 Ibid.
11 Equivalent to $426 in 2017 dollars.
12 LAC, RG 10, vol. 6747, file 420-8x, pt. 2, Marleau to MacInnes, 25 February 1938; MacInnes to Marleau, 1 March 1938.
13 Ibid., Charles Carswell to Deputy Minister of Justice, 4 March 1938.
14 AO, RG 4-32, file 797, year 1939, Memorandum for Mr. Snyder, 26 March 1938.
15 Ibid., Memorandum for the Honourable the Attorney General RE: Right of Indians to hunt and shoot, 25 March 1938.
16 Ibid., Memorandum Re. Rights of Indians to Hunt and Shoot. This was the second, longer document submitted with Magone's legal summary for Nixon.
17 Wesley faced three charges: killing deer out of season, using dogs to hunt deer, and killing a deer whose antlers were less than four inches long. He was acquitted of the first two charges and found guilty of the third. See *R. v. Wesley,* 1932 CanLII 267 (AB CA), http://canlii.ca/t/gch3m.

18 Cited in P.G. McHugh, "Maori Fishing Rights and the North American Indian," *Otago Law Review* 6, 1 (1985): 69. Section 12 of the Natural Resources Transfer Agreement states: "In order to secure to the Indians of the Province the continuance of the supply of game and fish for their support and subsistence, Canada agrees that the laws respecting game in force in the province from time to time shall apply to the Indians within the boundaries thereof, provided, however, that the said Indians shall have the right, which the Province hereby assures them, of hunting, trapping, and fishing game and fishing for food at all seasons of the year on all unoccupied Crown lands and on any other lands to which the said Indians may have a right of access." Cited in *R. v. Wesley*.
19 See Robert Normley, "Removing All Reasonable Cause of Discontent: Noteworthy Decisions of the Alberta Court of Appeal in Aboriginal Litigation." *Alberta Law Review* 52, 1 (2014): 102.
20 LAC, RG 10, vol. 6746, file 420-8, pt. 8, "Indians ask for Rights under old Hunting Pact," 23 April 1938.
21 Ibid. See also Sidney L. Harring, *White Man's Law*, particularly ch. 3, "'The Common Law Is Not Part Savage and Part Civilized': Chief Justice John Beverley Robinson and Native Rights," 62–90.
22 This clause stated that as the Crown made increasing profits from the resources within the treaty boundaries, the Anishinaabeg were to have an increase in their annual annuity payments.
23 Macdonald's brief can be found both in AO, RG 4-32, file 797, year 1939, and LAC, RG 10, vol. 6746, file 420-8, pt. 8. All subsequent references are from the latter source.
24 "*R. v. Commanda*," in *Ontario Weekly Notes*, ed. John J. Robinette ed. (Toronto: Carswell Company, 1939): 466–70.
25 Ibid., 468.
26 Ibid., 470.
27 Section 92(12) gave the provinces jurisdiction over "Property and Civil Rights in the Province," while section 92(16) gave them control "Generally with all Matters of a merely local or private nature in the Province." Ibid., 470.
28 LAC, RG 10, vol. 6747, file 420-8x, pt. 2, Nixon to Prime Minister Mackenzie King, 29 September 1939.
29 Ibid., Nixon to Thomas Crerar, 30 September 1939.
30 Ibid., King to Nixon, 4 October 1939.
31 Ibid., McGill to Nixon, 18 October 1939.
32 See John Saywell's *Just Call me Mitch: The Life and Times of Mitchell F. Hepburn* (Toronto: University of Toronto Press, 1991), and Neil McKenty, *Mitchell Hepburn* (Toronto: McClelland and Stewart, 1967).
33 LAC, RG 10, vol. 6747, file 420-8x, pt. 1, Draft letter, McGill to Nixon, 12 October 1939.
34 Ibid., Federal Deputy Minister of Mines to Nixon, 16 December 1939.
35 LAC, RG 10, vol. 6747, file 420-8x, pt. 3, Memorandum, 19 April 1944.
36 Ibid. These newspaper clippings can be found at LAC, RG 10, vol. 6747, file 420-8x, pt. 2.
37 Ibid.

Epilogue

1 John Leslie, "Assimilation, Integration or Termination? The Development of Canadian Indian Policy, 1943–1963" (PhD dissertation, Carleton University, 1999), 4.

2 See Sally Weaver, *Making Canadian Indian Policy: The Hidden Agenda, 1968–1970* (Toronto: University of Toronto Press, 1981); Weaver, "Federal Difficulties with Aboriginal Rights Demands," in *The Quest for Justice: Aboriginal Peoples and Aboriginal Rights,* ed. Menno Boldt and J. Anthony Long (Toronto: University of Toronto Press, 1985); Surtees, *Canadian Indian Policy.* Harold Cardinal offers a strong critique of the White Paper in *The Unjust Society: The Tragedy of Canada's Indians* (Edmonton: M.G. Hurtig, 1969).
3 Cited in Bradford W. Morse, "The Resolution of Land Claims," in Morse, *Aboriginal Peoples and the Law,* 620.
4 See A.H. Jakeman, "Indian Rights to Hunt for Food," *Canadian Bar Journal* 6, 3 (1963): 223–27; Norman F. Zlotkin, "Post-Confederation Treaties," in Morse, *Aboriginal Peoples and the Law,* 328–36 and 344–48.
5 See Indian-Eskimo Association of Canada, *Native Rights in Canada* (Calgary: Indian-Eskimo Association of Canada, 1970).
6 See Allan C. Cairns, *Citizens Plus: Aboriginal Peoples and the Canadian State* (Vancouver: UBC Press, 2000).
7 *Calder v. Attorney-General of British Columbia (AG,)* [1973] SCR 313.
8 Patrick Macklem makes this argument in *Indigenous Difference and the Constitution of Canada.*
9 Arthur Ray outlines how the adversarial nature of the courtroom makes it at times not a great venue for subtle historical arguments. See Ray, *Telling It to the Judge: Taking Native History to Court* (Montreal and Kingston: McGill-Queen's University Press, 2011). Peggy Blair outlines the limitations of historical research in legal settings, where the ambiguity of historical conclusions can be manipulated by lawyers (or misunderstood by judges). See Blair, *Lament for a First Nation.*
10 See Frances Widdowson and Albert Howard, *Disrobing the Aboriginal Industry: The Deception behind Indigenous Cultural Preservation* (Montreal and Kingston: McGill-Queen's University Press, 2008). Calvin Helin outlines potential changes facing both First Nations and Canada as a whole in *Dances with Dependency: Indigenous Success through Self-Reliance* (Vancouver: Orca Spirit Publishing and Communications, 2006). Jonathan Clapperton explores the connection between Aboriginal peoples and the environmental movement, and how Aboriginal peoples can become "inauthentic" in the eyes of the environmental movement if they don't adopt certain attitudes towards the environment. Clapperton notes that this image of the Indian as natural environmentalist has simultaneously empowered and disempowered First Nations. See "Stewards of the Earth? Aboriginal Peoples, Environmentalists and Historical Representation" (PhD dissertation, University of Saskatchewan, 2012). Margot Francis outlines how the concept of "Indianness" has constantly affected First Nations in Canada, and how First Nations have responded to this changing definition. See in particular ch. 4 on Banff National Park in *Creative Subversions: Whiteness, Indigeneity, and the National Imaginary* (Vancouver: UBC Press, 2011).

Bibliography

Early Records of the Game and Fish Commission and its later incarnations were destroyed in the 1950s when they were transferred to the Public Archives of Ontario (now the Archives of Ontario). Records of the Attorney General were similarly culled before their transfer to the Archives of Ontario in the 1960s. The individual assigned to this task removed many of the items pertaining to Aboriginal issues because they were deemed to be of little interest.

In the interests of full disclosure, files that were examined but did not reveal anything pertinent to this study have also been listed. I note them primarily to show that I did consult them. The fact that these sources contain nothing says much about how this was largely a battle between bureaucrats, with politicians appearing only at crucial moments. Premiers' papers, for example, contain nothing pertaining to First Nations hunting in Ontario. Other records were consulted to gain a broader understanding of Anishinaabeg harvesting activity in northern Ontario prior to 1850. I consulted these files in association with other work and research. Particularly important are the various post records and correspondence of the Hudson's Bay Company. These documents provided crucial context about how First Nations might have perceived the Robinson treaties, and how they understood the Ontario government's infringement of those treaties. Although I did not use all of these files for this book, they are listed here as they continue to inform my understanding of Anishinaabeg harvesting activity, treaty rights, and Ontario's game laws. They were particularly important for contextualizing the Ontario government's trap line system and how it conflicted with Anishinaabeg harvesting territories.

ARCHIVES

Library and Archives Canada
Record Group 1
    Series E-1, vol. 72
    Series E-1, Statebook "J"

Series E-1, Statebook "K"
Series E-1, Statebook "L"
Series L-3, vol. 263, bundle 5, #4
Landbook "C"
Census of Canada, Algoma District, 1861–91
Record Group 10, Records of Indian Affairs, vols. 11, 123, 151, 173, 718, 1028, 2405, 2406, 3033, 6743, 6745, 6746, 6747, 6748, 8865, 10751, 11194

Archives of Ontario
Record Group 1 (Ministry of Natural Resources/Commissioner of Crown Lands)
  Series A-I-6, vol. 25
Record Group 3 (Premier's Office)
  George Ross
  James Pliny Whitney
  William Hearst
  Ernest Charles Drury
  George Ferguson
  G.S. Henry
  Mitchell Hepburn
Record Group 4 (Attorney General of Ontario)
  Central Registry: Civil and Criminal Files
Fur Trade Records, MU 1392, F431
Miscellaneous Fur Trade Papers, MU 7848, F. 431
  Fort Matachewan Journal, parts 1 and 2, 1870–74
  Temiskaming District, Temagamingue Post, 1874–86
  Temiskaming District, Misc.
Duncan Cameron Papers, MU 2200, box 5–5c
Parry Island Reserve Papers
Sir Aemilius Irving Papers
  Report of Commissioners Anderson and Vidal, MU 1464, file 26/31/4
  Documents relating to Robinson Treaties annuity dispute, MU 1464, file 27/32/09, and file 27/32/13 to 14
  "Northwest Angle Treaty: Game and Fisheries," MU 1469, box 31, package 37
Sir John Beverly Robinson Papers
  William B. Robinson Diary

Indigenous and Northern Affairs Canada, Treaties and Historical Research Centre
Padjena v. Rex File, Unit Number P.92
Robinson Treaty File, Unit Number O.56
Commanda, Joe, and W. St. Pierre File, Unit Number P.18

University of Western Ontario Regional Room
Alexander Vidal Papers

Metropolitan Toronto Library, Baldwin Room
T.G. Anderson Papers

Queen's University Archives
Daniel McMartin Papers.

Hudson's Bay Company Archives

Fur Seizure Records
RG 2/2/7 and 2/2/8 – Sir Augustus Nanton Correspondence – Fur Seizures in Ontario and Quebec
RG 3/1A/1 – Fur Trade Department Annual Reports
RG 3/17E/1 to 4 – Hudson's Bay Company – Fur Trade Conference, 1934–36
A.6/104 – London Correspondence to Fur Trade Commissioner
A.12/FT230/1 – Game Acts – Provincial and Federal
A.12/FT319/1a – Fur Seizures
A.39/14 – Legal Opinions and Correspondence, Seizure of Furs
A.74/1 to 14 – Report on the Fur Trade, 1894–1905

Post Records
B.109/a/1 to 4 – La Cloche Post Journal
B.109/e/1 to 13 – La Cloche, Reports on District
B.129/a/1 to 20 – Michipicoten Post Journal
B.129/e/1 to 6 – Michipicoten, Report on District
B.149/e/1 to 2 – Nipigon, Report on District
B.162/a/1 to 6 – Pic Post Journals
B.162/e/1 – Pic, Report on District
B.231/a/1 to 10 – Fort William/Point Meurion Post Journal
B.364/e/1 to 2 – Whitefish Lake, Reports on District
B.488/a/1 to 3 – Temagami Post Journals
B.125/z/1 – Nipissing Post, Miscellaneous Items

PROVINCIAL AND FEDERAL SESSIONAL PAPERS

Annual Reports of the Department of Indian Affairs, 1890–1940. *Dominion Sessional Papers.*
Canada, Legislative Assembly. *Report on the Affairs of the Indians in Canada.* Section III, Journals, Legislative Assembly, Canada (1847), Appendix T.
Evans, Kelly. *Final Report of the Ontario Game and Fisheries Commission, 1909–1911.* Toronto: L.K. Cameron, 1912.
Joint Committee of the Senate and House of Commons on Indian Affairs: Minutes of Proceeding and Evidence, no. 11, 11 May 1961. Ottawa: Queen's Printer, 1961.
"Minutes of the Meetings of the Fish and Game Committee." In *Journals of the Legislative Assembly of the Province of Ontario.* Toronto: King's Printer, 1928–36.
Ontario. "Ontario Game and Fish Commission: Commissioners' Report." *Ontario Sessional Papers.* Toronto: Warwick and Sons, 1892–1940.
–. "Report of E.B. Borron, Stipendiary Magistrate, on that Part of the Basin of Hudson's Bay belonging to the Province of Ontario." *Ontario Sessional Papers.* Toronto: L.K. Cameron, 1885. [Borron's reports appear in the *Ontario Sessional Papers* between 1885 and 1890. The latter publication contains a condensed version of all five of Borron's reports.]

—. "Report of the Survey and Exploration of Northern Ontario, 1900." *Ontario Sessional Papers*. Toronto: L.K. Cameron, 1901.

Statutes of the Province of Ontario. Toronto: L.K. Cameron, 1892–1940.

Published Primary Sources

Blair, E.H. *The Indian Tribes of the Upper Mississippi and Region of the Great Lakes*. Cleveland: Arthur Clark, 1911.

Browne, G.P., ed. *Documents on the Confederation of British North America*. Toronto: McClelland and Stewart, 1969.

Canada. *Indian Treaties and Surrenders from 1680 to 1890, Treaty Numbers 1-138*, vol. 1. Ottawa: Brown, Chamberlin, 1891.

—. *Indian Treaties and Surrenders from 1680 to 1902. Treaty Numbers 218–482*, vol. 3. Ottawa: Brown and Chamberlain, 1891.

Caniff, William. *The Settlement of Upper Canada*. Toronto: Dudley and Burns, 1869; reprinted by Mika Silk Screening, 1971.

Colton, Charles. *Tour of the American Lakes and among the Indians of the North-West Territory: Disclosing the Character and Prospects of the Indian Race*. Vol. 1. New York: Kennikat Press, 1972. Originally published in 1833.

Contemporary Indian Legislation, 1951–1978. Ottawa: Department of Indian Affairs and Northern Development, Treaties and Historical Research Centre, 1981.

Cruickshank, E.A., ed. *The Correspondence of Lieutenant-Governor John Graves Simcoe, with Allied Documents Relating to his Administration of the Government of Upper Canada*. 5 vols. Toronto: Society, 1923.

Doughty, Sir Arthur G. *The Elgin-Grey Papers, 1846–1852*. 4 vols. Ottawa: J.O. Patenaude, 1937.

Firth, Edith G., ed. *The Town of York, 1793–1815: A Collection of Documents of Early Toronto*. Toronto: University of Toronto Press, 1962.

Guillet, E.G., ed. *The Valley of the Trent*. Toronto: University of Toronto Press, 1967.

Johnston, Charles. "Deserontyon, John." In *Dictionary of Canadian Biography*, vol. 5, *1801–1820*. Toronto: University of Toronto Press, 1983.

—, ed. *Valley of the Six Nations: A Collection of Documents on the Indian Lands of the Grand River*. Toronto: University of Toronto Press, 1964.

Kohl, J.G. *Kitchi-Gami. Wanderings around Lake Superior*. Minneapolis: Ross and Haines, 1956. Originally published in 1860.

Krech, Shephard III. *The Ecological Indian: Myth and History*. New York: W.W. Norton, 1999.

Morris, Alexander. *The Treaties of Canada with the Indians of Manitoba and the North-West Territories including the Negotiations on Which They Were Based*. Saskatoon: Fifth House Publishers, 1991.

Radcliff, Thomas. *Authentic Letters from Upper Canada: Including an account of Canadian Field Sports by Thomas William Magrath*. Toronto: Macmillan, 1952; originally published in 1833.

Theses

Chute, Janet. "A Century of Native Leadership: Shingwaukonse and His Heirs." PhD dissertation, McMaster University, 1987.

Clapperton, Jonathan. "Stewards of the Earth? Aboriginal Peoples, Environmentalists and Historical Representation." PhD dissertation, University of Saskatchewan, 2012.
Cottam, Barry. "An Historical Background of the *St. Catherine's Milling and Lumber Co.* Case." MA thesis, University of Western Ontario, 1987.
Cottam, Barry. "Federal/Provincial Disputes, Natural Resources and the Treaty #3 Ojibway, 1867–1924." PhD dissertation, University of Ottawa, 1994.
Davies, Eric Owen. "The Wilderness Myth: Wilderness in British Columbia." MA thesis, University of British Columbia, 1972.
Leighton, Douglas. "The Development of Federal Indian Policy in Canada, 1840–1890." PhD dissertation, University of Western Ontario, 1975.
Leslie, John. "Assimilation, Integration or Termination? The Development of Canadian Indian Policy, 1943–1963." PhD dissertation, Carleton University, 1999.
McNab, David J. "Herman Merivale and the British Empire, 1806–1874, with Special Reference to British North America, Southern Africa and India." PhD dissertation, University of Lancaster, 1978.
Milloy, John. "The Era of Civilization: British Policy for the Indians of Canada, 1830–1860." PhD dissertation, Oxford University, 1978.
Peterson, Jacqueline. "The People in Between: Indian-White Marriage and the Genesis of a Métis Society and Culture in the Great Lakes Region, 1680–1830." PhD dissertation, University of Illinois, 1981).
Smith, Donald B. "The Mississauga, Peter Jones and the White Man: The Algonquians' Adjustment to the Europeans on the North Shore of Lake Ontario to 1860." PhD dissertation, University of Toronto, 1975.
Surtees, Robert J. "Indian Land Cessions in Ontario, 1763–1862: The Evolution of a System." PhD dissertation, Carleton University, 1982.
–. "Indian Reserve Policy in Upper Canada." MA thesis, Carleton University, 1966.
Telford, Rhonda. "'The Sound of the Rustling of the Gold Is under My Feet Where I Stand; We Have a Rich Country': A History of Aboriginal Mineral Resources in Ontario. PhD dissertation, University of Toronto, 1996.
Thoms, J. Michael. "Illegal Conservation: Two Case Studies of Conflict between Indigenous and State Natural Resource Management Paradigms." MA thesis, Trent University, 1996.

SECONDARY SOURCES

Allen, Robert. *His Majesty's Indian Allies: British Indian Policy in the Defence of Canada, 1774–1815*. Toronto: Dundurn Press, 1992.
Anderson, J.W. *Fur Trader's Story*. Toronto: Ryerson Press, 1961.
Armstrong, Christopher. *The Politics of Federalism: Ontario's Relations with the Federal Government, 1867–1942*. Toronto: University of Toronto Press, 1981.
Backhouse, Constance. *Colour-Coded: A Legal History of Racism in Canada, 1900–1950*. Toronto: University of Toronto Press, 1999.
Baldwin, Douglas. *The Fur Trade in the Moose-Missinaibi River Valley, 1770–1917*. Toronto: Ministry of Culture and Recreation, 1975.
Belaney, Archie. *Pilgrims of the Wild*. London: Peter Davies, 1935.
Belanger, Dian Olson. *Managing American Wildlife: A History of the International Association of Fish and Wildlife Agencies*. Amherst: University of Massachusetts Press, 1988.

Bellfy, Phil. "The Anishnaabeg of the Lake Huron Borderlands." In *Lines Drawn upon Water: First Nations and the Great Lakes Borders and Borderlands,* ed. Karl Hele, 21–42. Waterloo, ON: Wilfrid Laurier University Press, 2008.

Benidickson, Jamie. *Idleness, Water, and a Canoe: Reflections on Paddling for Pleasure.* Toronto: University of Toronto Press, 1997.

Berger, Carl. *Science, God, and Nature in Victorian Canada.* Toronto: University of Toronto Press, 1983.

Binnema, Theodore, and Melanie Niemi. "'Let the Line be Drawn Now': Wilderness, Conservation and the Exclusion of Aboriginal Peoples from Banff National Park in Canada." *Environmental History* 11 (2006): 724–50.

Binnema, Ted, and Susan Neylan, eds. *New Histories for Old: Changing Perspectives on Canada's Native Pasts.* Vancouver: UBC Press, 2007.

Bishop, Charles. "The Emergence of Hunting Territories among the Northern Ojibwa." *Ethnology* 9 (1970): 1–15.

–. "The Emergence of the Northern Ojibwa: Social and Economic Consequences." *American Ethnologist* 3 (1976): 39–54.

–. *The Northern Ojibwa and the Fur Trade.* Toronto: Holt, Rinehart and Winston, 1974.

–. "The Question of Ojibwa Clans." In *Actes du Vingtième Congrès des Algonquinistes,* ed. William Cowan, 43–61. Ottawa: Carleton University Press, 1989.

Bishop, Charles, and M.E. Smith. "Early Historic Populations in Northwestern Ontario: Archaeological and Ethnohistorical Interpretations." *American Antiquity* 40 (1975): 54–63.

Blair, Peggy J. *Lament for a First Nation: The Williams Treaties of Southern Ontario.* Vancouver: UBC Press, 2008.

–. "Take for "Granted:" Aboriginal Title and Public Fishing Rights in Upper Canada." *Ontario History* 62, 2 (2000): 31–55.

Bleasdale, Ruth. "Manitowaning: An Experiment in Indian Settlement." *Ontario History* 66, 3 (1974): 147–57.

Brown, Jennifer, and C. Roderick Wilson. "The Eastern Subarctic: A Regional Overview." In *Native Peoples: The Canadian Experience,* ed. R. Bruce Morrison and C. Roderick Wilson. Toronto: McClelland and Stewart, 1986.

Brown, Robert Craig. "The Doctrine of Usefulness: Natural Resources and National Park Policy in Canada, 1887–1914." In *Canadian Parks in Perspective,* ed. J.G. Nelson. Montreal: Harvest House, 1970.

Brownlie, Robin. *A Fatherly Eye: Indian Agents, Government Power, and Aboriginal Resistance in Ontario, 1918–1939.* Don Mills: Oxford University Press, 2003.

–. "Man on the Spot: John Daly, Indian Agent for Parry Sound." *Journal of the Canadian Historical Association* 5 (1994): 63–86.

Burnett, J. Alexander. *A Passion for Wildlife: The History of the Canadian Wildlife Service.* Vancouver: UBC Press, 2003.

Cairns, Allan. *Citizens Plus: Aboriginal Peoples and the Canadian State.* Vancouver: UBC Press, 2000.

Calloway, Colin. *Crown and Calumet: British-Indian Relations, 1783–1815.* Norman: University of Oklahoma Press, 1987.

Calverley, David. "The Dispossession of the Northern Ojibwa and Cree: The Case of the Chapleau Game Preserve." *Ontario History* 101, 1 (2009): 83–103.

–. "The Impact of the Hudson's Bay Company on the Creation of Treaty Number Nine." *Ontario History* 98, 1 (2006): 30–51.
–. "Ojibwa Harvesting Rights and Family Hunting Territories: Rethinking Treaty Boundaries." In *This Is Indian Land: The 1850 Robinson Treaties,* ed. Karl S. Hele, 43–72. Winnipeg: University of Manitoba Press, 2016.
–. "The Poet and the Bureaucrat: Reconsidering Duncan Campbell Scott." In *Visions and Voices in Temagami,* ed. A.W. Plumstead., 63–75. NorthAy: Nipissing University, 2000.
–. "'When the Need No Longer Existed': Declining Wildlife and Native Hunting Rights in Ontario, 1791–1898." In *The Culture of Hunting in Canada,* ed. Jean L. Manore and Dale G. Miner. Vancouver: UBC Press, 2006.
Cammarate, Paul, and Kier P. Sterling. "Muir, John." In *Biographical Dictionary of American and Canadian Naturalists and Environmentalists,* ed. Keir B. Sterling, Richard P. Harmond, George A. Cevasco, and Lorne F. Hammond, 563–66. Westport, CT: Greenwood Publishing, 1997.
Canniff, William. *The Settlement of Upper Canada.* Toronto: Dudley and Burns, 1869. Reprint by Mika Silk Screening, Ltd., 1971.
Cardinal, Harold. *The Unjust Society: The Tragedy of Canada's Indians.* Edmonton: M.G. Hurtig, 1969.
Cartmill, Matt. *A View to Death in the Morning: Hunting and Nature through History.* Cambridge, MA: Harvard University Press, 1993.
Chochla, Mark. "Victorian Fly Fishers on the Nipigon." *Ontario History* 91, 2 (1999): 151–64.
Chute, Janet. *The Legacy of Shingwaukonse: A Century of Native Leadership.* Toronto: University of Toronto Press, 1998.
–. "Pursuing the Great Spirit's Plan: Nineteenth-Century Ojibwa Attitudes towards the Future of Logging and Mining on Unsurrendered Indian Lands North of Lakes Huron and Superior." In *Social Relations in Resource Hinterlands. Papers from the 27th Annual Meeting of the Western Association of Sociology and Anthropology,* ed. Thomas W. Dunk, 173–204. Thunder Bay: Lakehead University, Centre for Northern Studies, 1991.
–. "A Unifying Vision: Shingwaukonse's Plan for the Future of the Great Lakes Ojibwa." *Journal of the Canadian Historical Association* 7 (1997): 55–80.
Clepper, Henry. *Leaders of American Conservation.* New York: Ronald Press, 1971.
–. *Origins of American Conservationism.* New York: Ronald Press, 1966.
Craig, Gerald. *Upper Canada: The Formative Years, 1784–1841.* Toronto: McClelland and Stewart, 1963.
Cole, Curtis. "McCarthy, Osler and Hoskin, and Creelman, 1882–1902: Establishing a Reputation, Building a Practice." In *Essays in Canadian Law,* vol. 1, ed. David H. Flaherty, 149–66. Toronto: University of Toronto Press; Osgoode Society for Canadian Legal History, 1981.
Colpitts, George. *Game in the Garden: A Human History of Wildlife in Western Canada to 1940.* Vancouver: UBC Press, 2002.
Conway, Thor. *Archaeology in Northeastern Ontario: Searching for Our Past.* Toronto: Ministry of Culture and Recreation, n.d.
Cottam, Barry. "Indian Title as a 'Celestial Institution': David Mills and the *St. Catherine's Milling Case.*" In *Aboriginal Land Use in Canada: Historical and Legal Aspects,* ed. Kerry Abel and Jean Friesen, 247–66. Winnipeg: University of Manitoba Press, 1991.

–. "The Twentieth Century Legacy of the *St. Catherine's* Case: Thoughts on Aboriginal Title in the Common Law." In *Coexistence? Studies in Ontario–First Nation's Relations,* ed. Bruce W. Hodgins, Shawn Heard, and John S. Milloy, 118–27. Peterborough, ON: Frost Centre for Canadian Heritage and Development Studies, 1992.

Cox, Bruce Alden. "Whitemen Servants of Greed: Foreigners, Indians and Canada's Northwest Game Act of 1917." In *New Faces of the Fur Trade: Selected Papers of the North American Fur Trade Conference, Halifax, Nova Scotia, 1985,* ed. Jo-Anne Fiske, Susan Sleeper-Smith, and William Wicken, 121–35. East Lansing: Michigan State University, 1996.

Creighton, Donald. *Canada's First Century.* Toronto: Macmillan, 1970.

–. *John A. Macdonald: The Old Chieftain.* Toronto: Macmillan, 1955.

Cummins, Bryan. "Attawapiskat Cree Land Use and State Intervention." In *Papers of the Twenty-First Algonquian Conference,* ed. William Cowan, 100–13. Ottawa: Carleton University Press, 1990.

Dawson, K.C.A. *Prehistory of Northern Ontario.* Thunder Bay: Thunder Bay Historical Museum, 1983.

Densmore, Frances. *How Indians Use Wild Plants for Food, Medicine and Crafts.* Reprint. New York: Dover Publications, 1974.

Dickason, Olive P. *Canada's First Nations: A History of Founding Peoples from Earliest Times.* 3rd ed. Don Mills, ON: Oxford University Press, 2002.

Dorsey, Kurk. "Scientists, Citizens, and Statesmen: US-Canadian Wildlife Protection Treaties in the Progressive Era." *Diplomatic History* 19, 3 (1995): 407–29.

Doxtator, Deborah, and Jean Manore. "Research Report: Administrative History of Access by Native People to Quetico Provincial Park." Toronto: Ontario Native Affairs Directorate, 1988.

Dragland, Stan. *Floating Voice: Duncan Campbell Scott and the Literature of Treaty 9.* Concord, ON: House of Anansi Press, 1994.

Drummond, Ian. *Progress without Planning: The Economic History of Ontario from Confederation to the Second World War.* Toronto: University of Toronto Press, 1987.

Dunk, Thomas. "Indian Participation in the Industrial Economy on the North Shore of Lake Superior, 1869–1940." *Thunder Bay Historical Museum Society: Papers and Records* 15 (1987): 3–13.

Dunlap, Thomas. *Saving America's Wildlife.* Princeton, NJ: Princeton University Press, 1988.

Dunning, R.W. *Social and Economic Change among the Northern Ojibwa.* Toronto: University of Toronto Press, 1959.

Elliot, David W. "Aboriginal Title." In *Aboriginal Peoples and the Law: Indian, Métis and Inuit Rights in Canada,* ed. Bradford W. Morse, 48-121. Ottawa: Carleton University Press, 1991.

Evans, Margaret. *Sir Oliver Mowat.* Toronto: University of Toronto Press, 1992.

Fenton, William N., and Elisabeth Tooker. "Mohawk." In *Handbook of North American Indians,* vol. 15, *The Northeast,* ed. Bruce Trigger. Washington, DC: Smithsonian Institution, 1978.

Finlay, J.L., and D.N. Sprague. *The Structure of Canadian History.* 2nd ed. Scarborough: Prentice Hall, 1984.

Flanagan, Thomas. *First Nations? Second Thoughts.* Montreal and Kingston: McGill-Queen's University Press, 2000.

Forkey, Neil S. "Anglers, Fishers, and the St. Croix River: Conflict in a Canadian-American Borderland, 1867–1900." *Forest and Conservation History* 37 (October 1993): 179–87.
–. *Canadians and the Natural Environment to the Twenty-First Century.* Toronto: University of Toronto Press, 2012.
Foster, Janet. *Working for Wildlife: The Beginning of Preservation in Canada.* Toronto: University of Toronto Press, 1978.
Francis, Margot. *Creative Subversions: Whiteness, Indigeneity, and the National Imaginary.* Vancouver: UBC Press, 2011.
Funk, Robert. "Post-Pleistocene Adaptations." In *Handbook of North American Indians,* vol. 6, *The Northeast,* ed. Bruce Trigger. Washington, DC: Smithsonian Institution, 1986.
Gable, John Allen. "Roosevelt, Theodore." In *Dictionary of American and Canadian Naturalists and Environmentalists,* ed. Keir B. Sterling, Richard P. Harmond, George A. Cevasco, and Lorne F. Hammond, 683–85. Westport, CT: Greenwood Press, 1997.
Gentilcore, R. Louis, and David Wood. "A Military Colony in a Wilderness: The Upper Canada Frontier." In *Perspectives on Landscape and Settlement in Nineteenth Century Ontario,* ed. David Wood. Toronto: Macmillan, 1978.
George, Peter. "Ontario's Mining Industry, 1870–1940." In *Progress without Planning: The Economic History of Ontario from Confederation to the Second World War,* ed. Ian Drummond, 52–76. Toronto: University of Toronto Press, 1987.
Gillis, R. Peter, and Thomas R. Roach. "The American Influence on Conservation in Canada, 1899–1911." *Journal of Forest History* (October 1986): 160–74.
–. "The Beginnings of a Movement: The Montreal Congress and Its Aftermath, 1880–1896." In *Consuming Canada: Readings in Environmental History,* ed. Chad Gaffield and Pam Gaffield, 131–51. Toronto: Copp Clark, 1995.
Good, E. Reginald. "Colonizing a People: Mennonite Settlement in Waterloo Township." In *Earth, Water, Air and Fire: Studies in Canadian Ethnohistory,* ed. David T. McNab, 145–80. Waterloo, ON: Wilfrid Laurier University Press, 1998.
–. "Mississauga-Mennonite Relations in the Upper Grand River Valley." *Ontario History* 87, 2 (1995): 155–72.
Graham, Roger. *Arthur Meighen,* vol. 1, *The Door of Opportunity.* Toronto: Clark, Irwin, 1960.
Graymont, Barbara. "Thayendanega." In *Dictionary of Canadian Biography,* vol. 5, *1801–1820.* Toronto: University of Toronto Press, 1983.
Greer, Allan, and Ian Radforth. *Colonial Leviathan: State Formation in Mid-Nineteenth Century Canada.* Toronto: University of Toronto Press, 1992.
Hall, Anthony J. "*The St. Catherine's Milling and Lumber Company versus the Queen:* Indian Land Rights as a Factor in Federal-Provincial Relations in Nineteenth Century Canada." In *Aboriginal Land Use in Canada: Historical and Legal Aspects,* ed. Kerry Abel and Jean Friesen, 267–86. Winnipeg: University of Manitoba Press, 1991.
Hall, D.J. "Clifford Sifton and Canadian Indian Administration, 1896–1905." In *As Long as the Sun Shines and Water Flows,* ed. Ian A.L. Getty and Antoine S. Lussier. Nakoda Institute Occasional Paper No. 1. Vancouver: UBC Press, 1981.
Hallowell, A. Irving. *Culture and Experience.* Philadelphia: University of Pennsylvania Press, 1955.
–. "The Size of Algonkian Hunting Territories: A Function of Ecological Adjustment." *American Anthropologist* 51, 1 (1949): 35–45.

Hamori-Torok, Charles. "The Iroquois of Akwesasne (St. Regis), Mohawks of the Bay of Quinte (Tyendinaga), Onyota'a (the Oneida of the Thames), and Wahta Mohawk (Gibson), 1750-1945." In *Aboriginal Ontario: Historical Perspectives on the First Nations,* ed. Edward S. Rogers and Donald B. Smith, 258–72 . Toronto: Dundurn Press, 1994.

Hansen, Lise C. "The Anishinabek Land Claim and the Participation of the Indian People Living on the North Shore of Lake Superior in the Robinson Superior Treaty of 1850." Toronto: Ministry of Natural Resources, Office of Indian Resource Policy, 1985.

Hanson, L.C. "Chiefs and Principal Men: A Question of Leadership in Treaty Negotiations." *Anthropologica* 29, 1 (1987): 39–60.

Harring, Sidney L. "'The Liberal Treatment of Indians': Native Peoples in Nineteenth Century Ontario Law." *Saskatchewan Law Review* 56, 2 (1993): 297–371.

–. "The Six Nations Confederacy, Aboriginal Sovereignty and Ontario Aboriginal Law, 1790-1860." In *Earth, Water, Air and Fire: Studies in Canadian Ethnohistory,* ed. David T. McNab, 181–230. Waterloo: Wilfrid Laurier University Press, 1998.

–. *The White Man's Law: Native People in Nineteenth Century Canadian Jurisprudence.* Toronto: University of Toronto Press, 1998.

Hawthorn, Harold, ed. *A Survey of Contemporary Indians of Canada: Economic, Political, Educational Needs and Policies,* vol. 1. Ottawa: Indian Affairs Branch, 1966.

Haycock, Ronald Graham. *The Canadian Indian as a Subject and Concept in a Sampling of the Popular National Magazines Read in Canada, 1900–1970.* Waterloo, ON: Waterloo Lutheran University Press, 1971.

Hele, Karl S. "The Anishinabeg and Métis in the Sault Ste. Marie Borderlands: Confronting a Line Drawn upon the Water." In *Lines Drawn upon Water: First Nations and the Great Lakes Borders and Borderlands,* ed. Karl Hele, 65–84. Waterloo: Wilfrid Laurier University Press, 2008.

Helin, Calvin. *Dances with Dependency: Indigenous Success through Self-Reliance.* Vancouver: Orca Spirit Publishing and Communications, 2006.

Herrington, Eleanor M. "Captain John Deserontyon and the Mohawk Settlement at Desoronto." *Queen's Quarterly* 29 (1921): 165–80.

Hickerson, Harold. *The Chippewa and the Neighbours: A Study in Ethnohistory.* New York: Hold, Rinehart and Winston, 1970.

High, Steven. "Native Wage Labour and Independent Production during the Era of Irrelevance." *Labour/Le Travail* 37 (Spring 1996): 243–64.

Highsmith, Richard M. Jr., J. Granville Jensen, and Robert D. Rudd. *Conservation in the United States.* Chicago: Rand McNally, 1962.

Hobusch, Erich. *Fair Game: A History of Hunting, Shooting and Animal Conservation.* New York: Arco Publishing, 1980.

Hodgins, Bruce, and Jamie Benidickson. *The Temagami Experience: Recreation, Resources and Aboriginal Rights in the Northern Ontario Wilderness.* Toronto: University of Toronto Press, 1989.

Hodgins, Bruce, and K. Cannon. "The Aboriginal Presence in Provincial Parks and Other Protected Places." In *Changing Parks: The History, Future, and Cultural Context of Parks and Heritage Landscapes,* ed. Bruce Hodgins and John Marsh, 50–76. Toronto: Dundurn Press, 1998.

Hodgins, Bruce W., Shawn Heard, and John S. Milloy, eds. *Coexistence? Studies in Ontario–First Nations Relations.* Peterborough, ON: Frost Centre for Canadian Heritage and Development Studies, 1992.

Holzkam, Tim E. "Sturgeon Utilization by the Rainy River Ojibwa Bands." In *Papers of the Eighteenth Algonquian Conference,* ed. William Cowan, 155–63. Ottawa: Carleton University Press, 1987.

Holzkam, Tim E., Leo G. Waisberg, and Joan A. Lovisek. "'Stout Athletic Fellows': The Ojibwa during the 'Big Game Collapse' in Northwestern Ontario, 1821–71." In *Papers of the Twenty-Sixth Algonquian Conference,* ed. David H. Pentland, 169–82. Winnipeg: University of Manitoba Press, 1995.

Humphries, Charles W. *"Honest Enough to be Bold": The Life and Times of Sir James Pliny Whitney.* Toronto: University of Toronto Press, 1985.

Hunter, Martin. *Canadian Wilds.* Columbus: A.R. Harding Publishing, 1907.

Indian-Eskimo Association of Canada. *Native Rights in Canada.* Calgary: Indian-Eskimo Association of Canada, 1970.

Ireland, Brenda. "'Working a Great Hardship on Us': First Nations People, the State, and Fur-Bearer Conservation in British Columbia prior to 1930." *Native Studies Review* 11, 1 (1996): 65–90.

Isaac, Thomas. *Aboriginal Law: Cases, Material and Commentary.* Saskatoon: Purich Publishing, 1999.

Jacoby, Karl. *Crimes against Nature: Squatters, Poachers, Thieves, and the Hidden History of American Conservation.* Los Angeles: University of California Press, 2001.

Jakeman, A.H., "Indian Rights to Hunt for Food." *Canadian Bar Journal* 6, 3 (1963): 223–27.

Jarvis, Julia. "Robinson, William Benjamin." In *Dictionary of Canadian Biography,* vol. 10. Toronto/Laval: University of Toronto/Université Laval, 2003. http://www.biographi.ca/en/bio/robinson_william_benjamin_10E.html.

Jasen, Patricia. *Wild Things: Nature, Culture and Tourism in Ontario, 1790–1914.* Toronto: University of Toronto Press, 1995.

Johnson, Leo A. "The Mississauga–Lake Ontario Surrender of 1805." *Ontario History* 83, 3 (1990): 233–53.

Johnston, Charles M. "Deserontyon, John." In *Dictionary of Canadian Biography, Volume 5: 1801–1820.* Toronto: University of Toronto Press, 1983.

–. *E.C. Drury: Agrarian Idealist.* Toronto: University of Toronto Press, 1986.

Jones, Karen. "*Never Cry Wolf*: Science, Sentiment, and the Literary Rehabilitation of *Canis lupus.*" *Canadian Historical Review* 84, 1 (2003): 65–93.

Judd, Richard. *Common Lands, Common People: The Origins of Conservation in Northern New England.* Cambridge, MA: Harvard University Press, 1997.

Keller, Robert H., and Michael F. Turek. *American Indians and National Parks.* Tucson: University of Arizona Press, 1998.

Killam, Gerald. *Protected Places: A History of Ontario's Provincial Parks System.* Toronto: Dundurn Press, 1993.

Klinck, Carl F., and Reginald E. Watters, eds. *Canadian Anthology.* Toronto: Gage Educational Publishing, 1974.

Koenig, Edwin. "Fisheries Conflict on the Saugeen Peninsula: Toward a Historical Ecology." In *Papers of the Twenty-Eighth Algonquian Conference,* ed. David Pentland. Winnipeg: University of Manitoba Press, 1997.

Kuhlberg, Mark. "'Nothing It Seems Can Be Done about It': Charlie Cox, Indian Affairs' Timber Policy and the Long Lac Reserve, 1924–1940." *Canadian Historical Review* 84, 1 (2003): 33–63.

Kulchyski, Peter, and Frank Tester. *Kiumajut (Talking Back): Game Management and Inuit Rights, 1900–70*. Vancouver: UBC Press, 2007.
La Forest, Gérard V. *Natural Resources and Public Property under the Canadian Constitution*. Toronto: University of Toronto Press, 1969.
Lambert, Richard S., and Paul Pross. *Renewing Nature's Wealth: A Centennial History of the Public Management of Lands, Forests and Wildlife in Ontario, 1763–1967*. Toronto: Department of Lands and Forests, 1967.
Landon, Fred. *Western Ontario and the American Frontier*. Toronto: McClelland and Stewart, 1967.
LaPierre, Laurier. *Sir Wilfrid Laurier and the Romance of Canada*. Toronto: Stoddart Publishing, 1996.
Leighton, Douglas. "The Historical Importance of the Robinson Treaties of 1850." Paper presented to the Annual Meeting of the Canadian Historical Association, 9 June 1982.
–. "A Victorian Civil Servant at Work: Lawrence Vankoughnet and the Canadian Indian Department, 1874–1893." In *As Long as the Sun Shines and Water Flows*, ed. Ian A.L. Getty and Antoine S. Lussier. Nakoda Institute Occasional Paper No. 1. Vancouver: UBC Press, 1981.
Leslie, John. *A Historical Survey of Indian-Government Relations, 1940–1970*. Paper prepared for the Royal Commission on Aboriginal Peoples Liaison Office, Ottawa, 1993.
Leslie, John, and Ron Maguire, eds. *The Historical Development of the Indian Act*. Ottawa: Department of Indian Affairs and Northern Development, Treaties and Historical Research Centre, 1978.
Long, John S. "How the Commissioners Explained Treaty Number Nine to the Ojibwa and Cree in 1905," *Ontario History* 98, 1 (2006): 1–29.
–. "'No Basis for Argument?' The Signing of Treaty No. 9 in Northern Ontario, 1905–1906." *Native Studies Review* 5, 2 (1989): 19–54.
–. *Treaty No. 9: Making an Agreement to Share the Land in Far Northern Ontario in 1905*. Montreal and Kingston: McGill-Queen's University Press, 2013.
–. *Treaty No. 9: The Negotiations, 1901–1928*. Cobalt, ON: Cobalt Highway Book Shop, 1978.
Loo, Tina. *Making Law, Order, and Authority in British Columbia, 1821–1871*. Toronto: University of Toronto Press, 1994.
–. *States of Nature: Conserving Canada's Wildlife in the Twentieth Century*. Vancouver: UBC Press, 2006.
Lysyk, Kenneth. "The Unique Constitutional Position of the Canadian Indian." *Canadian Bar Review* 45 (1967): 513–53.
Lytwyn, Victor P. "Ojibwa and Ottawa Fisheries around Manitoulin Island: Historical and Geographical Perspectives on Aboriginal and Treaty Fishing Rights." *Native Studies Review* 6, 1 (1990): 1–30.
MacEachern, Alan. *Natural Selections: National Parks in Atlantic Canada, 1935–1970*. Montreal and Kingston: McGill-Queen's University Press, 2001.
Mackenzie, John M. *The Empire of Nature: Hunting, Conservation and British Imperialism*. New York: Manchester University Press, 1988.
Macklem, Patrick. "The Impact of Treaty 9 on Natural Resource Development in Northern Ontario." In *Aboriginal and Treaty Rights in Canada: Essays on Law, Equality and Respect for Difference*, ed. Michael Asch, 97–134. Vancouver: UBC Press, 1998.
–. *Indigenous Difference and the Constitution of Canada*. Toronto: University of Toronto Press, 2001.

Mahant, Edelgard E., and Graeme S. Mount. *An Introduction to Canadian-American Relations.* 2nd ed. Scarborough: Nelson Canada, 1989.

Manore, Jean. "Contested Terrains of Space and Place: Hunting and the Landscape Known as Algonquin Park, 1890–1950." In *The Culture of Hunting in Canada,* ed. Jean L. Manore and Dale G. Miner, 121–47. Vancouver: UBC Press, 2007.

–. *Cross Currents: Hydroelectricity and the Engineering of Northern Ontario.* Waterloo: Wilfrid Laurier University Press, 1999.

Martin, Brad. "Negotiating a Partnership of Interests: Inuvialuit Land Claims and the Establishment of Northern Yukon (Ivvavik) National Park." In *A Century of Parks Canada, 1911–2011,* ed. Claire Campbell, 273–301. Calgary: University of Calgary Press, 2011.

Mason, Courtney. *Spirits of the Rockies: Reasserting an Indigenous Presence in Banff National Park.* Toronto; University of Toronto Press, 2014.

McCalla, Douglas. *Planting the Province: The Economic History of Upper Canada, 1784–1870.* Toronto: University of Toronto Press, 1993.

McCandless, Robert G. *Yukon Wildlife: A Social History.* Edmonton: University of Alberta Press, 1985.

McHugh, P.G. "Maori Fishing Rights and the North American Indian." *Otago Law Review* 6, 1 (1985): 62–94.

McKay, Ian. "The Liberal Order Framework: A Prospectus for a Reconnaissance of Canadian History." *Canadian Historical Review* 81, 4 (2004): 616–45.

McKenty, Neil. *Mitchell Hepburn.* Toronto: McClelland and Stewart, 1967.

McNab, David J. *Research Report on the Chapleau Game Preserve and New Brunswick House Indian Reserve #76, Treaty #9.* Toronto: Ministry of Natural Resources, 1980.

McNeil, Kent. *Emerging Justice: Essays on Indigenous Rights in Canada and Australia.* Saskatoon: Native Law Centre, University of Saskatchewan, 2001.

Miller, Char. *Gifford Pinchot and the Making of Modern Environmentalism.* Washington, DC: Island Press, 2001.

Millman, T.R. "Anderson, Thomas Gummersall." In *Dictionary of Canadian Biography,* vol. 10. Toronto/Laval: University of Toronto/Université Laval, 2003. http://www.biographi.ca/en/bio/anderson_thomas_gummersall_10E.html.

Morantz, Toby. "The Probability of Family Hunting Territories in Eighteenth Century James Bay: Old Evidence Newly Presented." In *Papers of the Ninth Algonquian Conference,* ed. William Cowan, 224–36. Ottawa: Carleton University Press, 1978.

–. *The White Man's Gonna Getcha: The Colonial Challenge to the Crees in Quebec.* Montreal and Kingston: McGill-Queen's University Press, 2002.

Morrison, James. *The Robinson Treaties: A Case Study.* Prepared for the Royal Commission on Aboriginal Peoples, 1996.

–. *Treaty Research Report: Treaty No. 9.* Ottawa: DIAND, T&HRC, 1986.

Morse, Bradford, ed. *Aboriginal Peoples and the Law: Indian, Métis and Inuit Rights in Canada.* Ottawa: Carleton University Press, 1991.

Munsche, P.B. *Gentlemen and Poachers: The English Game Laws, 1671–1831.* Cambridge: Cambridge University Press, 1981.

Nash, Roderick. "The Cultural Significance of the American Wilderness." In *Wilderness and the Quality of Life,* ed. Maxine E. McClosky and James P. Gilligan, 66–73. New York: Sierra Club, 1969.

–. *Wilderness and the American Mind.* Rev. ed. New Haven, CT: Yale University Press, 1973.

Nash, Roderick, ed. *The Call of the Wild (1900–1916)*. New York: George Braziller, 1970.
Nelles, H.V. *The Politics of Development: Forest, Mines and Hydro-Electric Development in Ontario, 1849–1941*. Toronto: Macmillan of Canada, 1974.
Newell, Dianne. *Tangled Webs of History: Indians and the Laws in Canada's Pacific Coast Fisheries*. Toronto: University of Toronto Press, 1993.
Normley, Robert. "Removing All Reasonable Cause of Discontent: Noteworthy Decisions of the Alberta Court of Appeal in Aboriginal Litigation." *Alberta Law Review* 52, 1 (2014): 99–110.
Oliver, Peter. *G. Howard Ferguson: Ontario Tory*. Toronto: University of Toronto Press, 1977.
Osburn, Michael. "Pinchot, Gifford." In *Biographical Dictionary of American and Canadian Naturalists and Environmentalists,* ed. Keir B. Sterling, Richard P. Harmond, George A. Cevasco, and Lorne F. Hammond. Westport, CT: Greenwood Publishing, 1997.
Owen, A.L. Riesch. *Conservation under F.D.R.* New York: Praeger Publishers, 1983.
Pain, S.A. *The Way North: Men, Mines and Minerals*. Toronto: Ryerson Press, 1964.
Putnam, D.F., and R.G. Putnam. *Canada: A Regional Analysis*. Toronto: J.M. Dent and Sons, 1970.
Quimby, G. *Indian Life in the Upper Lakes Region, 11,000 B.C. to A.D. 1800*. Chicago: University of Chicago Press, 1960.
Ray, Arthur. *The Canadian Fur Trade in the Industrial Age*. Toronto: University of Toronto Press, 1990.
–. *I Have Lived Here since the World Began: An Illustrated History of Canada's Native People*. Toronto: Key Porter Books, 1996.
–. *Telling It to the Judge: Taking Native History to Court*. Montreal and Kingston: McGill-Queen's University Press, 2011.
Ray, Arthur J., and Donald Freeman. *Give Us Good Measure: An Economic Analysis of Relations between the Indians and the Hudson's Bay Company*. Toronto: University of Toronto Press, 1978.
Ray, Arthur, Jim Miller, and Frank Tough. *Bounty and Benevolence: A History of Saskatchewan Treaties*. Montreal and Kingston: McGill-Queen's University Press, 2000.
Rea, K.J. *The Prosperous Years: The Economic History of Ontario, 1939–1975*. Toronto: University of Toronto Press, 1985.
Reiger, John F. *American Sportsmen and the Origins of Conservation*. New York: Winchester Press, 1975.
Richardson, Arthur Herbert. *Conservation by the People: The History of the Conservation Movement in Ontario to 1970*. Toronto: University of Toronto Press, for the Conservation Authority of Ontario, 1974.
Riley, John L. *The Once and Future Great Lakes Country: An Ecological History*. Montreal and Kingston: McGill-Queen's University Press, 2014.
Rogers, Edward S. "The Algonquian Farmers of Southern Ontario, 1830–1945." In *Aboriginal Ontario: Historical Perspectives on the First Nations,* ed. Edward S. Rogers and Donald B. Smith, 122–66. Toronto: Dundurn Press, 1994.
–. "Band Organization among the Indians of Eastern Subarctic Canada." In *Contributions to Anthropology: Band Societies,* ed. David Damas, 21–50. Anthropological Series 84, Bulletin 228. Ottawa: Queen's Printer, 1969.
–. "Changing Settlement Patterns of the Cree-Ojibwa of Northern Ontario." *Southwestern Journal of Anthropology* 19, 1 (1963): 64–88.

–. "Cultural Adaptations: The Northern Ojibway of the Boreal Forest, 1670–1980." In *Boreal Forest Adaptations*, ed. A.T. Steegman, 85–141. New York: Plenum Press, 1983.

Rogers, Edward S., and Mary Black. "Subsistence Strategy in the Fish and Hare Period, Northern Ontario: The Weagamow Ojibway, 1880–1920." *Journal of Anthropological Research* 32, 1 (1976): 1–43.

Rogers, Edward S., and J. Garth Taylor. "Northern Ojibwa." In *The Handbook of North American Indians*, vol. 6, *Subarctic*, ed. Helm J. Washington, 231–43. Washington, DC: Smithsonian Institution, 1981.

Rogers, Edward, and Flora Tobobondung. "Parry Island Farmers: A Period of Change in the Way of Life of the Algonkians of Southern Ontario." National Museum of Man Mercury Series, Canadian Ethnology Service Paper No. 31. Ottawa: National Museum of Man, 1975.

Romney, Paul. "Mowat, Sir Oliver." In *Dictionary of Canadian Biography, 1901–1910*, vol. 13. Toronto/Laval: University of Toronto/Université Laval, 2003. http://www.biographi.ca/en/bio/mowat_oliver_13E.html.

Rotman, Leonard Ian. *Parallel Paths: Fiduciary Doctrine and the Crown-Native Relationship in Canada*. Toronto: University of Toronto Press, 1996.

Sanders, D.E. "Indian Hunting and Fishing Rights." *Saskatchewan Law Review* 38, 1 (1973–74): 45–62.

Saywell, John. *Just Call me Mitch: The Life and Times of Mitchell F. Hepburn*. Toronto: University of Toronto Press, 1991.

–. *The Lawmakers: Judicial Power and the Shaping of Canadian Federalism*. Toronto: University of Toronto Press, 2002.

Schmalz, Peter. *The History of the Saugeen Indians*. Toronto: Ontario Historical Research Publication No. 5, 1977.

–. *The Ojibwa of Southern Ontario*. Toronto: University of Toronto Press, 1991.

Schull, Joseph. *Laurier*. Toronto: Macmillan, 1965.

Scott, D.C. "The Forsaken." In *Canadian Anthology*, ed. Carl F. Klink and Reginald E. Watters, 151–53. Toronto: Gage Publishing, 1974.

–. "The Last of the Indian Treaties." *Scribner's Magazine* 40 (November 1906): 573–83.

–. "The Onondaga Madonna." In *Canadian Anthology*, ed. Carl F. Klink and Reginald E. Watters, 149–50. Toronto: Gage Publishing, 1974.

Sherwood, Morgan. *Big Game in Alaska: A History of Wildlife and People*. New Haven, CT: Yale University Press, 1981.

Sinclair, Peter W. "The North and North-West: Forestry and Agriculture." In *Progress without Planning: The Economic History of Ontario from Confederation to the Second World War*, ed. Ian Drummond, 77–90. Toronto: University of Toronto Press, 1987.

Slatterly, Brian, et al. *Canadian Native Law Cases with Comprehensive Subject and Statute Indexes*. Saskatoon: University of Saskatchewan Native Law Centre, 1986.

Smith, Donald. "Aboriginal Rights a Century Ago: Were the Indians Cheated in 1885? An Old Case Re-examined." *The Beaver* 67, 1 (1987): 4–15.

–. "The Dispossession of the Mississauga Indians: A Missing Chapter in the Early History of Upper Canada." In *Historical Essays on Upper Canada: New Perspectives*, ed. J.K. Johnson and Bruce G. Wilson, 23-52. Ottawa: Carleton University Press, 1991.

–. *From the Land of Shadows: The Making of Grey Owl*. Saskatoon: Western Producer Prairie Books, 1990.

–. "Jones, Peter." In *Dictionary of Canadian Biography,* vol. 8. Toronto/Laval: University of Toronto/Université Laval, 2003. http://www.biographi.ca/en/bio/jones_peter_8E.html.
–. *Mississauga Portraits: Ojibwe Voices from Nineteenth Century Canada.* Toronto: University of Toronto Press, 2013.
–. *Sacred Feathers: The Reverend Peter Jones (Kahkewaquonaby) and the Mississauga Indians.* 2nd ed. Toronto: University of Toronto Press, 2013.
Smith, W.L., *The Makers of Canada: The Pioneers of Old Ontario.* Toronto: George N. Morang, 1923.
Speck, Frank. *Family Hunting Territories and Social Life of the Various Algonquian Bands of the Ottawa Valley.* Memoir 70, no. 8. Ottawa: Department of Mines, Geological Survey, 1915.
–. "The Family Hunting Band as the Basis of Algonkian Social Organization." *American Anthropologist,* New Series, 17, 2 (1915): 289–305.
Speck, Frank, and Loren C. Eiseley. "Significance of Hunting Territory Systems of the Algonkian in Social Theory." *American Anthropologist,* New Series, 41, 2 (1939): 269–80.
Spence, Mark David. *Dispossessing the Wilderness: Indian Removal and the Making of the National Parks.* New York: Oxford University Press, 1999.
Stagg, Jack. *Anglo-Indian Relations in North America to 1763, and an Analysis of the Royal Proclamation of 7 October, 1763.* Ottawa: Department of Indian Affairs and Northern Development, Treaties and Historical Research Centre, 1981.
Stevenson, Garth. *Ex Uno Plures: Federal-Provincial Relations in Canada, 1867–1896.* Montreal and Kingston: McGill-Queen's University Press, 1993.
Sterling, Keir B., Richard P. Harmond, George A. Cevasco, and Lorne F. Hammond, eds. *Biographical Dictionary of American and Canadian Naturalists and Environmentalists.* Westport, CT: Greenwood Press, 1997.
Sterling, Lori, and Peter Lemmond. "*R. v. Powley:* Building a Foundation for the Constitutional Recognition of Métis and Aboriginal Rights." *Supreme Court Law Review* 24 (2004): 243–67.
Surtees, Robert J. *Canadian Indian Policy: A Critical Bibliography.* Bloomington: Indiana University Press, 1982.
–. "Canadian Indian Policies." In *Handbook of North American Indians,* vol. 4, *History of Indian-White Relations,* ed. Wilcomb E. Washburn, 81–95. Washington, DC: Smithsonian Institution, 1988.
– "Canadian Indian Treaties." In *Handbook of North American Indians,* vol.4, *History of Indian-White Relations,* ed. Wilcomb E. Washburn, 202–10. Washington, DC: Smithsonian Institution, 1988.
–. "Land Cessions, 1763-1830." In *Aboriginal Ontario: Historical Perspectives on the First Nations,* ed. Edward S. Rogers and Donald B. Smith, 92–121. Toronto: Dundurn Press, 1994.
–. "The Development of an Indian Reserve Policy in Canada." *Ontario History* 61, 2 (1969): 87–98.
–. *Indian Land Surrenders in Ontario, 1763–1867.* Ottawa: Department of Indian Affairs and Northern Development, Treaties and Historical Research Centre, 1984.
–. *The Northern Connection: Ontario Northland since 1902.* North York: Captus Press, 1992.

–. *The Original People.* Toronto: Holt, Rinehart and Winston of Canada, 1971.
–. *Treaty Research Report: Manitoulin Island Treaties.* Ottawa: Department of Indian Affairs and Northern Development, Treaties and Historical Research Centre, 1986.
–. *Treaty Research Report: The Robinson Treaties.* Ottawa: Department of Indian Affairs and Northern Development, Treaties and Historical Research Centre, 1984.
Tanner, Helen Hornbeck, et al. *Atlas of Great Lakes Indian History.* Norman: University of Oklahoma Press, 1982.
Theriault, Madeline Katt. *Moose to Moccasins: The Story of Ka Kita Wa Pa No Kwe.* Toronto: Natural Heritage/Natural History, 1992.
Thomas, Philip D. "Thoreau, Henry David." In *Biographical Dictionary of American and Canadian Naturalists and Environmentalists,* ed. Keir B. Sterling, Richard P. Harmond, George A. Cevasco, and Lorne F. Hammond. Westport, CT: Greenwood Publishing, 1997.
Thoreau, Henry David. *Walden.* Ottawa: Prospero Books, 1999 (reprint).
Titley, E. Brian. *A Narrow Vision: Duncan Campbell Scott and the Administration of Indian Affairs in Canada.* Vancouver: UBC Press, 1986.
Tober, James. *Who Owns the Wildlife? The Political Economy of Conservation in Nineteenth-Century America.* Westport, CT: Greenwood Press, 1981.
Tobias, John. "Protection, Civilization, Assimilation: An Outline History of Canada's Indian Policy." In *As Long as the Sun Shines and Water Flows: A Reader on Canadian Native Studies,* ed. Ian A.L. Gettey and Antoine S. Lussier. Nakoda Institute Occasional Paper No. 1. Vancouver: UBC Press, 1981.
Tough, Frank. "Conservation and the Indian: Clifford Sifton's Commission of Conservation, 1910–1919." *Native Studies Review* 8, 1 (1992): 61–73.
–. "Ontario Appropriation of Indian Hunting: Provincial Conservation Policies vs. Aboriginal and Treaty Rights, ca. 1892–1930." Prepared for the Ontario Native Affairs Secretariat, January 1991.
Tucker, Albert. *Steam into Wilderness.* Toronto: Fitzhenry and Whiteside, 1978.
Vanasse, Joseph L. "The White Dog Feast." *Canadian Magazine* (November 1907): 62–64.
Waisberg, Leo, and Tim Holzkamm. "'A Tendency to Discourage Them from Cultivating': Ojibwa Agriculture and Indian Affairs Administration in Northwestern Ontario." *Ethnohistory* 40, 2 (1993): 175–211.
Waldram, James B. *As Long as the Rivers Run: Hydroelectric Development and Native Communities in Western Canada.* Winnipeg: University of Manitoba Press, 1988.
Wall, Sharon. *The Nurture of Nature: Childhood, Antimodernism, and Ontario Summer Camps, 1920–1955.* Vancouver: UBC Press, 2010.
–. "Totem Poles, Teepees, and Token Traditions: 'Playing Indian' at Ontario Summer Camps, 1920–1955." *Canadian Historical Review* 86, 3 (2005): 513–44.
Warecki, George. *Protecting Ontario's Wilderness: A History of Changing Ideas and Preservation Politics, 1927–1973.* New York: Peter Lang, 2000.
Warren, Louis S. *The Hunter's Game: Poachers and Conservationists in Twentieth Century America.* New Haven, CT: Yale University Press, 1997.
Weaver, Sally. "Federal Difficulties with Aboriginal Rights Demands." In *The Quest for Justice: Aboriginal Peoples and Aboriginal Rights,* ed. Menno Boldt and J. Anthony Long, 139–47. Toronto: University of Toronto Press, 1985.

—. "The Iroquois: The Grand River Reserve in the Late Nineteenth and Early Twentieth Centuries, 1875–1945." In *Aboriginal Ontario: Historical Perspectives on the First Nations*, ed. Edward S. Rogers and Donald B. Smith, 213–57. Toronto: Dundurn Press, 1994.

—. *Making Canadian Indian Policy: The Hidden Agenda, 1968–1970*. Toronto: University of Toronto Press, 1981.

—. "Six Nations of the Grand River, Ontario." In *Handbook of North American Indians*, vol. 15, *Northeast*, ed. Bruce Trigger, 525–37. Washington, DC: Smithsonian Institution, 1987.

Webber, Jeremy. "Relations of Force and Relations of Justice: The Emergence of Normative Community between Colonists and Aboriginal Peoples." *Osgoode Hall Law Journal* 33: 623–60.

West, John J. Van. "Ojibwa Fisheries, Commercial Fisheries Development and Fisheries Administration, 1873–1915: An Examination of Conflicting Interest and the Collapse of the Sturgeon Fisheries of the Lake of the Woods." *Native Studies Review* 6, 1 (1990): 31–65.

White, J. "Place-Names of Georgian Bay including the North Channel." *Ontario History* (1911): 5–81.

White, Richard. *The Middle Ground: Indians, Empires, and Republics in the Great Lakes Region, 1650–1815*. 2nd ed. Cambridge: Cambridge University Press, 2011.

Widdowson, Frances, and Albert Howard. *Disrobing the Aboriginal Industry: The Deception behind Indigenous Cultural Preservation*. Montreal and Kingston: McGill-Queen's University Press, 2008.

Wightman, W.R. *Forever on the Fringe: Six Studies in the Development of Manitoulin Island*. Toronto: University of Toronto Press, 1982.

Wightman, W. Robert, and Nancy M. Wightman. "Changing Patterns of Rural Peopling in Northeastern Ontario, 1901–1941." *Ontario History* 62, 2 (2000): 161–81.

Wightman, W. Robert, and Nancy M. Wightman. *The Land Between: Northwestern Ontario Resource Development, 1800 to the 1990s*. Toronto: University of Toronto Press, 1997.

Wightman, W. Robert, and Nancy M. Wightman. "The Mica Bay Affair: Conflict on the Upper Lakes Mining Frontier, 1840–1850." *Ontario History* 83, 3 (1991): 193–208.

Wilson, Barbara M. *Ontario and the First World War, 1914–1918: A Collection of Documents*. Toronto: University of Toronto Press, 1977.

Wise, S.F. "Sir Francis Bond Head." In *Dictionary of Canadian Biography*, vol. 10, *1871–1880*, ed. Marc la Terreur, 342–45. Toronto: University of Toronto Press, 1972.

Wood, J. David. *Making Ontario: Agricultural Colonization and Landscape Re-creation before the Railway*. Montreal and Kingston: McGill-Queen's University Press, 2000.

Woodward, Jack. *Native Law*. Toronto: Carswell, 1989.

Worster, Donald, *A Passion for Nature: The Life of John Muir*. Oxford: Oxford University Press, 2008.

Wright, J.V. *Ontario Prehistory: An Eleven Thousand Year Archaeological Outline*. Ottawa: National Museum of Man, 1972.

Wright, Roland. "The Public Right of Fishing, Government Fishing Policy and Indian Fishing Rights in Upper Canada." *Ontario History* 86 (1994): 337–62.

Young, Stanley P. "The Deer, the Indians, and the American Pioneers." In *The Deer of North America: The White-tailed, Mule and Black-tailed Deer, Genus Odocoileus – Their History and Management*, ed. Walter P. Taylor, 1–28. Washington, DC: Wildlife Management Institute, 1956.

Zaslow, Morris. "Edward Barnes Borron, 1820–1915: Northern Pioneer and Public Servant Extraordinary." In *Aspects of Nineteenth Century Ontario,* ed. F.H. Armstrong et al., 297–311. Toronto: University of Toronto Press, 1974.
–. *The Expansion of Northern Canada, 1914–1967.* Toronto: McClelland and Stewart, 1988.
–. *The Opening of the Canadian North, 1870–1914* . Toronto: McClelland and Stewart, 1971.
Zlotkin, Norman F. "Post-Confederation Treaties." In *Aboriginal Peoples and the Law: Indian, Métis and Inuit Rights in Canada,* ed. Bradford Morse, 272–407. Ottawa: Carleton University Press, 1991.

Case Law

Attorney-General of Canada v. Attorney-General of Ontario (1896), [1897] A.C. 199 (P.C.), affirming (sub nom. *Province of Ontario v. Dominion of Canada and Province of Quebec; In re Indian Claims*) [1895] 25 S.C.R. 434

Calder v. Attorney-General of British Columbia, [1973] S.C.R. 313, [1973] 4 W.W.R. 1

Ontario Mining Company v. Seybold (1901), 32 S.C.R. 1, affirmed (1902), [1903] A.C. 73, 3 C.N.L.C. 203 (P.C.)

R. v. Commanda, [1939] 3 D.L.R. 635, 72 C.C.C. 246 (Ont. H.C.)

R. v. Hill (1907), 15 O.L.R. 406 (C.A.)

R. v. Martin (1917), 41 O.L.R. 79, 39 D.L.R. 635, 29 C.C.C. 189 (C.A.)

R. v. Padjena (1930), 4 C.N.L.C. 411 (Ont. Div. Ct.)

R. v. Rodgers, [1923] 3 D.L.R. 414, [1923] 2 W.W.R. 353, 40 C.C.C. 51, 33 Man. R. 139 (C.A.)

R. v. Syliboy (1928), [1929] 1 D.L.R. 307, 50 C.C.C. 389 (N.S. Co. Ct.)

R. v. Wesley, [1932] 2 W.W.R. 337, 26 Alta. L.R. 433 (C.A.)

Sero v. Gault (1921), 50 O.L.R. 27, 64 D.L.R. 327 (H.C.)

St. Catherine's Milling and Lumber Co. v. R. (1888), 14 A.C. 46 (P.C.), affirming (1887), 13 S.C.R. 577

Index

Note: Game Act stands for the Ontario Game Act; HBC stands for Hudson's Bay Company; Indian Affairs stands for the federal Department of Indian Affairs.

Aboriginal peoples. *See* First Nations; Inuit; Métis; *see also* Anishinaabeg; Haudenosaunee (Six Nations); Mushkegowuk
acculturation, 5–6, 8–9, 50, 52–53, 122–23, 135*n*9; and "civilization," 8, 18, 37–38, 41, 62–63, 66, 73, 75, 86–87; and farming/wage labour, 10, 18, 25, 31, 37, 52, 63, 75, 77, 91, 102; and leniency, 9, 41, 49–50, 73–75, 83–87, 107–8; motivation for, 72
An Act to Amend the Act for the Protection of Game and Fur-Bearing Animals (Ontario, 1892), 28. *See also* Game Act (Ontario)
An Act the Better to Protect the Mississauga Tribes, Living on the Indian Reserve of the River Credit (Upper Canada, 1829), 30
Allan, D.J., 119
Anderson, J.W., 77
Anderson, Thomas, 13–14, 19, 22, 27, 31, 142*n*44. *See also* Vidal-Anderson Commission and Report
Anishinaabeg, 11, 12; early colonial treaties with, 15–18; and knowledge/recognition of treaty importance, 13–14, 20–27; post-War of 1812 resettlement of, 20, 140*n*26; and Robinson Treaties, 5, 6, 9, 14, 18–27; Scott's early interactions with, 74; traplines of, 6, 90–93, 104–8, 160*n*53. *See also* hunting rights of Anishinaabeg, *and entry following*; traplines, Anishinaabeg; treaties between Anishinaabeg and Crown, in Ontario
Armstrong, Christopher: *The Politics of Federalism*, 8
Attorney-General for the Dominion of Canada v. Attorney-General for Ontario, 114–15, 117

Bacon, N.H., 68–70
Bagot, Charles: report commissioned by, 22, 31
Baldwin-Lafontaine Reform government, 14, 19, 20, 21, 24
bears, 77–78, 104
beaver, hunting/trapping of: Anishinaabeg practices of, as misrepresented, 104; for food, 48, 77–78, 92–93; for HBC, 51,

54–55, 56, 58, 65, 70; quota/seasonal regulation of, 33, 48, 79, 107; in *R. v. Padjena*, 88, 91–93, 96
Belaney, Archie, 91–92
Bibbs, Corporal (RCMP), 103, 104
Biscotasing (ON), 91–92; HBC warehouse at, 55, 59, 64
Black, W.D., 88, 101–3
Black Committee, 88–89, 90, 100–4, 110, 111
Borden, Robert, 66, 70, 85–86
British North America Act, 7, 62, 94; [s. 91(24)], 82, 95, 116, 117; [s. 109], 44, 95, 116
Brown, William, 79–81, 85, 155*n*20
Browning, A.G., and H.D. Leask, 43
Burke, J.G., 91–94, 97, 159*n*27

Calder v. Attorney-General of British Columbia, 124
Canadian Charter of Rights and Freedoms, 124
Canadian Expeditionary Force, 83–84, 156*n*34
Canadian National Railway (CNR), 81; as boundary marker, 103, 120
Canadian Pacific Railway (CPR), 55, 67, 91, 106; and Commanda/Ottawaska case, 40, 45–46
caribou, 34, 47, 77, 93
Carswell, Charles, 112
Cartwright, John Robinson, 67
Chapleau, Samuel, 79
Chapleau Game Preserve, 91, 98, 102, 159*n*28
Chapleau Indian Agency, 98, 103–4, 106–7
Charles II, 56
Cherokee, US treatment of, 18
Chipman, C.C., 51, 54–57, 59, 63–66, 70–71
Chitty, George, 40, 45
Christianson, Michael, 105–6
Clarke, Alfred H., 113
Cockburn, George, 48
Commanda, Barnaby, and Wilson Ottawaska, 40, 42–47, 49, 76–77, 121, 124

Commanda, Francis, 46, 60
Commanda, Joseph, and case of, 11, 111–21
Commanda, Semo (chief), 40, 43, 44, 45
Confederation, 4–5
Conn, Hugh, 3, 109, 119–21, 124, 125
conservation, wildlife, 4, 5–7, 8, 10–11, 28–39, 51–53, 146*n*28; animals detrimental to, 35–36; animals protected by, 33–34; First Nations as perceived threat to, 28, 36–39, 40–41, 46–47, 100–4; transcendentalism and, 31, 32, 147*n*31; utilitarianism and, 29, 31, 32, 33, 37, 147*n*31, 148*n*41
Constitution Act, 1982, 4, 12
Cook, George, 79
Cory, T.L., 112
Couture, Joseph-Marie, Fr., 103
Crawford, William Redford, 17
Cree of Treaty 9. *See* Mushkegowuk
Crerar, Thomas, 110, 118–19
crust hunting, 36–37, 149*n*57

Daly, John, 106, 160*n*55
Davis, E.J., 44–45
deer hunting: Anishinaabeg practices of, as misrepresented, 35–37, 104, 118; in colonial era, 29–30; court cases involving, 111, 113, 161*n*17; quota/seasonal regulation of, 28, 30, 33–37, 47, 49, 77, 83, 107, 148*n*46; for sport, 33–37, 47, 78; by wolves, 35–36
Depew, Joseph E., 88
Desmoulin, Ellis (chief), 91–93
Diefenbaker, John, 122
Dominion-Provincial Wildlife Conference (1919), 86
Drayton, H.L., 57–58
Dundas, Henry, 30

Edwards, Frank (Indian agent), 97, 103–4, 159*n*27
Edwards, Frank (provincial enforcement officer), 68, 79–82, 83, 155*n*20
Edwards, William, 84
Elgin, James Bruce, Eighth Earl of, 13–14, 21–24

Index

Evans, Kelly: and Indian Affairs, 61–63; Ontario Game Commission report by, 61, 75–78

Fanning, George, 79–80
Ferguson, George, 85, 156*n*38
First Nations: as early military allies, 15, 18; later military service by, 83–84, 156*n*34; perceived coddling of, through treaties, 37–39; as perceived threat to wildlife conservation, 28, 36–39, 40–41, 46–47, 100–4. *See also* acculturation; Anishinaabeg; Haudenosaunee (Six Nations); Mushkegowuk
Fisher, John, 111–12, 117
fishing: early treaty access to, 137*n*11; Game Act restrictions on, 48, 151*n*44; in *Sero v. Gault*, 93–94, 95, 152*n*13. *See also* sport hunting and fishing
Fleming, John, 93
Fort Frances Indian Agency, 106, 107
Fort William, 13, 21; HBC post at, 23, 65, 80, 153*n*42
Fort William Band: enforcement abuse complaints by, 78–85, 155*n*20; and Hunter death, 78–79, 83; and Ogima case, 48–50
Fort William Indian Agency, 79–81, 85
Foubert, Wilfred, 92–93
Foy, J.J., 58–59, 67, 69
fur trade: railways and, 54, 80–81, 91–92; as threatened by Game Act, 51–54. *See also* Hudson's Bay Company (HBC), *and entries following*

Game Act (Ontario), 28–29, 31–39; colonial precursors of, 30–31; constables' search/seizure powers under, 80–81; enforcement abuses of, 8–9, 38, 72, 76–82, 85, 98; HBC's challenge of, 51–71, 82, 96, 98, 115, 153*n*45; Indian Affairs and, 7, 8–9, 40–50; Scott's willingness to challenge, 9, 82–87, 89, 118. *See also entries below*
Game Act (Ontario), test cases for Indian Affairs challenges of. See *R. v. Commanda; R. v. Padjena*
Game Act (Ontario), versions of: (1892), 28–29, 31–39; (1893), 148*n*46; (1900), 47–48, 151*n*38, 151*n*49; (1905), 48; (1907), 48, 83, 151*n*44; (1913), 38, 80–81, 83
Game Commission (Ontario), 4, 10–11, 33–39, 81, 100, 107, 148*n*41; and Commanda/Ottawaska case, 40, 42–47, 76–77; on First Nations as wolves, 28, 36–38, 101; Game Act as response to, 28–29; and HBC, 52–71; and Indian Affairs, 40–50; and privileging of sport hunting, 28, 32–35, 36; unchanging policy of, 38–39, 73, 75–77, 90
game preserves, 10–11, 102–3, 111; at Chapleau, 91, 98, 102, 159*n*28
Garvey, Charles, 98–99
Gault, Thomas, 93. *See also Sero v. Gault*
Gauthier, David, 111–12
geese, 10, 101–2
George V, 5, 83–84
Gibson, J.M., 45–47
Godfrey, T.J., 98, 103, 106–7
Greene, Ainslie W., 116, 117–18
Grey, Henry Grey, Third Earl, 21
Grey Owl. *See* Belaney, Archie

Haldimand, Frederick, 15, 17
Hall, R.H., 63–65, 67–68
Hanna, W.J., 69, 78–79
Harper, James, 19–20, 139*n*22
Harring, Sidney, 6, 152*n*13, 158*n*18
Harrison, Harold, 92
Haudenosaunee (Six Nations), 11, 20, 30, 114; at Bay of Quinte, 31, 93–94, 95–96, 137*n*8
Hawthorn, Harold, 109–10
Hawthorn Report (also known as Hawthorn-Tremblay Report), 109–10, 123, 124
Head, Francis Bond, 18
Hearst, William, 69–70, 85
Hepburn, Mitchell, 119
Hodgins, Frank, 67, 68–69, 98
Hudson's Bay Company (HBC), 4, 20, 74, 77, 100, 119; and relationship with Anishinaabeg, 51–53, 152*n*2. *See also entries below*

Index

Hudson's Bay Company posts, 13, 23, 25, 80, 135*n*8, 142*n*41, 153*n*42; Ontario government raids/fur seizures at, 52, 54–55, 58–59, 63–70, 79

Hudson's Bay Company's challenge of Game Act, 51–71, 82, 96, 98, 115, 153*n*45; arrest/fur seizures as catalysts for, 54–55; Court of Appeal's refusal to rule on, 68–69; Indian Affairs and, 52, 53, 54, 56–57, 59–66, 70; negotiated settlement of, 69–70; political factors affecting, 65–69

Hunter, Pierre, 78–79, 83

hunting, Indigenous, 6–7; as conscientious/sustainable, 103, 104, 105–6; and food/nutritional needs, 77–78, 103; as food source for colonial settlers, 7, 16–17, 29–31, 38; increased settlement vs, 15–18; misrepresentations of, 36–39, 100–4; resource development vs, 18–27; traplines for, 6, 90–93, 104–8, 160*n*53. *See also* hunting rights of Anishinaabeg, *and entry following*

hunting, non-Indigenous: licensing/seasonal regulation of, 6–7, 34–35, 100, 103, 105; for sport, 28, 32–37, 46–47, 61, 78, 86, 100–1, 102, 159*n*27; as supplemental activity, 30–31, 77; and trapline takeovers, 79, 91–92, 93, 104, 106, 107, 120. *See also* sport hunting and fishing

hunting rights of Anishinaabeg, 3–11; complexity of, 3–5; early recognition of need to codify, 13–14, 20–27; HBC and, 51–71, 82; historiographical issues of, 10–11; as ignored at Confederation, 4–5; Indian Affairs' inability/unwillingness to defend, 7, 8–9, 40–50; Indian agents' support of, 9, 43, 48–49, 78, 89, 91–93, 94, 97–98, 101, 103, 108, 109, 111; Ontario government's undercutting of, 5–7, 28–41, 75–77; Ontario legislation affecting, 28–29, 31–39; petitions to Crown to uphold, 5, 83–85; in *R. v. Commanda*, 109–21; in *R. v. Padjena*, 88–108; under Robinson Treaties, 5, 6, 14, 26–27, 40, 43, 44, 48–49, 78, 82–83, 99, 102–3; Scott's appreciation of, 73–75, 76, 86–87, 108, 110; Scott's willingness to defend, 82–87; as supported by Martin memo, 82–83; after Second World War, 122–25; treaty boundaries and, 88, 89, 99, 105, 111–12. *See also entry below*; Robinson Treaties (1850), *and entries following*

hunting rights of Anishinaabeg, threats to: acculturation, 5–6, 8–9, 50, 52–53, 62–63, 66, 73, 122–23, 135*n*9; government enforcement abuses, 8–9, 38, 72, 76–82, 85, 98; government trapline system, 88–91, 103–8; liberalism/equality, 4, 5–9, 76, 123; racism, 61–63, 73, 78–80, 90, 102, 107; resource development, 7, 8, 14, 15, 18–27, 31–32; settlement, 17–18; sport hunting, 28, 32–36, 46–47, 61, 78, 86, 102, 159*n*27; tourism/recreation, 32–35, 37, 100–2, 147*n*33, 151*n*44, 159*n*27; wildlife conservation, 4, 5–7, 8, 10–11, 28–39, 51–53. *See also individual topics*

Indian Act, amendments to: (1890), 41; (1951), 122

Indian Affairs, Department of: acculturation/leniency approach of, 9, 41, 49–50, 73–75, 83–87, 107–8; administration/bureaucracy of, 41–42; evolving attitude of, toward First Nations, 9, 72–87, 89; First Nations advocacy within, 119–21; and HBC, 52, 53, 54, 56–57, 59–66, 70; and Ontario game laws, 7, 8–9, 40–50, 82–87; and Ontario trapline system, 104–5, 110, 118, 119–20; after Second World War, 122–23. *See also* McLean, J.D.; Scott, Duncan Campbell

Indian Affairs test cases, for challenge of Game Act. *See R. v. Commanda*; *R. v. Padjena*

Indian agencies: Chapleau, 98, 103–4, 106–7; Fort Frances, 106, 107; Fort William, 79–80; Nipissing, 105–6; Port Arthur, 91–92; Sault Ste. Marie, 106; Thessalon, 106

Indian agents, 73, 75, 83, 86; enforcement abuses reported by, 8–9, 72, 78–79, 98;

Index

trapline system information gathering by, 105–6; treaty hunting rights supported by, 9, 43, 48–49, 78, 89, 91–93, 94, 97–98, 101, 103, 108, 109, 111
Indian Department (later Indian Affairs), 4, 13, 15, 18, 26, 31, 137n7, 138n12, 140n26
Indian-Eskimo Association of Canada: *Native Rights in Canada*, 124
Indians. *See* First Nations; *entries for specific nations*
Indigenous peoples. *See* First Nations; Inuit; Métis; *see also* Anishinaabeg; Haudenosaunee (Six Nations); Mushkegowuk
Interior, Department of the, 41, 42
Inuit, 10, 12
Iroquois. *See* Haudenosaunee (Six Nations)

Johnson, George, 25–26

Keating, William, 26
Kehoe, J.J., 57–58
Kelly, Hugh, 67
King, William Lyon Mackenzie, 118–19
Kulchyski, Peter, and Frank Tester: *Kiumajut (Talking Back)*, 10
Kwisiwa, Paul. *See* Quesawa, Paul

La Forest, Gérard, 124
Langworthy, W.F., 49, 95–97
LaRose, Fred, 54
Latchford, Frank, 85, 156n38
Laurier, Wilfrid, 42, 50, 66
Leslie, John, 109–10, 122
liberalism and equality, concepts of, 4, 5–9, 76, 123
Lockhart, J.F., 107
Long Lake Band, 79
Loo, Tina, 53, 146n28
Ludwig, M.H., 97, 98–99
Lysyk, Kenneth, 3, 124

MacCallum, G.A., 148n41
Macaulay, J.B.: report of, 22
Macdonald, J.H., 112, 116–17

Macdonald, John A., 32, 145n25
MacInnes, T.R.L., 88, 100–3, 105, 110–12, 117, 119
Mackenzie, A.F., 98
MacKinnon, F.D., 65, 67, 153n45
Macklem, Patrick, 4, 141n36
Maclaren, John J., 67
Magee, James, 67
Magone, C.R., 113–16
Magrath, Thomas William, 29
Manitoba Game Act, 97
Marleau, J.A., 111–12
marsh or jack-light hunting, 36–37
Martin, Joe, 83–84
Martin, Professor (author of memorandum to Scott), 82–83, 84, 85
Matthews, J.B., 100
McCarthy, Frank, 100
McCarthy, Leighton, 54–70, 100
McComber, A.J., 49
McComber, Arthur, 88, 94–97
McCoy, Alexander (chief), 78, 83–85
McCoy, Moses (chief), 48–49
McCrea, Charles, 98
McCurry, J.H., 111–12
McDonald, D.M., 105
McDougall, William, 48–49
McGill, Harold, 110–11, 117–21
McGillivray, Alexander A., 113–14
McGookin, Thomas, 105–6, 160n53
McKay, Ian, 5, 8
McKay, John, 88, 94, 96–98, 115
McKenzie, N.M.W.J., 68
McLean, J.D., 42–50, 98; and Commanda/Ottawaska case, 43–50; as contrasted with Scott, 84–85, 94, 110; and enforcement abuse complaints, 79–82; and HBC case, 59–63, 65–66
McMartin, Daniel G., 74
Meighen, Arthur, 85–86
Meredith, William, 67, 69, 70
Metcalfe, Charles, First Baron Metcalfe, 14, 21
Métis, 12, 24, 26, 75, 139n22, 143n57
Mica Bay (ON): occupation of mine at, 24, 142n44
Michano, Louis (chief), 79

Michipicoten: Anishinaabeg of, 20, 25, 98, 106, 159*n*28; HBC post in, 23
Migratory Birds Convention Act, 10, 123, 146*n*27
Miner, Jack, 101–2, 104
minerals and timber, 5, 6, 7, 8, 18–20, 22, 31–32, 117; Anishinaabeg awareness of value of, 23–24, 142*n*39
mining: in colonial era, 13–14; court case involving, 43–44; as impetus for Robinson Treaties, 18–27, 136*n*3; licences/leases for, 14, 18–19, 20, 139*n*19, 140*n*26; and Mica Bay incident, 24, 142*n*44; after silver discovery, 54
Missanabie (ON), HBC post at, 68
Mitchell, Charles R., 113
Mohawk, 31, 93–94. *See also* Haudenosaunee (Six Nations)
Montizambert (ON), HBC post at, 58–59, 65, 68
moose hunting: Anishinaabeg practices of, as misrepresented, 36–37, 80, 81, 104, 118; as Anishinaabeg treaty right, 3, 40, 43, 44; in Commanda/Ottawaska case, 40–46; for food, 40, 45, 77–78, 83, 93, 107, 111–12; in Hunter case, 78; in Ogima case, 48–49; quota/seasonal regulation of, 3, 28, 30, 33–37, 46–48, 76–77, 83, 107, 125
Morrison, James, 20
Mowat, Oliver, 7, 31–32, 42, 50, 145*n*25
Murray, James, Governor of Quebec, 113–14, 116
Mushkegowuk, 12, 70, 135*n*8, 157*n*5; Conn's support of, 119, 120–21; government harassment of, 159*n*27; Miner's antipathy to, 101–2; Scott's early interactions with, 74; treaty rights of, 99, 102, 150*n*7, 151*n*49; winter food needs of, 77–78, 103, 155*n*15
muskrat, 51, 58, 67, 77, 107

Nanton, Augustus, 65–66, 68, 69
National Transcontinental Railway, 96
Naval Aid Bill (1912), 66, 85
Nebenaigoching (chief), 20–21, 24, 26, 127

Newcombe, E.L., 42, 84
Nichols, Arthur Henry, 80
Nicholson, G.B., 103, 160*n*46
Nipissing Band, 40–47, 56, 60. *See also* Commanda, Barnaby, and Wilson Ottawaska
Nipissing Indian Agency, 105–6
Nixon, Harry C., 112–13, 115–16, 118–19

O'Connor, J.J., 79, 81, 155*n*20
Ogima, Frank, 48–49
O'Jeek, John, 111
Ojibwa. *See* Anishinaabeg
Ontario: early treaties/laws in, 5, 6, 9, 14, 15–27, 29–31; vs HBC, 51–71, 79, 82, 96, 98, 115, 153*n*45; and provincial rights/jurisdictional issues, 7, 8, 31–32, 40–44, 49–50, 62–63; trapline system of, 88–91, 103–8; and undercutting of treaty hunting rights, 5–7, 28–41, 75–77. *See also* Game Act (Ontario), *and entries following*; Game Commission (Ontario); traplines, Ontario government system of
Ontario Game and Fisheries Commission: report of (1912), 61, 75–78
Ontario Game Protective Association, 61
Ontario Medical Act, 115
Ontario Mining Company v. Seybold, 43–44
Ontario Provincial Police (OPP), 79, 81
Ontario Temperance Act, 115
Osler, Featherston, 115
Osler, H.S., 37, 38, 59
Ottawaska, Wilson. *See* Commanda, Barnaby, and Wilson Ottawaska
otter, 48, 54, 58, 65, 70, 77, 78, 91

Padjena, Joe, 88–90, 91–100. *See also R. v. Padjena*
Papineau, Denis Benjamin, 20–21
parks, national/provincial, 10–11, 91. *See also* Chapleau Game Preserve
Peau de Chat, Joseph (chief), 25–26, 126
Pedley, Frank, 57, 65–66
Peetawabano, Robert, 77
Peltier, Frank, 78, 83–85
Pennefather, Richard: report of, 31

Perdue, William Edgerton, 97
Pic River Band, 79–80, 104, 126; and *R. v. Padjena*, 91–100
Port Arthur Indian Agency, 91–92
Power, Augustus, 42
Prendergast, James, 115
Prewar, George, 106

Quebec, 54, 64, 66, 113–14; game laws in, 56, 69; Mushkegowuk of, 77, 157*n*5
Quebec Mining Company (Mica Bay), 24, 142*n*44
Quesawa, Paul, 88, 90, 91–92, 94, 95, 97–99, 104

R. v. Commanda, 11, 111–21; arrests/initial conviction in, 111–12; case law referred to in, 113–15, 116–17; Indian Affairs' appeal of, 112–17; Ontario's interest/involvement in, 112–13, 115–19; political factors affecting, 118–20; as test case, 110–12
R. v. Hill, 115, 116–17
R. v. Martin, 115
R. v. Padjena, 88–108, 112; arrests/initial conviction in, 88, 91–94; Divisional Court's overturning of, 88, 94–97; as failing on boundary issue, 88, 97–100, 111; and Hodgins's participation in HBC case, 68–69, 98, 115; as imperfect test case, 99–100, 111
R. v. Rodgers, 97, 115
R. v. Syliboy, 96, 159*n*24
R. v. Wesley, 113–14, 161*n*17
rabbits, 77, 93
racism, 61–63, 73, 78–80, 90, 102, 107
Radcliff, Thomas, 29
Radcliff, William, 29
railway crews, Anishinaabeg hunters' sale of meat to, 40, 46, 81
railways, 32, 34, 41, 66; fur trade and, 54, 80–81, 91–92. *See also specific railway lines*
Report on the Affairs of the Indians of Canada (Bagot Report, 1845), 22, 31
"Report on the Indians of Upper Canada" (Macaulay Report, 1839), 22

resource development, 7, 8, 14, 15, 18–27, 31–32. *See also* minerals and timber; mining
Revillon Frères, 55
Riddell, William Renwick, 93–94, 96
Robinson, William Benjamin, 13, 19, 20, 24–27, 87, 121
Robinson Treaties (1850), 18–27; as agreements between nations, 21, 22–23, 82, 114, 117, 141*n*36; Anishinaabeg hunting rights under, 5, 6, 14, 26–27, 40, 43, 44, 48–49, 78, 82–83, 99, 102–3; Anishinaabeg knowledge of/efforts to enforce, 40, 44, 48–49, 78, 83–84, 93; and Anishinaabeg recognition of treaty importance, 13–14, 20–27; background to, 18–24; creation/terms of, 24–27; HBC and, 52–53, 56, 58, 60–61, 64–65, 70–71, 82; Indian Affairs and, 8–9, 40, 44, 85, 87; Indian agents' support of, 9, 43, 48–49, 78, 91–93; map of territories under, 16(i); Ontario's view of, 5–7, 38–41, 75–77; in *R. v. Commanda*, 110–17, 121; in *R. v. Padjena*, 88, 90, 92–97, 99, 108; Scott and, 74, 78, 82–83, 85, 87, 99
Robinson-Huron Treaty (1850), 26, 56; in *R. v. Commanda*, 111–12, 117
Robinson-Superior Treaty (1850), 26, 48–49, 78, 83; in *R. v. Padjena*, 88, 91–93, 96–97, 99
Rod and Gun (magazine), 33, 35, 36
Rogers, Joseph E., 40, 46, 81
Rogers, Robert, 66
Rothera, C.F., 106
Routledge, John, 65
Royal Commission on Game and Fish (Ontario). *See* Game Commission (Ontario)
Royal Proclamation (1763), 14, 15, 18, 43, 113, 116, 140*n*26

Sanders, Douglas, 124
Sartre, Jean-Paul, 10
Sault Ste. Marie, 13, 19–25, 106, 121
Scott, Duncan Campbell, 72–87, 150*n*7, 155*n*10, 156*n*34, 159*n*27; and appreciation of Anishinaabeg treaty rights,

73–75, 76, 86–87, 108, 110; poetry of, 74–75, 155n4; and *R. v. Padjena*, 92, 94, 97–100; on "transitional Indian," 72, 74–75; as willing to challenge Game Act, 9, 82–87, 89, 118
Sero, Eliza, 93. See also *Sero v. Gault*
Sero v. Gault, 93–94, 95, 96, 115, 116, 152n13, 158n17
Shabogesic, Angus, 111
Shabogesic, Louis, 111
Shingwaukonse (chief), 20–21, 24, 25–26, 141n38, 142n46
Sifton, Clifford, 41–42, 43
Simcoe, Elizabeth, 29
Simcoe, John Graves, 29–30, 144n12
Sims, G.H., 106
Smart, James, 42–50
Snyder, C.L., 113
Soulier, Walter, 98
Spence, Mark David, 11, 136n18
Spencer, Albert, 103–4, 106
sport hunting and fishing, 32–37, 46–47, 61, 78, 159n27; First Nations considered only as guides for, 46–47, 102, 147n33, 151n44; by foreigners, 28, 34–35, 86; revenue from, 34–35, 100–1, 102
St. Catherine's Milling and Lumber v. R., 8, 31–32, 43–44, 114, 117, 145n23
St. Laurent, Louis, 122
St. Pierre, William, 111–12
Stanger, J.S.H.S., 68
Stoker, Bram: *Dracula*, 36
Stone, E.L., 100
A Survey of the Contemporary Indians of Canada (Hawthorn Report), 109–10, 123, 124

Taylor, D.J., 120, 121
Telford, Rhonda, 19, 136n3
Temiskaming and Northern Ontario Railway, 33, 54, 66
Thoreau, Henry David, 32
Tilley, E.A., 111
timber. *See* minerals and timber
Tinsley, Edwin, 37, 60
Tokeney, Joe, 104
Totomenai (chief), 25, 126

Tough, Frank, 86–87
tourism and recreation, 32–35, 37, 100–2, 147n33, 151n44, 159n 27
Train, George, 55, 58–59
transcendentalism, 31, 32, 147n31
traplines, Anishinaabeg, 6, 104–8; as based on family territories, 90, 104–5; rotation of, 105, 160n53; white hunters' takeover of, 79, 91–92, 93, 104, 106, 107, 120
traplines, Ontario government system of, 88–91, 103–8; displacement/lost access caused by, 90–91, 98, 104–5, 108; Indian Affairs' attempts to work with, 104–5, 110, 118, 119–20; Indian agents' involvement in, 89, 105–6
treaties between Anishinaabeg and Crown, in Ontario: as agreements between nations, 21, 22–23, 82, 114, 117, 141n36; Anishinaabeg recognition of need for, 13–14, 20–27; boundaries of, 88, 89, 99, 105, 111–12; early, 15–17, 16(i); presents given with, 17, 138n12, 141n38; Robinson, 5, 6, 9, 14, 18–27; as threat to wildlife conservation, 37–39, 40–41. *See also* Robinson Treaties, *and entries following*
Treaty 3 (1873), 31–32, 43–44, 70, 78, 117, 159n27; on map, 16(i)
Treaty 7 (1877), 117
Treaty 9 (1905–6), 12, 70, 159n27, 159n35; on map, 16(i); in *R. v. Padjena*, 90, 159n28; Scott's involvement in, 74
Trudeau, Pierre Elliott, 123

United States, 15, 17–18, 19, 20, 82, 95, 156n31; sport hunters from, 86; wildlife conservation in, 7, 11, 32, 146n28, 147n31
utilitarianism, 29, 31, 32, 33, 37, 140n31, 148n41

Vankoughnet, Lawrence, 42
Vidal, Alexander, 13–14, 19, 20, 22, 27, 31, 141n38, 142n44
Vidal-Anderson Commission and Report, 22–24, 27, 31; chart prepared for, 23, 126–27; and different perceptions of land value, 23–24

Wabinoo, Charles, 74–75
Wall, J.J., 92
War of 1812, 15, 20, 140*n*26
Warnica, J.L., 29
Watson, Lord William, 31–32, 114–15, 117, 145*n*23
Webster-Ashburton Treaty, 82, 156*n*31
Wesley, William, and court case of, 113–14, 161*n*17
white hunters. *See* hunting, non-Indigenous; sport hunting
White Paper on Indian policy (1969), 123
Whitney, James Pliny, 65, 66–67, 68, 69, 70
wildlife conservation. *See* conservation, wildlife
Williams, A.S., 99
Wilson, R.C., 58–59
wolves, 33, 35–38; First Nations compared to, 28, 36–38, 101

Younger, Robert, 65, 67, 153*n*45

NATURE | HISTORY | SOCIETY
GENERAL EDITOR: GRAEME WYNN

Claire Elizabeth Campbell, *Shaped by the West Wind: Nature and History in Georgian Bay*
Tina Loo, *States of Nature: Conserving Canada's Wildlife in the Twentieth Century*
Jamie Benidickson, *The Culture of Flushing: A Social and Legal History of Sewage*
William J. Turkel, *The Archive of Place: Unearthing the Pasts of the Chilcotin Plateau*
John Sandlos, *Hunters at the Margin: Native People and Wildlife Conservation in the Northwest Territories*
James Murton, *Creating a Modern Countryside: Liberalism and Land Resettlement in British Columbia*
Greg Gillespie, *Hunting for Empire: Narratives of Sport in Rupert's Land, 1840–70*
Stephen J. Pyne, *Awful Splendour: A Fire History of Canada*
Hans M. Carlson, *Home Is the Hunter: The James Bay Cree and Their Land*
Liza Piper, *The Industrial Transformation of Subarctic Canada*
Sharon Wall, *The Nurture of Nature: Childhood, Antimodernism, and Ontario Summer Camps, 1920–55*
Joy Parr, *Sensing Changes: Technologies, Environments, and the Everyday, 1953–2003*
Jamie Linton, *What Is Water? The History of a Modern Abstraction*
Dean Bavington, *Managed Annihilation: An Unnatural History of the Newfoundland Cod Collapse*
Shannon Stunden Bower, *Wet Prairie: People, Land, and Water in Agricultural Manitoba*
J. Keri Cronin, *Manufacturing National Park Nature: Photography, Ecology, and the Wilderness Industry of Jasper*
Jocelyn Thorpe, *Temagami's Tangled Wild: Race, Gender, and the Making of Canadian Nature*
Darcy Ingram, *Wildlife, Conservation, and Conflict in Quebec, 1840–1914*
Caroline Desbiens, *Power from the North: Territory, Identity, and the Culture of Hydroelectricity in Quebec*
Sean Kheraj, *Inventing Stanley Park: An Environmental History*

Justin Page, *Tracking the Great Bear: How Environmentalists Recreated British Columbia's Coastal Rainforest*

Daniel Macfarlane, *Negotiating a River: Canada, the US, and the Creation of the St. Lawrence Seaway*

Ryan O'Connor, *The First Green Wave: Pollution Probe and the Origins of Environmental Activism in Ontario*

John Thistle, *Resettling the Range: Animals, Ecologies, and Human Communities in British Columbia*

Carly A. Dokis, *Where the Rivers Meet: Pipelines, Participatory Resource Management, and Aboriginal-State Relations in the Northwest Territories*

Jessica van Horssen, *A Town Called Asbestos: Environmental Contamination, Health, and Resilience in a Resource Community*

Nancy B. Bouchier and Ken Cruikshank, *The People and the Bay: A Social and Environmental History of Hamilton Harbour*

Jonathan Peyton, *Unbuilt Environments: Tracing Postwar Development in Northwest British Columbia*

Mark R. Leeming, *In Defence of Home Places: Environmental Activism in Nova Scotia*

Jim Clifford, *West Ham and the River Lea: A Social and Environmental History of London's Industrialized Marshland, 1839-1914*

Michèle Dagenais, *Montreal, City of Water: An Environmental History*

Printed and bound in Canada by Friesens
Set in Garamond by Artegraphica Design Co. Ltd.
Copy editor: Frank Chow
Proofreader: Carmen Tiampo
Indexer: Cheryl Lemmens
Cartographer: Eric Leinberger